Revolution in Penology

Revolution in Penology

Rethinking the Society of Captives

Bruce A. Arrigo & Dragan Milovanovic

ROWMAN & LITTLEFIELD PUBLISHERS, INC.
Lanham • Boulder • New York • Toronto • Plymouth, UK

ROWMAN & LITTLEFIELD PUBLISHERS, INC.

Published in the United States of America
by Rowman & Littlefield Publishers, Inc.
A wholly owned subsidary of The Rowman & Littlefield Publishing Group, Inc.
4501 Forbes Boulevard, Suite 200, Lanham, Maryland 20706
www.rowmanlittlefield.com

Estover Road
Plymouth PL6 7PY
United Kingdom

British Library Cataloguing in Publication Information Available

Library of Congress Cataloging-in-Publication Data

The hardback edition of this book was previously catalogued by the Library of
Congress as follows:

Arrigo, Bruce A.
  Revolution in penology : rethinking the society of captives / Bruce A. Arrigo
and Dragan Milovanovic.
    p. cm.
  Includes bibliographical references.
  [etc.]
  1. Criminology. 2. Punishment. 3. Criminal justice, Administration of I.
Milovanovic, Dragan, II. Title.
  HV6025.A77 2009
  365'.7—dc22   2008027781

ISBN: 978-0-7425-6362-9 (cloth : alk. paper)
ISBN: 978-0-7425-6363-6 (pbk. : alk. paper)
ISBN: 978-1-4422-0259-7 (electronic)

Printed in the United States of America

For Michael Swisher:

You understood my capture;
you made it speakable;
you helped to set me free.

BAA

Contents

Foreword

The number of people serving sentences in state and federal prisons in the United States has grown from 196,000 in 1972 to more than 1.4 million today, with an additional 750,000 Americans in jails, amounting to 2.4 million people incarcerated. Indeed, according to a recent JFA Institute report, *Unlocking America*, the American prison-industrial complex is a "self-fuelling system" with a 40 percent recidivism rate for the 650,000 prisoners released each year that results from "a range of policies that increase surveillance over people released from prison, impose obstacles to their reentry into society, and eliminate support systems that ease their transition from prison to the streets" (Austin et al., 2007, 1). Moreover, the report states, "prison policy has exacerbated the festering national problem of social and racial inequality. Incarceration rates for blacks and Latinos are now more than six times higher than for whites; 60% of America's prison population is either African-American or Latino. A shocking eight percent of black men of working age are now behind bars, and 21% of those between the ages of 25 and 44 have served a sentence at some point in their lives" (Austin et al., 2007, 1). This is the stark culmination of prison policy informed by modernist penology. Clearly, something is fundamentally wrong with our current ways of dealing with criminal offenders, and it is toward a total reframing of penology that the authors of *Revolution in Penology* aim.

At first, it might seem strange that a book ostensibly about penology, the systematic study of penal systems, is founded in a theoretical framework, "constitutive thinking," that extols the potential of human liberation, and not just for prisoners or the punished but for us all. Of course, that is the point, for this radically provocative book is the antithesis of modernist penology. It screams for a revolution in our thinking about and practice of dealing with those who offend, not least to take down the prison-industrial complex that has resulted in the well-documented explosion of the prison population. As the book's authors say in their introduction, "*Revolution in Penology* intends to be a flash of light, a poetic spark, a fleeting epiphany, a coupling moment. It intends to communicate that subjectivity can be recovered for any one or group in which dispossession or alienation prevails. It intends to communicate that becoming other can be resuscitated for any one or group in which oppression and disenfranchisement triumphs." The prospect is for transformation to become more fully human, not as an endpoint but through an ongoing process of becoming.

Bruce Arrigo and Dragan Milovanovic—each highly accomplished critical criminologists with a penchant for postmodernist, particularly French, social theory (Jacques Lacan, Gilles Deleuze, and Felix Guattari)—cast off from our 1990s collaborations, which established a postmodernist-influenced constitutive criminology, to chart this new territory. Nurtured on the theoretical milk of social constructionist ideas about reification and objectification, as well as the seemingly indigestible 1960s assertion that reality, not least prison, is socially constructed through the ideologies of penology, these authors set out to deconstruct penological thinking and challenge us to reconstruct our world in nonpunitive, less harmful ways. To do so, they draw on often unfamiliar concepts, such as "molar and larval selves," and difficult-to-comprehend terms, such as "rhizome" and "Möbius," embodied in postmodernism, poststructuralism, chaos theory, and dynamic systems theory, which lead us into new ways of seeing, doing, and being. They draw on Deleuze and Guattari's concept of "a molecular subject" with "the capacity to mutate, transform, metamorphosize, and to always dwell in the process of becoming" as a way of "breaking free from restrictions placed on free-flowing desire."

At its core, their vision is premised on a holistic conception of humans-in-the-world that resists false separations from it, whether these are manifest in the form of autonomous individuals, groups, or institutions. Rather, following the coconstitutive, coproductive concepts from constitutive theory, they come to see that prison and its complicit coconspirator penology are internal human social and symbolic processes that have real external harmful consequences on those of us in and out of prison, regardless of whether we mask this control in seemingly less limiting aspects of disciplinary apparatuses, such as rehabilitation or restorative justice. In this revolutionary vision, Arrigo and Milovanovic share Loïc Wacquant's view of penality as the ensemble of categories, discourses, practices, and institutions concerned with enforcement of the sociocultural order that has become a major engine of urban and social change in the twenty-first century. In countering this historical development, Arrigo and Milovanovic "suggest a replacement vision of crime control that reconnects the components, parts, and segments to the whole in dynamic configurations rather than furthering the analytical and institutional separation that conventional penology prescribes."

After outlining their core assumptions, the authors explore the way expressions of power "emerge from within historically mediated sociocultural conditions," which give rise to penal forms that sustain the social structures that produce them in a dynamic relationship of mutual coproduction. This is not so much replication as it is reproduction in multiple and manifest forms that reflect and resonate with the whole of which they are parts. They outline, particularly in chapters 2 and 3, how the discourse of penology, penal policy, and penal practice play a pivotal role in this regenerative process and, through them, how all in society are victimized as they are limited from what they might otherwise have become. To avoid their own engagement in this ongoing pattern of destructive development, Arrigo and Milovanovic adopt the reflexive strategies of the "criminology of the shadow" and the "criminology of the stranger" in what they call the phenomenology of penal harm. The criminology of the shadow unveils the structural harms that are embodied in all that is penal. Within this analysis, the authors take a critical psychoanalytical turn, drawing on Erich Fromm, Jacques Derrida, Jacques Lacan, and Gilles Deleuze and Felix Guattari, among others, to "demonstrate how the recursive activities of existing correctional abstractions, categories, and practices work to coproduce and reify the prison-form, its constitutive parts, and the whole of society that legitimizes and essentializes the discourse of penology." For example, Fromm is mined for his insight into mechanisms of escape from automaton conformity toward realizing positive freedom of self, one without regulation of thought by the state. Symptomatic of this desire to escape their own powerlessness is the public's "habitually uncritical regard for penal harm," reflecting their insignificance and simultaneously insulating them from that reality. The public's *unconscious mind* could be shaken from this complacency by exposing it to the reality of penal harm. Here, the authors ingeniously draw on Derrida's deconstruction, particularly his hierarchical oppositions and reversal of hierarchies, to do the heavy linguistic lifting of exposing the ideological positions amid a contested terrain buried beneath the penological shadow. Through applying the work of Lacan, they reveal the absence of a philosophy of the human subject in penology, but with Deleuze and Guattari, the endless process of change and becoming is unlocked, freed from stasis, the reactive and resistive forces that curb human desire; this is the molecular rather than the molar. Applying this analysis to desistance theory, whereby over time many offenders mature out of crime, Arrigo and Milovanovic go beyond the view that prison disrupts the process of going straight to show that such analysis is merely reconstitutive of the existing molar (static) institutional forms that smother human desire. In contrast, the criminology of the stranger offers a "transdesistance" approach that "examines how the activities of the recovering subject (being) and the transformative subject (becoming) recast the character of human agency as constituents of a replacement discourse and logic." Here, in a radical, indeed revolutionary, approach, the authors are able to untangle the difficult problem of acknowledging the harm of offence without bringing harm to the offender. In exploring the possibilities of becoming that overcomes the limits of existing approaches to prisoner release, they state, "Each subject, then, in accord with Deleuze and Guattari, must be seen as a multiplicity, not a subject that lives only within the narrow diagrams of the release plan. . . . What needs to be sought are the imminent forces of deterritorialization, of desires captured in one set of assemblages rather than another, of the body and its multiple forms of expression, only some aspects of which are allowed materialization." In other words, radical transdesistance theory seeks to open up the multiplicity of avenues for desire to make connections, rather than to restrict these to investing energy into reconstituting the dead skin of the existing order.

In chapter 4 the authors examine the self-fueling system of incarceration-release-reincarceration known as the "pains-of-imprisonment" thesis. In a critical assessment of modernist penology's account of the punitive violence of prison, they show how the roles of prison actors (prisoners, correctional officers, public officials, and the general public) take center stage in the production of their violent conditions of confinement. Whether it is the systems approach to violence prediction of actuarial science with its multicausal analysis of violence or the progressive liberal analysis "that stresses violence as an artifact of social disorganization," these approaches offer an inadequate account of the penological problem. In contrast, Arrigo and Milovanovic apply a probing constitutive critique that feeds on Michel Foucault's concepts of the microtechnologies of disciplinary power and institutional surveillance, Deleuze and Guattari's concept of continuous control that pervades the informational pathways of our "socius" and that is embodied through discourse as our subject identity, and Jean Baudrillard's consumption of simulacra in which the prisonization process engulfs society through film, video, and computer gaming that elevates us to controllers and violent oppressors of fictional others: "Rapaciously devoured by an insatiable society hungry for more sights and sounds, the various messages these hyperreal images convey leave no room for distinguishing between what is real and what is illusion, between what is authentic and what is representational. Thus, reality implodes. Foundations disappear and with them the grounding of truth, the factual, the real, and, more troubling, the self and the social." The authors go on to demonstrate the key role that existing institutional processes play in normalizing violence and limiting the process of human transformation into a continuous state of becoming, thereby amplifying the criminological shadow. This curtailing of possibilities affects not only prisoners but all those involved in prison work and, ultimately, the whole society for failing to realize its own transcendent potential.

Unlike the pessimistic social theorists on whose work they draw, Arrigo and Milovanovic offer a way out through acknowledging "indigenous forces, minor narratives, and subaltern voices," which can displace, replace, and resist homeostasis and equilibrium conditions that are characteristic of the molar forces. This analysis is given concrete form in chapter 5 through a detailed and vivid microanalysis of the case of "Mary," a homeless woman of color, whose struggles to emerge from the cocoon of her oppressive existence overwhelm her glimpses of an alternative future.

Overall, Arrigo and Milovanovic have challenged penology to stand outside itself and, in doing so, to herald the possibility of the postpenological society, one that calls for us to "accept the potentials that inhere within each of us" and to resist the tendency to "limit these becomings." In their radical, provocative, and complex analysis, we are freed to envision not only a *Revolution in Penology* but a release of possibility toward the liberation of humanity. As a reader, your reentry into society has just ended; your release from it has just begun.

Stuart Henry
Director, School of Public Affairs
San Diego State University

Acknowledgments

The authors gratefully acknowledge the uncompromising support and generosity of Stuart Henry throughout the conceptualization and writing of this book. We especially thank him for his willingness to allow us to reproduce in verbatim form portions of chapters 1 and 2 and, in modified form, sections of the same. We thank the publisher of this material, Global Options, for granting us permission to reproduce excerpts from D. Milovanovic and S. Henry, "Constitutive Penology," which appeared in *Social Justice* 18 (1991): 204–24. We are also greatly indebted to Stuart's numerous keen insights in chapters 1 and 2. Additionally, the authors thank the publisher Taylor & Francis for granting us permission to reprint selected portions of B. Arrigo, "Crime, Justice, and the Under-laborer: On the Criminology of the Shadow and the Search for Disciplinary Legitimacy and Identity," published in *Justice Quarterly* 25(2008): 439–68). Excerpts of this material are found in chapter 3. We also thank Ms. Heather Bersot, who worked diligently to prepare the index, mindful of the need for thoroughness, accuracy, and clarity.

Introduction

Revolution: from whence does it come? It emerges in unconscious desire and is echoed in one's assemblages. It is given birth in an imperceptible whisper or in a shadow's desperate glow. And when it first appears, it is like a stranger calling: unrecognizable, inaccessible, and unspeakable. But when it is movement, a movement for the masses, it is an active line of flight: productive, mutating, transforming.

And so it is with penology, the molecular revolution in penology. Its journey of becoming, of becoming other, begins with a hushed, nearly undetectable call for change. But this change is not static, fixed, or certain. It is not axiomatic, hierarchical, or categorical. The changes we envision in penology are about absences made present; about freedoms without mechanisms of escape; about the lack in speech that finds expression, embodiment, and temporary narrative coherence; about simulated (and stultifying) hyperreality undone by images, thoughts, and languages of the possible; about the hermeneutics of suspicion and panoptic biopower displaced by a flourishing of being; and about rhizomatic deterritorialization and reterritorialization that makes becoming other that much more realizable. These are the constitutive roots of transpraxis; they await our thoughtful cultivation.

Revolution in Penology makes no apologies for its active lines of flight. It intends resistance but not negation. It intends disassembling static regularities and reactive singularities but affirms reassembling dynamic flows in nonlinear form. It intends to recover the subject, to promote human excellence, but it seeks to fan the productive forces of resuscitation, the agency/structure duality yet to come. This is a daunting task indeed. We make this challenge speakable and therefore knowable and transmutable in the pages of this book.

But do not be easily fooled. We do not merely propose the repast of poetry. Ours is a warlike machine: a nomadic expedition undertaken to specify, nay experience, penological transpraxis. For this journey, poet warriors must emerge rhizomatically. If productively mobilized, these nomads can describe the space/time processes through which the pains of imprisonment are cyclically reified, the normalization of violence is repetitively enacted, and the essentializing prisonization discourse that imagines, names, and regulates its abstract machines is recursively sustained. These are the reactive flows of the correctional industrial edifice that must be (dis)located. These (dis)locations are perceptible only in those transitory, but lucid, moments (fleeting epiphanies) when difference is not reduced to sameness, when knowing is not homogenized, when being is not vanquished, and when becoming is not reduced to or repressed by molar, larval forces.

It is here, then, where coupling moments appear as emergents. As (dis)locations, they give rise to ambulant, mutating (dis)identities, to (dis)continuities in which metamorphosis is rendered possible. Hence, the revolution unfolds accordingly.

Revolution in Penology is not the last word or the final line of active flight. It is a novel beginning that awaits further deconstruction and reconstruction. It is productive; thus, it must evolve—undergo dissipations and bifurcations—much like all complex adaptive (dynamic) systems. But this is to be expected; our war machine is always already nomadic. It wanders! The search continues apace.

Given that it is in motion, a productive energy flow, *Revolution in Penology* does not signify a major discourse or a totalizing logic. It is a minor literature, sensitive to dynamic symmetry-breaking perturbations, the perspective of schizoanalysis, the nonpermanent reversal of hierarchies, the presence of far-from-equilibrium conditions, and the *discourse of the hysteric/analyst*. As minor literature, it is not situated in closure, completion, or capture. These are the conditions that foster point, limit, and cyclical attractors whose effects gravitate toward and settle into nominal categories of sense making and finite renditions of narrative coherence. Ours is a transmutating text: active in its flight, bilinear in its direction, strange in its attractors, and intending, spontaneous, and hence more authentic, in its interrelational agency/structure mutuality. The revolution is forever a departure, rather than a destination, in its unfolding meaning.

But the *Revolution in Penology*, like the stranger calling, is not merely about us, about you, or about reactionary prisonization energy flows. It is about the socius: SOCIETY + I + US. We: SOCIETY + I + US, as the socius, are always already interconnected and deeply rooted. The socius is made of intersecting and overlapping assemblages. Some are more reactive, some more active; some dissipate and assume repetitive molar rigidities, while others dissipate and follow molecular pathways as novel developments. How each of us energizes our will to power such that this "overcoming" finds expression in our assemblages is the challenge that awaits radical reconceptualization. This engaged work of reauthoring the socius in dynamic adaptive form seeks images of thought that demythologize the shadow as well as mental visualizations that reontologize and reepistemologize the transient stranger, expressed in provisional, relational, and positional ways. And so it is with penology, the molecular revolution in penology.

This journey of which we speak does not simply rest with or in penology. The shadow slumbers in darkness elsewhere; it awaits mobilization and movement everywhere. The biophysics of power and surveillance, materialist culture overly technologized as sign-exchange simulacra, the metaphysics of presence, negative freedom, and the subjectification of the Body-without-Organs are increasingly omnipresent. But they are not omniscient. Hence, we seek other molecular revolutions. From whence do they come? They are borne in resistance to the status quo about society, about I, and about us. This opposition is not filled with hate, rage, or revenge: we do not envision the inversion of the master-slave dialectic. Reversing the relations of libidinal production does not give rise to (does not make possible) transformative politics. But it is a metamorphosizing political agenda to which we are most assuredly drawn. Oedipal and capital logic must be disassembled and reassembled in the socius elsewhere everywhere if our war machine is to usher in much-needed change.

Thus, *Revolution in Penology* intends to be a flash of light, a poetic spark, a fleeting epiphany, a coupling moment. It intends to communicate that subjectivity can be recovered for any one or group in which dispossession or alienation prevails. It intends to communicate that becoming other can be resuscitated for any one or group in which oppression and disenfranchisement triumphs. This minor literature is about experimental and pragmatic insight, kaleidoscopic movement, a will to overcome for the masses now, again, anew.

And so, the journey commences. . . .

ORGANIZATION OF THE BOOK

Revolution in Penology is divided into two parts. Part 1 emphasizes developments in constitutive theory and consists of chapters 1 to 3. Part 2 features developments in constitutive practice and encompasses chapters 4 and 5 and the conclusion. Both portions of the book draw attention to the critical potential of a postmodernist-inspired inquiry to advance our understanding of penology proper, discursive manifestations of penal harm, and the possibility of transformative justice. To accomplish these objectives, contributions from continental philosophy, cultural studies, psychoanalysis, and complex systems science figure prominently into the overall inquiry.

In chapter 1, the linkages between constitutive criminology and constitutive penology are delineated and examined. Of particular interest is the context in which the latter emerged in parallel with the conceptual insights of the former. Emphasis is placed on demonstrating where and how postmodern theory underpins the emergence and development of a new way of conceiving of and responding to the harms that constitute crime. Informing the analysis is commentary on the core assumptions of constitutive theory. These presuppositions include coproduction, dynamics systems/complexity theory, and the reification process. The implications of these broad-based assumptions are assessed in relation to understanding the subject's potential recovery (being) and transformative revival (becoming).

Chapter 2 examines several philosophies of punishment and demonstrates that, rather than justify the use of prison as punishment, they add additional harm to society and conceal the continuing crimes that they facilitate. In particular, the chapter critiques the modernist philosophies of (1) incapacitation/social defense, (2) retribution/just deserts, (3) deterrence, and (4) rehabilitation/treatment. Additionally, several progressive, though certainly modernist, perspectives are also enumerated that challenge the extant mainstream correctional ideologies. These more radical approaches include (1) abolitionism, (2) diversion, (3) decarceration, and (4) peacemaking/restorative justice. The latter is recognized as representing a way out of the quagmire of existent justifications for state investment in harm production but, nonetheless, is acknowledged for its contribution to reifying the prison-form. The development of a "new penology" movement is also reviewed, especially in its epistemological commitment to actuarial justice. Additionally, chapter 2 outlines the unique conceptual facets of constitutive penology, emphasizing a semiotic analysis of correctional policy. Observations on human agency, social structure, discourse, reality construction, and the discursive practices that inform these notions are considered. The manner in which the constitutive agenda extends and deepens the prevailing and critical literatures in penology is also reviewed.

Chapter 3 addresses the phenomenology of penal harm. This is a reference to the *criminology of the shadow* and the breadth and depth of injury recursively and cyclically reproduced through the agency/structure duality that sustains and legitimizes prison philosophies, practices, and policies and the correctional complex that is informed by and stands above them all. These crimes as the power to harm are rooted in the psychoanalytic contours of penology's cultural identity, as well as its capture (and closure) of multiple identities reduced/repressed in nominal, static form through the reification process. Chapter 3 also proposes a protean strategy for transcending the limitations of the criminological shadow. This is an allusion to the *criminology of the stranger* and how the activities of the recovering subject (being) and the transformative subject (becoming) possess the liberating capacity to recast the nature of human agency as constituents of a replacement discourse and logic. This replacement or alternative schema endeavors to affirm the oppressor in the act of negating the oppression, always already in provisional, positional, and relational ways. The relevance of this strategy in penology is linked to a radicalized desistance theory or to a *transdesistance model* of becoming, mutating, and evolving. The radicality of this approach as a dimension of the criminological stranger is provisionally delineated.

Chapter 4 examines the "pains-of-imprisonment" thesis. This is a reference to the incarceration-release-reincarceration machine nurtured, sustained, and reified by those human agents and structural/organizational forces that appropriate its totalizing and oppressive logic. This analysis includes a summary review of the prevailing modernist paradigms that account for the expanse of violence that is imprisonment. More specifically, however, the pains-of-imprisonment thesis implicates the discursive work of the kept, their keepers (prison workers), correctional administrators (or other governmental officials), and the punitive public who excessively invest in the harm-producing activities that essentialize prison and that *normalize* violence. Thus, chapter 4 demonstrates how human flourishing and becoming for all participants is profoundly reduced and repressed. The manner in which the coproduction of penological reality illustrates and amplifies the criminological shadow is discussed. The contexts consistent with the criminological stranger in which such molar, reactive forces can be resisted, destabilized, and deconstructed are specified.

Unlike chapter 4 and its targeted application at the "macrosociological" level, chapter 5 undertakes its application at the "microsociological" level. Of particular focus is the case study of Mary, a poor (and street-dwelling) woman of color. The various ways in which the homeless shelter and correctional systems defined her identity are featured. As the chapter reveals, Mary's (dis)identities (her multiple and ambulant standpoints) and her (dis)continuities (the manifold locations from which she could experience a becoming, a molecular revolution) were reduced/repressed. Several strategies for overcoming this harm (in which difference is reconstituted as sameness) consistent with our position on transpraxis and transformative justice are explored.

The conclusion suggestively outlines a number of additional observations regarding the ongoing revolution in penology. These include techniques and tactics that advance our "war machine" but from within a holistic framework. These comments, conditional and speculative, address critical engagement at the macro-, meso-, and microlevels of analysis. Collectively, they represent some possible directions in sustaining change that privilege active molecular forces/flows and becoming.

I

DEVELOPMENTS IN CONSTITUTIVE THEORY AND PENOLOGY

1

✛

From Constitutive Criminology to Constitutive Penology

As co-constitutive, not one is acceptable without the other; they stand to-gether in a web of experiences. As co-resonating, one points to the next and the next points to another. . . . "Being" does not have to win out over "being," or "Being" does not have to conquer "Time." The two parts of the pairing can be mutually conditioning or co-constitutive as in *yin* and *yang*. This constitutes *dao*. . . . Both truth and method, both ontology and hermeneutics, both the whole and the parts are co-constitutive. . . . Since *yin* and *yang* are primordial polarities that are mutually conditioning and eternally linked, they represent co-constitutive elements in the dialectics of harmonization. Conflict is part of harmony and harmony part of con-flict; *yang* is part of *yin* and *yin* is part of *yang*.

—Goulding 2007, 100, 109, 115

INTRODUCTION: CONSTITUTIVE THINKING

Constitutive theory, or, more accurately, as employed in the quote above, coconstitutive thinking, underlies constitutive criminology and penology. It starts from the assumption that society is a whole con-taining within it "parts" that together sustain the whole, while the whole simultaneously and reciprocally shapes its parts. Parts of a society can range from its structure and culture to its organizations, institutions, and communities; from its networks, groups, and families to its human agents; from the behavior, personality, and attitude of individuals to their organs, cells, chromosomes, and genes. Since each of these parts is itself a

3

part of something else and also contains other parts, yet each also exists on a different order of magnitude, it is helpful to conceive of the parts of society as segments, containing parts, that themselves contain components. Each of these segments exists in integral relationship to the parts that constitute it, as do the components that constitute the part, yet each also exists in relation to other segments and to the wider societal whole (Deleuze and Guattari 1987; DeLanda 2006; Robinson 2004). As such, components, parts, segments, and whole exist in a dynamic, mutually interdependent coproductive relationship. The segments constitute the whole, as the whole constitutes the segments, the segments its parts, and the parts their components. Still further, by "parts" we do not mean some stable essence. Rather, parts have been conceptualized as COREL sets, which are historically situated configurations of relatively stable, relatively autonomous constitutive interrelational sets (Henry and Milovanovic 1996).[1] By "wholes" we do not mean totalities; rather, we refer to dynamic systems in process of continuous construction and deconstruction with only relatively stable moments of coherence and longevity, the consequence of which implicates nonlinear dynamics.

This relationship between components, parts, segments, and wholes is not to imply, therefore, a functional system in a Parsonian sense; rather, it is a dynamic set of converging and diverging associations and assemblages between the constitutive units. Consequently, wholes, segments, parts, and components must be studied not as separate "levels," such as the "micro," "meso," and "macro." Rather, components of parts may reconnect with wider segments; parts, in turn, can reconnect with other parts or other components, producing effects that do not necessarily follow linear dynamics. The effects of a component in one part do not necessarily have similar and predictable dynamics when reassembled in other segments (see particularly DeLanda 2006, 8–46). Both unintentional consequences and disproportional effects can result from these emergent properties of alignment and dissociation, convergence and divergence, synthesis and antithesis.

While components, parts, segments, and whole are implicated in each other, and while each contains aspects of the other, the components, parts, segments, and whole are not identical. Because of their multiple alignments, they do not exactly mirror that in which they are embedded but converge and diverge with it as they converge and diverge with other assemblages. Differences between aspects of each of the components, parts, and segments contribute to changes in the whole, as well as to changes in the other parts and segments with which they are related, and produce an ongoing ecological transformation to whole and parts over time. Analysis of any part of society extracted from the whole or from its interrelated components or segments ignores the importance of these multiple convergent and divergent connections, differential and nonlinear movements, thresholds, critical values, singularities, disproportional effects, conflicts and tensions, and variable capacities to affect some thing/one and to be affected by some thing/one. A comprehensive analysis of any component, part, or segment of society must understand each in relation to the others and in relation to the whole that they constitute. Thus, crime and its control are each constitutive parts of society that must be understood in relation to the other parts and segments and the social whole, and they must be understood in the framework of dynamic change.

Constitutive thinking, as outlined above, gave rise to constitutive criminology, a postmodernist-influenced theoretical perspective on crime, crime control, and justice that builds on these fundamental assumptions about the constitutive relationship of components, parts, segments, and wholes. The core of the constitutive argument is that "crime" and its control—as actions, social processes, and parts of a society—cannot be separated from the totality of segments and emergent qualities that comprise the structural and cultural contexts in which they are produced or from the components that comprise human agents' contribution to those contexts (Henry and Milovanovic 1996, 1999; Milovanovic and Henry 1991). In order to understand crime, it is necessary to comprehend the relationships that coproduce it, as well as the ways in which crime contributes to the production of other parts and segments of the society and to the production of the totality that is society. Totality is not to be understood as some static entity; rather, it has emergent properties or potentials that are not necessarily attributable to the sum of the parts. Moreover, in order to understand crime control, it, too, must be examined, not only in relation to crime but in relation to the whole society of which it is a part and to the segments of that society with which it interrelates. Thus, instead of identifying "causes" of offending, constitutive criminology examines relations that coproduce crime with a view toward questioning taken-for-granted assumptions about it and the actions that sustain it.

The various ways in which mundane language (i.e., discourse) is used to create distinctions that identify social objects as separate from the human agents that produce them comprise an essential dynamic within this totality. Additionally, integral to this coproduction are the manifold ways in which discursive distinctions are acted toward as though they exist independently of those who produced them and separate from the society in which they are embedded (reification).

Thus, we ground our view of constitutive penology within three broad-based assumptions of constitutive theory: (1) coproduction, (2) dynamic systems/complexity theory, and (3) reification. We examine how these notions apply to crime and its control and how each embodies the possibility of *transforming* the human subject (Henry and Milovanovic 1996, 1999;

Milovanovic and Henry 1991). This emphasis on the *transformative* possibilities of the human subject represents something of a departure from the original notion of the *recovering subject* as developed in constitutive criminology. In their earlier work, Stuart Henry and Dragan Milovanovic (1996) acknowledged the considerable struggle individuals confront when endeavoring to express their humanity (i.e., to make a difference), given the multiple ways in which it is denied (whether through harms of repression or reduction) by existing structures of discourse and expressions of power. As such, they noted that more fully retrieving or reclaiming or recovering the subject involved a particular understanding about one's humanity. As they suggested, "The substance of being human must . . . entail what precede[s] us as biography, what looms ahead as prospect, caught in the contingent moment of the here and how, plowed by the discordant strands of unconscious processes" (1996, 36). This is a movement away from what constrains the subject (as expressed through language, which names the self, society, and its part to which one is connected) toward a more robust expression of what the subject could *be*. However, here we take the position that the notion of a transformative subject extends and deepens the human agent's possible *becoming*. It directs human agents to the discursive processes that regenerate or revitalize. We might think of the subject who transcends existing categories of identity. This is the individual who continuously reconstitutes his or her humanity—a subject-in-process (Kristeva 1984) always in movement and actively mutating—in order to become more fully human (Deleuze and Guattari 1987).[2] As such, the subject, once having experienced restoration, reclamation, and recovery in being, is only then able to surpass the limitations of even these finite characterizations, categories, and codifications. This transformation entails both the ability to recover the potential of being human and to generate processes that allow for perpetual becoming rather than being or, as Gilles Deleuze (1983) would say, "a people yet to come" (see also Deleuze and Guattari 1986).[3]

Let us then summarize how the main assumptions we make inform this argument. First, human agents, acting in a sociopolitical context, shaped by historical forces of the time, are the active coproducers and reproducers of their dynamic worlds. To the extent that human subjects are the coarchitects of the worlds they define and inhabit and that shape them, the possibility exists of recovering, reclaiming, and transforming one's sense of self, of expanding the capacities to affect others, to be affected, and to experience a continual metamorphosis as a becoming self. This is a vibrant transition from the "idle chatter" (Milovanovic 2003, 230) of modernity[4] and from the idea that humans are somehow unitary selves, operating independently of the structuring effects of the discursive medium through which they act and of which they are embodied.

Assuming an active, though not necessarily unitary, agency—whether or not human subjects are aware of their contribution to that which they produce—foreshadows the possibility of humanity's liberation from its own oppression by the totality of what it produces and by the unity of how it appears.

Second, understanding the interactions of components, parts, segments, and wholes is informed by dynamic systems theory (i.e. chaos/complexity theory). Rather than essences, we have COREL sets or assemblages with various threshold values, at which point they exhibit different capacities to affect others and to be affected (Deleuze 1983; see also Massumi 1992 and DeLanda 2002). For example, Manuel DeLanda, following Deleuze, specifies that *nonlinear* rather than linear causality best explains these occurrences.[5] As he tells us, nonlinearity is "defined by thresholds below or above which external causes fail to produce an effect, that is, thresholds determining the capacities of an entity to be causally affected" (2006, 20; 1997).[6] Similarly, in his work *Becoming Deviant*, David Matza (1969) draws attention to the process of objectification (becoming the assigned label) in which the person's capacity to self-author is rendered less effective. In the extreme, this results in the subject reacting as circumstances suggest (appropriating and acting upon the stigma). In other words, configurations of interrelational sets, which the subject represents, have varying capacities to influence the identity of self and the experience of others. Contrary to much of the modernist analysis that views the subject or the forces within which he or she is immersed as static, constitutive theory sees ongoing change, transformation, mutation, metamorphosis. At certain points, indeed, systems may "jump" to different states (attractor basins), which become the locus from which qualitatively different actions may follow.

The third assumption in our perspective concerns reification. The conceptual and institutional control apparatus of society, being part of the social structure (segment) that we produce, appears to continuously stand above us, disciplining us in accord with the prevailing political economy (Foucault 1977a), and yet its totalizing effects result not from any inherent quality of this apparatus. More recently, Deleuze (1995) has identified a postdisciplinary society, a "control" society, whereby sites of confinement, such as prisons, factories, schools, hospitals, and the family, are all undergoing change increasingly connected to a ubiquitous digital age where differential access to information and subservience to marketing logic reign supreme (see, e.g., the emergence of the actuarial model in criminal justice discussed in Feeley and Simon 2004). These effects are the ongoing outcome of our elevation of this panoptic-control machinery through a continual process of engagement and disengagement with our own agency, which ultimately gives way to the very institutional structures that its creative engagement produces. In other words, human creative agency loses sight of its contribution to what it produces as the reified object of its own subjectivity.

Social constructionists laid the foundation for an understanding of this view of reification (Berger and Luckmann 1967; Quinney 1970; for a review, see Henry 2007). They recognized that reification is part of the constitutive work undertaken when human agents objectify their social relations through discursive practices. To the extent that these constructed realities (i.e., the social and organizational structures of materialist culture that foster harm) can be deconstructed to expose what they signify (technologies of discipline), they also can be reconstructed for what they could be (languages or grammars or vocabularies of possibility). Deleuze and Felix Guattari (1987) also have informed us that in the process of creating strata—more permanent structures ("molar structures")—there always remain deterritorializing forces that tend toward their undoing.[7] With such deconstruction and reconstruction, prospects for alternative and replacement forms of human experience and structural arrangements (always defined in provisional, relational, and positional ways) that humanize the subject are made that much more realizable.[8]

This chapter explores how the implications stemming from these three broad-based assumptions pertaining to constitutive theory inform our understanding of the subject's transformational process. This metamorphosis includes alternative ways in which to define crime as harm. As such, these three presuppositions (i.e., coproduction, nonlinear dynamics, and reification) underscore the perspective on constitutive penology developed throughout this book.

First, we examine constitutive criminology's assessment of the transforming subject, that is, the subject of becoming rather than being. Following the insights of affirmative postmodern inquiry (Rosenau 1992; Henry and Milovanovic 1996; Arrigo, Milovanovic, and Schehr 2005), this includes examining the forces that render the human subject the unitary locus of thought and action and that more aptly redefine the individual as decentered and unstable, although ultimately retrievable, mutable, and transformational. Next, we review the constitutive criminological approach to social structure. Of particular interest are the destabilizing and restabilizing activities by which the institutional and organizational facets of the social are (or can be) fashioned. Once again, insights derived from affirmative postmodern theory inform the analysis.

We then explain how these collective observations on human agency and social structure contribute to an emergent conception of, and response to, the harms that constitute crime. Specifically, by relying on constitutive criminology's definition of crime as the power to harm (Milovanovic and Henry 2001; Henry and Milovanovic 2003), we propose that penological discourses and practices are both the material and symbolic forces that nurture and sustain, reify and legitimize such injury. Moreover, we offer some provisional observations on how human agency as reconstituted in the form of a becoming (i.e., "people yet to come") and social structure as reconstructed represent an alternative and more liberating basis from which to speak about and name harm, including those injuries that occur through the discourse of penology and the prison practices to which this language system is inextricably connected. We suggest a replacement vision of crime control that reconnects the components, parts, and segments to the whole in dynamic configurations rather than furthering the analytical and institutional separation that conventional penology prescribes. However, before we address each of these matters, some general comments on how we view the relationship between penology (including prison life) and the constitutive enterprise are warranted.[9]

CONSTITUTIVE PENOLOGY AND ITS PRESUPPOSITIONS

In so far as it provides the discursive reference for actions that create, develop, and sustain prisons, penology also provides some of the constitutive work that gives form, sustenance, and permanence to the subordination of human agency. Penology, as it is conventionally practiced, is an exercise in separation, categorization, exclusion, isolation, and reification. It is a partial analysis of the societal response to crime, as though the institutions and philosophy of punishing offenders can be precipitously removed from the social order of the disciplinary-control society in whose medium they are suspended. In its broadest sense, traditional penology refers to the systematic study of penal systems, including consideration of their abolition. In a narrower sense, penology is the focused study of the effectiveness of correctional sentencing in preventing reoffending, or the microscopic examination of penal institutions and their routine practices of violence and discrimination impacting those confined. In each instance, the productive content of discursive work in framing, describing, evaluating, and conceptualizing the penal is a crucial aspect of how prisons are maintained and how society conceives of itself as ordered.

With these observations in mind, we follow Deleuze and Guattari (1987) in searching for the appropriate question to ponder. Thus, we ask, to what problem does "prison" respond? In answering this question, as Michel Foucault (1977a) showed, a prison is just one manifestation of a solution to a problem, namely, delinquency and crime as harm. However, we need to identify the way the changing notions of crime and delinquency become connected to a form of prison (Deleuze and Guattari 1987, 66), which is similar to other institutional forms (factories, barracks,

schools, hospitals). We argue that this connection becomes more apparent
when crime and delinquency are redefined as one kind of harm production related to a range of similar institutional forms. We examine the issue
of crime as harm later in this chapter.

Debates over being in and out of prison, over building more or fewer
facilities, about prison overcrowding and prison overspending, about
abuses in prison rather than the abuse that is prison, about alternatives to
incarceration and challenges to those defending prison, all essentialize
PRISON. Moreover, the participants to these prison debates neglect to
consider the continuous and reconstitutive effects that this historically
structured disciplinary discourse legitimizes through their ongoing and
excessive elaboration. Indeed, as John Sloop (1996, 4) notes in *The Cultural
Prison*,

> rhetoric acts as an extraordinary powerful and historical basis by and
> through which cultures and "individuals" are constituted. . . . As discourses
> and definitions become generally accepted within a culture, they are as-
> sumed and hence act as sedimented practices. Particular orders of discourse,
> shared definitions, must exist if human beings are to have consciousness of
> themselves and the world around them. Yet, the need for regularity gives
> such discourses a solidified nature in which change or transition becomes
> difficult.

Theorists (critical or otherwise), penal policymakers, correctional practitioners, and those engaged in the criminal harm of others all coproduce
a discourse that gives form and permanence to the very entity that they
(and we) collectively despise, yet each, as discursively constituted, implicates the necessity of the other.[10] As such, all are *imprisoned* by the language of penology, as we are by the language of crime. Richard Sparks
(2001, 207) incisively observes that "however much penologists have historically claimed to stand on the progressive side of every engagement,
the subject cannot evade complicity in or responsibility for the disciplinary apparatuses erected in its name and especially their regressive consequences for stigmatized and dispossessed people."

It is our contention that the verbalized goals and policies at the manifest level of penology and "corrections," the discursively structured routine of prison life, and the meaning of being behind bars must be understood in relation to various and oftentimes contradictory discursive
practices that sustain, oppose, and attempt to replace them. Moreover,
these discursive constitutive practices are embodied in the disciplinary
whole, the wider discourse of crime and punishment throughout society
and the social order. Correspondingly, these discursive practices constitute the framework that shapes and conveys structures of meaning. But,
as concentrations or iterations of discursively structured meaning, pris-

ons and correctional life can only be adequately discussed in the context of other developments in a given political economy. Indeed, we share Loïc Wacquant's (2005) view of penality, namely, that it is the ensemble of categories, discourses, practices, and institutions concerned with enforcement of the sociocultural order. He argues that it is necessary to understand the intersections between these discursive elements and practices and the major social cleavages of constructed categories[11] of class, race, and gender if we are to explain why it is that the penal has become a major engine of urban and social change in the twenty-first century.

Accordingly, throughout this book, we critically analyze the discursive practices that constitute both penology and the reality of prison existence, while also relating these to the discursive practices that constitute daily life and the structural divisions that separate us from our fellow human subjects.[12] We explore the extent to which all of us are our own jailers, sentenced by our sentences, imprisoned by our words. This is not linguistic determinism since we do not give priority to discourse; rather, we argue that meaning is *both* preconstituted by historically contingent, situated structural processes and shaped by human agents in their recursive use of established discourse in everyday interaction.[13]

However, we argue that the very act of recursivity also allows moments of agency to be mobilized; we *can* escape our sentences. This is because, while repetition tends to produce statistical regularities, ongoing iteration may also produce disproportional effects as suggested by dynamic systems theory. This is also so because emerging forms implicate both stratifying and destratifying processes with often one more dominant, but nevertheless with the other remaining with potential effects. Consider, for example, the position offered by Mary Bosworth (1999a) in her account of women's human agency amid the oppressive prison milieu. As she comments, female incarcerates

> fashion . . . acts of resistance, from positions of weakness. . . . Their resistance occurs in a variety of ways, including religious, cultural or ethnic practices, lesbian activity, education and the idealization of motherhood. . . . They are each an expression of agency, and one which is possible, despite the rigors of confinement. They illustrate that the ability to be an agent transcends the range of choices available, and rests on other, more diffuse, elements which are embedded in the material and symbolic world of the community in which the prison is situated. (1999a, 206–207)

Consistent with this view, the trajectory of this book entertains what an alternative direction might encompass, one that provides an opportunity for the development of new "replacement discourses" (Henry 1994; Milovanovic 2003, 259); that is, how more enabling expressive forms are connected with developing content.[14] These are ways of reconnecting the severed parts of our lives toward integrating them with the wider whole, ways of thinking and acting toward others that affirm their (our) humanity, mutuality, and interdependence. This direction is explored throughout Part I of this volume in which the relationship between constitutive theory and constitutive penology is rendered more complete. Moreover, this direction is illustrated throughout Part II of this volume in which the utility of constitutive penology for specific penological practices/problems is made clearer through relevant applications.

Finally, we note that in our interpretation of replacement discourses, we do not regard the phenomenon as merely another packaged set of ways to talk about and make sense of the world. Rather, replacement discourses embody the logic of Friedrich Nietzsche's "transpraxis" (Henry and Milovanovic 1996). This is a nonreifying and affirmative strategy of engagement, allowing human subjects to speak about their social relations and institutions while speaking through them, conceiving of them not as externalities or objects but as emergent processes closely bound up with our creative being and becoming. By appropriating the strategy of transpraxis, individuals are continuously made aware of the interrelatedness of their agency and the structures they reproduce through the constitutive activity of talking, perceiving, conceptualizing, and theorizing. Thus, as Bruce Arrigo (2001, 220) explains,

> Transpraxis retains the Marxist conviction that theory and practice need to be linked to produce change; however, it also addresses the role of language in such transformations. Transpraxis involves the dialectics of linguistic struggle in which the new, reconstituted order does not recreate conditions of alienation and oppression. Transpraxis is a deliberate and affirmative attempt not to reverse hierarchies but, instead, to affirm those who victimize, marginalize and criminalize while renouncing their victimizing, marginalizing and criminalizing practices. Transpraxis is an effort to validate in the act of resistance. The key to transpraxis is speech, words, grammar and how we talk about (and then act upon) emancipation.

As this chapter subsequently explains, the possibility for transpraxis resides in the constitutive approach to human agency and social structure, and it is to these matters that we now turn.

CONSTITUTIVE CRIMINOLOGY AND HUMAN AGENCY

In order to explain the constitutive approach to "recovering" or reclaiming human agency, including its significance for rethinking the discourse of penology, the notion of the "decentered" or divided subject warrants some consideration. Put simply, humans have a sense of their own self-identity, which appears for the most part through experience and belief as a unified whole, even referred to as the individual, the person. But constitutive theory sees this unity of self as an illusion: humans are multiple selves, even though they desire to be whole and seek to fulfill this desire through often fruitlessly pursuing and receiving recognition from objects of desire and "semiotic fictions" (Nietzsche). Two conceptions of the subject are particularly noteworthy to ground constitutive theory, even though they are both, in many important respects, quite distinct. Jacques Lacan's work in psychoanalytic semiotics represents one understanding; the other is based on the insights of Gilles Deleuze, often in collaboration with Felix Guattari.

Jacques Lacan

Constitutive theory's reliance on the notion of the divided or slashed subject originates in the psychoanalytic semiotic formulations of Jacques Lacan (e.g., 1977, 1981, 1985, 1991; Ragland and Milovanovic 2005).[15] Lacan was a Freudian revisionist who reconsidered Sigmund Freud's developmental theory as taking account of language and symbolic representation. Lacan (1977) made use of Ferdinand de Saussure's (1966) two-part nature of the signifier: the signifier represented an acoustic-image; the signified, the concept (say the word "tree" and a mental representation for a tree materializes). Lacan (1981) also focused on a Hegelian notion of desire. In reworking Freud's (1965) formulations on the unconscious, Lacan (1977) recognized that the subject (the self) was inexorably connected to discourse (to language). For Lacan, language functioned as a "stand-in," a substitute, for the identity of the individual; it spoke for or on behalf of the self (Arrigo and Schehr 1998, 632–33; Henry and Milovanovic 1996, 28–34). Consistent with this, Lacan (1977) argued that the unconscious was structured much like a language. Not surprisingly, then, he examined "the inner workings of that discourse located within the . . . unconscious. For Lacan, this [domain was] the repository of knowledge, power, agency, and desire" (Arrigo 2002, 133).[16]

Lacan's (1981) attention to the unconscious and to the desire embodied in language that spoke for the person[17] led him to identify two planes of subjectivity or two levels of the self: the *subject of speech* and *the speaking subject*. The first of these represents the content or narrative of what the "I" (the person) says or writes. It is the text itself. But, following Jacques Derrida (1977, 1978), the *subject of speech* also represents the metaphysics of presence (the unspoken and obscured subtext) (Arrigo, Milovanovic, and Schehr 2005, 2–3). In other words, when a person speaks, "another plane is hidden which is the locus of the actual producer of the narrative or text" (Milovanovic 2003, 230). This is the concealed, postponed, or deferred self, absent in the spoken or written narrative. The second plane of subjectivity is the *speaking subject*. It signifies the "scripted" meaning that is uttered. Psychoanalytically, it is the language of the "Other" (of the unconscious) that often passes through and functions as a substitute for the identity, individuality, and humanity of the one who speaks or writes. This "Other" is not directly or immediately accessible. Despite this, the question Lacan (1977, 1981) explored throughout the course of his considerable career was one of identifying the voice (language) and way of knowing (desire) that spoke for and on behalf of the subject (the self).[18]

Lacan's (1977, 193–94, 310–16) position that language speaks us, or that it often represents a stand-in for the "real" subject whose identity, regrettably, remains dormant, silenced, and repressed, significantly recasts the established view of human agency (see also Lacan 1988, 243). In effect, contrary to the modernist conception of the purposeful, rational subject developed through the insights of Enlightenment philosophy and Cartesian epistemology (Descartes 1999), the subject is not so much in control of his or her thoughts, whose effects include purposeful and utilitarian action; rather, the subject is much more decentered, divided, and unstable. The force and significance of these observations are particularly apparent in the realm of penology.

Gilles Deleuze

The work of Deleuze, often coauthored with Felix Guattari, initially began in deference to Jacques Lacan (see *Logic of Sense*, 1990a) but evolved into an antipsychoanalytic stance. *Anti-Oedipus* (1983) and *A Thousand Plateaus* (1987) highlighted a polemic against the Freudian edifice. Deleuze subsequently wrote a number of works that transcended the Lacanian notion of the subject. For Deleuze, following Nietzsche, the cosmos signified dynamic forces, some active and some reactive, that were put in relation by a will to power. Some forms were productive: they expanded the capacities of the subject to both affect and be affected in the direction of becoming. Other forms were not productive: they led to nihilism, *ressentiment*, despair, and the creation of semiotic fictions in order to overcome one's existential position of hopelessness. In their two-volume epic work, Deleuze and Guattari (1983, 1987) argued that Lacan's (1977, 1981) subject was mobilized to activity by an inherent lack (*manque d'être*) established through its inauguration into the symbolic order. Hence, desire was based on the not-all (*pas tout/e*). Contrastingly, they argued that desire was active and productive, not reactive. As such, it did not lack anything.

Following Deleuze and Guattari (1983, 1987), desire's natural state was to make connections, to expand its capacities. Similarly to the Lacanian version of subjectivity, they asserted that the self was caught in symbolic play, arising after three syntheses (connective, dealing with libidinal investments; disjunctive, dealing with recording; and conjunctive, dealing with consumption). The subject appeared at a conjunctive synthesis: "So that was me"! "The subject emerges only as an after-effect of the selections made by desire among various disjunctive and connective syntheses, not as the agent of selection" (Holland 1999, 33; Massumi 1992, 75–76). The "I" that emerges, much like in Lacan, often finds itself captured in nominal forms: for Lacan, in the *discourse of the master and university*; for Deleuze, in particular regimes of signs replete with "order words" (akin to Lacan's master signifiers) that are molar and majoritarian.

Accordingly, Deleuze and Guattari (1983, 1987) talked about "larval" selves, the continued development of connections, and the realizations that followed after the fact. At times, however, a concept of self became molar in the sense that it became a statistically predictable event. This is the territorialized, molar self that Deleuze and Guattari (1983, 1986, 1987) and Deleuze (e.g., 1983, 1986, 1989) critiqued throughout their writing. In contrast, they advocated a self in continuous process, a molecular subject that had the capacity to mutate, transform, metamorphosize, and always dwell in the process of becoming. Minor discourses offered maximal potential for this emergent.

The larval subject was always subject to "capture," to being fixed in identity, to having connections repressed or denied, to finding itself in a continuous feedback loop[19] where a static notion of identity was self-reinforced. Thus, the larval subject was further molded by the "socius" (the particular historically situated social formation) and various strata (fixed, molar structures) that formed identities in rigid categories.

Deleuze's notion of the signifier, developed in his early *Logic of Sense* (1990a), was further refined by Felix Guattari and reached its clearest expression in the former's volume on Proust (2000) and in his late two-volume work on the cinema (1986, 1989). Rather than being informed by Saussure, it was inspired by Louis Hjelmslev (later works on the cinema witnessed a focus on C. S. Peirce and Henri Bergson). Rather than a dualistic relationship between the signifier and signified, Deleuze, informed by Guattari, saw a much more dynamic situation of expression and content.[20] Not all was semiotics in the strictest sense; rather, much of what was communicated was nonverbal.

Deleuze and Guattari (1983, 1987) described how certain "regimes of signs" (e.g., one form of expression) became stratified, territorialized, fixing dynamic movement. In their view, stratified society generated "abstract machines," certain logics (e.g., panopticism, rationalization, formal rationality, the equivalent form, capital logic) that tended to create linear outcomes best accounted for by Euclidean geometry. Additionally, stratified society tended to produce "apparatuses of capture," abstract machines that fixed the flow of desire into statistical regularities, establishing the molar subject. It was the oedipal myth that fit quite congruently with the notion of capital logic. Accordingly, their work undermined this connection, a strategy Deleuze and Guattari (1983) termed "schizoanalysis." This concept suggested a new vision of the subject. Their attack was directed toward the molar and major discourses/literatures (Deleuze and Guattari 1986). Their antidote: remain molecular; invest in the molecular, both with regard to the human being and at every "level" of society.

Deleuze and Guattari (1983, 1986, and 1987) accepted Lacan's schematizations on desire as mostly descriptive analyses of how the larval subject became captured in the logic of the Oedipus and capital. Their argument was that Lacan (except for his commentary on the four discourses, 1991) offered little guidance in breaking free from restrictions placed on free-flowing desire. Thus, researchers interested in the contributions of constitutive criminology and penology could gain considerable insight into the plight of the subject by remaining within the Lacanian edifice, especially at the descriptive level. However, as we subsequently demonstrate, Deleuze and Guattari (1983, 1986, 1987) and Deleuze (e.g., 1983, 1986, 1989) provide the bases for an alternative, more complete reading of constitutive criminology and penology. In particular, they went significantly beyond Lacan (1977, 1985, and 1988) in articulating the notion of becoming. This point is addressed more fully throughout other sections of this chapter. For now, though, some examples of the construction of human agency warrant consideration. For illustrative purposes, let us consider the confinement of persons diagnosed with psychiatric disorders.

Applications

The process of civil (Arrigo 1993) and criminal (Arrigo 1996a) incarceration for mental health systems users requires that a separate forensic hearing be conducted in which determinations of one's competency or psychiatric status are assessed. Medicolegal decision brokers (e.g., doctors, psychiatrists, social workers, and therapists) use words or expressions such as "dangerous," "incompetent to stand trial," "psychotic," "guilty but mentally ill," "diseased," "in need of treatment," and "criminally insane" to render judgments about the confinement of "disordered" citizens (Arrigo 2006a). These terms, however, as part of a coordinated and specialized language system (i.e., psycholegal discourse) represent a "master (juridical) narrative . . . produc[ing] a circumscribed knowledge understood [to be] *psychiatric justice*" (Arrigo 2002, 108).[21] Indeed, the joint operation of the medical and legal establishment fills in these terms with selected contents, consistent with their unstated values, effectively reducing the otherwise manifold (and more affirming) meanings (expressions) of these terms to limited possibilities (Arrigo 1996a, 174–75).

For example, to define a person as "diseased" or "in need of treatment" is to imply[22] that the individual is not well and is not able to care for her- or himself. The hidden value unconsciously at work with these descriptors, then, is that the person is a passive, rather than an active, architect of her or his life and, therefore, is not responsible for it. Corrective action is necessary so that the individual can normatively function and be made well (Arrigo 2006a; Arrigo and Williams 1999).

Troubling about this conclusion is that alternative interpretations (minor discourses) for persons with psychiatric (dis)abilities do not find their way into psycholegal discourse. Words or expressions such as "consumer," "mental health systems user," "psychiatric survivor," "disordered citizen," and "one with problems in living," with their corresponding assumptions and values, are denied affirmative recognition within the context of civil and criminal mental health law. Indeed, as a practical matter, in order for persons with psychiatric (dis)abilities to petition for release from civil and/or criminal custody, they must adopt the preexisting parameters of meaning that already define them. They must take up residence in molar categories as a nominalized "I." To resist these linguistically structured medicolegal categories of sense making is to risk sustained confinement in the prison or the hospital (Arrigo 1994, 25–31; 1996b, 151–73). In this particular instance, then, disordered subjects contribute, knowingly or not, to the very victimization of self and the denial of identity they seek to renounce.

However, and importantly, the denial and concealment of the human subject by the disembodied scripting of their identities is not limited to those subject to such classification and processing schemes. Indeed, those medicolegal decision brokers whose discursive productions cloak the identity of their "clients" through the psychiatric reality they utter and weave also objectify those who create such narrative constructions as differently ordered and normally constructed. Medicolegal decision makers become trapped in the caricature that stands in opposition to that which they describe. Indeed, with each layer of diagnostic category, with every turn of the *Diagnostic and Statistical Manual of Mental Disorders-IV-TR* (APA 2001), they are thrown farther into the false, incomplete other that their humanity does not represent and cannot embody. The flow of discourse that enables medicolegal experts to define and manage those mental health consumers subject to corrections and treatment *imprisons* the architects of this very discourse! Their humanity remains concealed; their identity goes unspoken. Those who appropriate the grammar of psychiatric justice (i.e., "professionalese" or "medicolegalese") do so without communicating their own unique subjectivity. Thus, they, too, are unfulfilled, and their speech (and action) endlessly signifies a desire for more complete recognition and understanding.

According to Lacan (1977, 1981), this struggle in discourse is how the concealment of one's true or authentic (albeit fragmented) self occurs. Similarly, with Deleuze and Guattari (1983, 1987), regimes of signs that become stratified in a socius also tend to restrict alternative codifications. The after-the-fact realization, "Ah, that is me," now gets framed in reference to molar categories and identities. For both Lacan (1977, 1985) and Deleuze and Guattari (1983, 1987), the subject emerges as an aftereffect. This is the presence of hegemony (Laclau and Mouffe 2001) assuming a discursive linguistic form (Henry and Milovanovic 1996, 158, 160–62). The subject in speech is therefore *unstable* rather than stable, *decentered* rather than centered (MacCabe 2002, 153). Thus, the mental health citizen, exposed to the machinery of the psychiatric hospital or the correctional facility, is "the embodiment of multiple, overlapping, and contradictory expressions of desire, representing discordant voices [that are] temporarily unified by way of a dominant grammar and language system" (Arrigo 1996b, 168). Simultaneously, mental health professionals who utilize the discourse of psychiatric or penal control for its apparent unity are no less fragmented and decentered. Their human agency becomes subordinated to their "expert" identity, smothered by its order, authority, and hegemony, shattered by the organization of its professional concepts, categories, and treatment regimes, as they ply these disciplinary techniques in the name of helping others.

Although language, as a stand-in, speaks the subject (e.g., Silverman 1983; Pecheux and Nagpal 1982; Deleuze and Guattari 1987), it does not follow that human agency is without implication in the activity of naming or defining reality. Indeed, the divided or decentered subject may actively confront the dialectics of (linguistic) struggle (Henry and Milovanovic 1996, 170–77). For example, while structural forces and their associated social processes (e.g., the criminal justice and mental health systems) announce the humanity of mentally ill offenders (Arrigo 2002), "disordered citizens" can and do contribute to that which defines them (e.g., participation in consumer self-help groups). As Pierre Bourdieu and Wacquant explain (1992, 167–68), "Social agents are knowing agents who, even when they are subjected to determinisms, contribute to producing the efficacy of that which determines them in so far as they structure what determines them." Thus, subjects help to develop or to produce the very social forms of which they are a part. Recovering subjects, however, are not necessarily cognizant of the world that they coshape.[23]

Indeed, "the world produced by human agency is only episodically perceived as the outcome of its own authorship: much of the time we are forgetful producers of our world" (Henry and Milovanovic 1996, 37). This forgetfulness returns us to the power of those social and structural forces that define our existences and mark our realities (subject us to various forms of "capture") in ways that are never neutral, saturated as they are in cloaked values and concealed assumptions, the ideological discourses that inconspicuously convey something more or something other about our identities. The stock of our cultural and personal experiences, the expanse of our philosophical, political, and religious alliances, the magnitude of our institutional, organizational, and corporate allegiances all constitute our "habitus" (Bourdieu 1984; Rosenau 1992, 59), our socius (Deleuze and Guattari 1987). Therefore, the substance of human agency and of becoming must entail something more.

Indeed, in this scripted process of being endlessly decentered, the subject can be reconstituted into a mutating, becoming subject. Without ongoing, active engagement from individuals, there would be no world, no cultures, no social conditions, and no socius. "Human agency is connected to the structures that it makes, as are the human agents [connected] to each other in making those structures" (Henry and Milovanovic 1996, 39). Discourse is pivotal to how agents transcend their historically mediated, discursively constituted, and structurally situated existences. Recovering agency and the dynamics of becoming, then, involves reclaiming one's affirmative place in the dialectical play of speech. As Paulo Freire (1973, 76) observed, "To exist, humanly, is to *name* the world [and then] to change it. Once named[,] the world . . . reappears to the namers as a problem and requires of them a new *naming*. Men [and women] are not built in silence[; they are built] in word, in work, in action-reflection."

The constitutive challenge for the revitalizing and rejuvenating subject is to resist the organizing parameters of meaning that "speak" the person; that is, through discourse, human investment in the linguistic (and therefore social) reproduction of established molar structures must be displaced and become, in short, molecular rather than molar. To accomplish this, human agency, thus one's potential liberation, must be in flux, mutable, and in process (Kristeva 1984). The molar and molecular, not in practice dichotomous, must appear as tendencies with tensions remaining where each may, as historically contingent emergents, become more dominant or subservient. Transformation for the regenerating subject necessarily includes the development of alternative vocabularies of meaning. These are "replacement discourses" (Henry and Milovanovic 1996, 41, 214–29), "minor literatures" (Deleuze and Guattari 1986) that embody the disparate voices of, and ways of knowing for, those marginalized by the prevailing language system in use (e.g., penological, medical, or legal discourse). Through these alternative vocabularies, "the aim is to [replace] an inchoate life narrative [with] a congruent one, and [to] transform . . . [the] meanings that previously blocked the person's story with new ones" (Omer and Strenger 1992, 253). This approach acknowledges that people are "their own authors and can become [their own] poets" (Parry and

Doan 1994, 47). We can be the jazz players making meaning that is the music of becoming.

Thus, reclaiming one's rightful place as the architect of one's life means that people must be given the requisite (reflective) space within which to create and speak "true words" (Freire 1973, 56–67) about themselves, about their interpersonal exchanges, and about the social world humans develop. Expressive forms of the nonlinguistic variety, too, must be expanded. Ironically, the most difficult challenge in this regard is the recovery of the human subject from the confines of certain professional (health care) discourses. The assembling of more and more ways to define and claim truth about the world—the enterprise embodied in the Enlightenment and the colossus that is modernism—is, for those subjected to its authority and for those espousing its deity, the tomb that must be lifted from the struggling, despairing subject.

As this discussion on human agency reveals, the decentered subject can be retrieved. This retrieval or recovery entails an active, deliberate effort to fashion new or alternative vocabularies of meaning in which one's identity, one's being, is more fully embodied in various discourses and other forms of expression. However, as delineated in this section, the potential of human agency entails much more than this. Ultimately, that which is recovered also must be open to processes of revitalization, renewal, and transformation. Thus, the metamorphosis of being is directed toward the future becoming or continual evolution of the person. This is the realm of the transformative subject. However, human agency is inexorably connected to the material world in which it exists. Therefore, constitutive theory must address the dynamics of social structure at whose interstices are found the spaces for departure from its grip. It is to this matter that we now turn.

CONSTITUTIVE CRIMINOLOGY AND SOCIAL STRUCTURE

The constitutive position on social structure or form does not subscribe to an objective, reductionistic, or historically fixed characterization for social order. Nor does a dualistic base-superstructure capture its direction. Rather, "social structure is a cluster of ideas and images about order and its maintenance, a collection of humans oriented to uphold their version of these images, the reality of the outcomes that follow from actions they take to bring this about, and the potential to transform these images, actions and outcomes" (Henry and Milovanovic 1996, 65). Thus, the construction of social reality is a *coproduction* in which "structure (the individual-social) and agency (active-passive) are mutually implicated in any production of knowledge" (Henry and Milovanovic 1996, 65; see also Giddens 1984).

Constitutive theory acknowledges that the principal means by which structural or organizational forces are given expressive form is through language,[24] and it is through the spoken or written word that the dialectical play of meanings (and their differential effects) embedded in these phenomena receive (circumscribed) narrative coherence (e.g., Derrida 1977, 1978; Jackson 1995; Deleuze and Guattari 1987). The prison system—the prison-form as we have previously suggested—responds to a problem; however, it is but one possible response, one possible coherent narrative and structured reality (Deleuze and Guattari 1987, 66–67; Foucault 1977a, 231–33). Indeed, as Foucault (1977a, 231) has argued,

> it had already been constituted outside the legal apparatus when, throughout the social body, procedures were being elaborated for distributing individuals, fixing them in space, classifying them, extracting from them the maximum in time and forces, training their bodies, coding their continuous behaviour, maintaining them in perfect visibility, forming around them an apparatus of observation, registration and recording, constituting on them a body of knowledge that is accumulated and centralized.

The notion of delinquency and the delinquent, then, as forms of expression lies in "reciprocal presupposition" with the prison-form (Deleuze and Guattari 1987, 66). The emergent content (prisonization discourse) and its signification "is reducible not to a thing but to a complex state of things as a formation of power (architecture, regimentation, etc.)" (Deleuze and Guattari 1987, 55–67). Consistent with this position, constitutive penology maintains that distinctions, boundaries, and divides created between prison and nonprison (e.g., the kept and their keepers, the public and those punished) belie the underlying constitutive process. Fictional binaries such as these ignore or dismiss the coconstitutive, mutually dependent, and reciprocal nature of structure and agency in which distinctiveness and separateness are not assumed. Instead, coproduction exists.[25]

To illustrate, consider the execution of persons with mental illness who invoke a right to refuse treatment (Arrigo 2006a; Arrigo and Taska 1999). The narrative that coheres in this instance is intimately linked to how the *prison system* and its *agents* interpret competency, treatment refusal, and mental illness (Arrigo and Williams 1999). As a constructed text, the structural response (i.e., execution or stay of execution) is laden with a multitude of meanings anchored, however, in a coordinated, stratified language system (i.e., medicolegal discourse),[26] producing circumscribed images about mentally ill offenders on death row (prisoners as diseased, deviant, and dangerous) taken to be de facto reality (Arrigo 2002).

In this instance, human beings with capacities to affect and to be affected are interpreted through restrictive expressive forms and a bounded locus of signification within which to coproduce their identities. This narrower locus enables medicolegal technicians, professionals, and specialists to utilize their classificatory and reductionistic agendas, a locus with which even the subjected often come to identify in their ongoing coproductions of reality. These are summary representations (Knorr Cetina 1982, 36–37; see also Knorr Cetina 1999) in which spoken meanings become everyday constructions, given the behavior organized around them (e.g., forensic psychiatrists assessing competency for execution and predicting dangerousness, approaching mental illness as a disease, and testifying in court as "experts" about both). As a result, these images and selected meanings establish themselves as concrete entities, that is, "real" categories of classification, notwithstanding the provisional, relational, positional, and thus unstable nature of social forms and structures (Arrigo 1995, 452–54).

Constitutive theorists argue, therefore, that society's molar statistical regularities (e.g., institutions, culture, socius), as energized by human actions and as organized around their discursive categories, are relations of the power to define others and, in the process, also define their users. Constitutive theorists deconstruct the psycho-social-cultural matrix (COREL sets) of a given society to assess how each relationship and each relational set is embodied in an order (e.g., a prison-form). Moreover, such theorists consider what maintains and sustains that order and how crime and its control are microcosms of the relations of power that constitute the wider order in which they, too, are situated. It is not that crime, as a relation of power, is separate from the broader institutional realm to which it is connected; rather, it is both an extreme representation and a mundane manifestation of those very same relations. A similar logic obtains with respect to crime control.

Indeed, the punishment meted out to those who inflict harm on others, especially when that injury is separated out and identified in criminal law as warranting penalties, is comparable in form to the daily sanctioning children receive when violating the patriarchal/matriarchal rules of their families.[27] It is similar in form to the discipline exercised by the teacher over the student for disobedient behavior or for failure to complete assignments. Consider, as well, workplace employees who receive verbal reprimands, write-ups, or other supervisory warnings by employers for poor productivity, absenteeism/tardiness, ethical misconduct, or other job-related infractions. These examples from education and work represent the exercise of power and exclusion over those who violate prevailing definitions of acceptable or normative conduct wherein the institutional displays of power and exclusion demonstrably affect others. Most especially, however, these are instances in which decision makers and power brokers utilize their position of authority when feeling challenged, threatened, demeaned, or somehow disrespected by the behavior of those lacking such standing.

These day-to-day relations of power that order society and its institutional and organizational structures are left out of the definitions of crime and punishment. These routine interactions, as constitutive of the definition of harm, demonstrate how the vast number of individuals in subordinate relations to others (teachers, bosses) are injured by the authority (the power) that these superiors have over them as subordinates wield harm against those who have authority over them. This is the cycle of human destructiveness in which both agency and various structures are, in far too many instances, coproduced. The resultant coercive conditions of inequality, structured along multiple criteria or created categories of division (e.g., class, race, gender, ethnicity, ability, age, and weight, as well as their intersectional nature) are sustained in daily microinteractions and reified through major institutional entities. These entities, including the educational and employment sectors, embrace the view and send the message that one's liberation through another's oppression will foster progress and change. However, this logic merely characterizes the hierarchical societal form. To illustrate, consider the classic Stanford "Prison Experiment" (Haney, Banks, and Zimbardo 1973; Zimbardo 2007).

Social psychologist Philip Zimbardo extended the experimental research of colleague Stanley Milgram (1974) on authority and obedience. Zimbardo showed how groups of people could become empowered to abuse those similar to them simply by being defined as having authority through their role in an organizational structure (a prison). Zimbardo designed his experiment to examine how far a structured situation could affect the actions of its incumbents, especially when these persons became anonymous. He used a sample of twenty-four of the "best and brightest" Stanford University students, who were all in good physical and mental health and had no history of crime or violence, and randomly assigned them to play the roles of prisoner and guard. Those designated prisoners were "arrested," booked, given IDs, stripped, deloused, and assigned institutional smocks. Those designated guards patrolled, in groups of three, the captive "prisoners," who were to be held in confinement for two weeks. During the second day, the "prisoners" resisted their confinement by barricading themselves in their cells by putting their beds against their doors. Zimbardo (2007, B6) describes what happened next:

> Suddenly the guards perceived the prisoners as "dangerous"; they had to be dealt with harshly to demonstrate who was boss and who was powerless. At first, guard abuses were retaliation for taunts and disobedience. Over time the guards became ever more abusive, and some even delighted in sadistically tormenting their prisoners. Though physical punishment was restricted, the

guards on each shift were free to make up their own rules, and they invented a variety of psychological tactics to demonstrate their dominance over their powerless charges. . . . The actual behaviors that were enacted in the prison simulation . . . are a lesson in "creative evil," in how certain social settings can transform intelligent young men into perpetrators of psychological abuse.

The abuse was so bad that the mock prison experiment had to be stopped after six days, and after five days, students had to be released early because of extreme stress. Most of those who remained "adopt[ed] a zombie-like attitude and posture, totally obedient to escalating guard demands" (Zimbardo 2007, B6). Zimbardo reflects on how "the situational forces in that 'bad barrel' had overwhelmed the goodness of most of those infected by their viral power." He asks how the experiment could have descended into a hellhole, how good personalities could become so dominated by a bad situation, and how it was possible that human character could be so dramatically transformed in a matter of days. He considers how psychologists, researchers, and parents could fall under the spell of the experimenter's authority and how they allowed the experiment to continue as long as it did, subsequently resulting in full-blown emotional meltdown for several of the students. Zimbardo (2007, B7) continues,

> We had created a dominating behavioral context whose power insidiously frayed the seemingly impervious values of compassion, fair play, and belief in a just world. The situation won; humanity lost. . . . I believe that most of us tend to be fascinated with evil not because of its consequences but because evil is a demonstration of power and domination over others. . . . The Stanford prison experiment is but one of a host of studies in psychology that reveal the extent to which our behavior can be transformed . . . to deviate in unimaginable ways, even to readily accepting a dehumanized conception of others as "animals," and to accepting spurious rationales for why pain will be good for them. . . . We humans exaggerate the extent to which our actions are voluntary and rationally chosen—or to put it differently, we all underestimate the power of the situation. My claim is not that individuals are incapable of criminal culpability; rather it is that . . . the situation and the system creating it also must share in the responsibility for illegal and immoral behavior. . . . Veiled behind the power of the situation is the greater power of the system which creates and maintains complicity at the highest military and government levels.

Unlike Zimbardo, we believe that what became apparent in his prison experiment—widely revealed through the realities of the recent abuses at the Abu Ghraib and Guantanamo Bay prisons—is simply an extreme manifestation of all hierarchical power relations. As he warns, "Evil is a demonstration of power and domination over others" (Zimbardo 2007,

B7). Indeed, we argue that more or less evil can be equated to more or less power and domination. Thus, constitutive theorists maintain that relationships of inequality established throughout the whole society and embedded in and reflected throughout its organizational and cultural arrangements translate into specific harmful relationships between the powerful and the powerless. Social processes of inequality not only produce directly harmful outcomes but also provide a blueprint, a "diagram" (Deleuze 1988), for how relationships operate. Zimbardo's (Haney, Banks, and Zimbardo 1973) college students did not have to create the concept of abuse in response to resistance to their authority; they simply had to create new and situationally constructed forms. They moved so readily to this abuse because evil or harm, as a demonstration of power, is inimical to power differentials. For the constitutive theorist, human relationships in hierarchically ordered societies as different as those in the United States, Europe, China, or India, for example, are first and foremost relationships of and about unequal power. Accordingly, these relationships represent relations of harm in which only some are defined as crime.

The power that frames or diagrams human relationships may be formal and stabilized as in corporations, organizations, or government agencies or in social institutions, such as marriage and family. This power may be traditionally established as part of a historical and cultural context, as in relations between different races, ethnicities, and genders. Moreover, it may be informal and fluctuating, as in subcultural groups or within interpersonal relationships among otherwise similar individuals. A brief reflection on harmful relationships, whether encountered in families through male-dominated patriarchal households impacting children, or experienced in the workplace by abusive organizational structures, or witnessed in race-divided neighborhoods or ethnically divided communities, reveals the range and extent to which normal relations are relations of power. As such, they are relations of greater or lesser harm.

In any of these frames of power, harm is either a manifest or latent outcome. Harm is not so much caused by inequality as it is embedded in relations of inequality. Constitutive theory seeks to demonstrate the ways in which harm is the frequent expression of unequal power relationships, to reveal the ways that some of this harm is labeled as crime while some is not, and to expose the ways in which some of this harm is labeled as control.

This analysis of the discursive coproduction of reality—that is, of hierarchically ordered relations of power sustained through discursive activity—leaves open the door to possible symbolic and material transformation. Constitutive theory allows us to comment critically on what "is" and to suggest reflexively what "could be." Organizational and social conditions, as relations of power, once constituted as summary representations, depend on the investment of humans to sustain these constructions in everyday discourse, with their implied values and hidden assumptions (Henry and Milovanovic 1996, 68). However, these constructions—particularly those that are marginalizing and alienating, oppressive and subordinating—can be exposed, reversed, destabilized, or dismantled. The activity of deconstruction (e.g., Derrida 1977) allows us to decode the meanings embedded in the words or phrases used to name the very oppressive forms or images we help to create. In addition, a reidentification with nonterritorialized modes of communication or "minor literature/discourses" (Deleuze and Guattari 1987, 1986), more fully affirming of the speaking being, is possible provided we accept the "relative autonomy of structures and subject as well as their dependence in the coproduction of social reality" (Henry and Milovanovic 1996, 69). This is what Anthony Giddens (1984) means when describing the *duality* or mutuality of structure and agency. Both have meaning apart from, and because of, one another. This is why our notion of COREL sets, combined with assemblage theory and our notion of coproduction, provides strategies for going beyond the dualism of structure and agency.

Thus, in relation to the deconstructive/reconstructive possibilities for structure, "the social properties of social systems are both medium and outcome of the practices they recursively organize. Structure is not 'external' to individuals. . . . [It] is in a certain sense more 'internal' than exterior to their activities. Structure is not to be equated with constraint but is always [to be understood as] both constraining and enabling" (Giddens 1984, 25). Parts, however, with some qualification to Giddens, are not somehow stitched together into a "seamless whole" (DeLanda 2006, 10); rather, components of parts can disengage and reengage in ever-new configurations (diagrams) with nonlinear effects. Moreover, parts do not necessarily have similar effects if reconfigured in a different COREL set. Still further, what appears as a seamless whole is only one moment of possible manifestation; each moment is an instance of becoming that can be captured within the logic of a particular political economy within a historical formation; tensions within, however, tend to realignment. Thus, every moment, in the form of a distinct stratum, exhibits both territorializations and deterritorializations, and each seamless whole tends toward change.[28]

A fundamental series of questions follows from the constitutive position on social structure. In particular, who is enabled, in what ways, and at whose expense, given existing structural arrangements and cultural practices? Are there ways in which existing structures of power could be reconstituted such that their relations of power were less harmful in the sense of being less exploitative, less oppressive, and, in the broadest sense of the term, less criminogenic, more enabling, and more generating of active forces? Stated differently, "If . . . the goal is actually to reduce the behavior that we now call 'criminal' (and its resultant suffering) . . . then [isn't] the criminal justice system . . . obligated . . . to confront the situation and our role in creating and perpetuating it?" (Zimbardo 2007, B7). In order to examine this set of questions and, indeed, to focus on what needs confronting, it is important first to explore the idea of crime as power since, if crime is restricted to only those expressions of power defined by criminal law, then we will not have addressed the underlying problem but only an extreme manifestation of it.

In short, an examination is needed not only of expressive forms (labels for harm) but also of their content (how emerging configurations or diagrams of hierarchical power can translate into harm). Thus, unlike a Saussurian (1966) dualistic analysis of signifier (legalistic definition) and signified (traditionally understood harms), an alternative inquiry would open discussion to various forms of expression and various forms of content. The key question, then, would be focused on how the two come to be connected in distinct strata, soci, and regimes of signs.

CONSTITUTIVE CRIMINOLOGY AND CRIME AS THE POWER TO HARM

Constitutive criminology sees current legalistically defined crime as a subset of harmful behavior/action. It is but one expressive form. It is that set of behavior that has been defined by governmental processes and the politics implied in these as sufficiently offensive to those having the power and occasionally the authority to warrant state sanction. Similar insidious behavior that is likewise harmful is excluded from this definition. Theorists, dating back at least to Edwin Sutherland, have argued for a more expansive definition, one that would include white-collar, corporate, and state crime, as well as crimes against humanity (Sullivan and Tifft 2005). We are not exploring how or why that occurs (for an overview of approaches to the definition of crime, see Henry and Lanier 1998, 2001). Instead, we simply want to clarify that of the three principal elements that define crime—extent of harm, severity of official sanctions as defined by a government process, and consensus about seriousness—the element of harm is the most critical. This is because it is independent of the political process (though harm may be brought about through it), unlike official responses/sanctions, which can be manipulated by powerful interest groups, and consensus, which can be manipulated by the interests operating through the media. In contrast, "harm" can be measured by its impact on victims as they experience its pain and undergo suffering from its infliction.[29] From this expansive definition, any actions or processes that produce harm can be redefined as "crime." So what is harm?

From the constitutive perspective, harm is the investment of energy in injury-producing, socially constructed relations of power based on inequalities constructed around differences. Harms are actions and processes that deny or prevent us from being or becoming fully human. Being human means to make a difference in/to the world, to act on it, to interact with others and together to transform the environment and ourselves; it is the capacity to affect and to be affected; it is becoming (mutating, evolving, transforming) and not merely existing. If this process is prevented or limited, we become less than human; as such, we are harmed. Thus, constitutive criminologists define crime from the point of view of harm as "the power to deny others their ability to make a difference" (Henry and Milovanovic 1996, 116). The paradox of constitutive criminology is that while the making of difference constitutes what it is to be human, the use of difference (often expressed through such categories as race, gender, age, ability, and the like) that denies or compromises another's right to be different or to make a difference is what constitutes the harm that is crime.

Moreover, going beyond critics of this position, which on its surface seems purely normative, some draw attention to Deleuze's and Nietzsche's discussions of active and reactive forces to locate potential evaluative criteria. Reactive forces are "forces of adaptation or conservation" (Deleuze 1983, 41); active forces are those of mutation and transformation (Nietzsche 1969; see also Patton 2000, 60–67). It is will to power that activates the interplay between the two. Accordingly, where reactive forces dominate, nihilism, resentment, despair, and Thanatos predominate; where active forces dominate, mutation, transformation, becoming, and Eros predominate. Each can then become the locus of "lines of flight," flows of either reactive or active energy. The former (reactive) tends toward molar structures; the latter (active) tends toward molecular structures. Thus, evaluation hinges on genealogically discerning the alignment of historically contingent forces, and this alignment cannot be predicted in advance to necessarily produce "good" results in the long run. Indeed, as Paul Patton (2000, 67, 68) reminds us, we should always be vigilant as to how lines of flight actually manifest themselves in historically specific political economies (relatively stable configurations of COREL sets).

The nucleus of crime, then, is harm. However, in so far as harm is an act that denies another's humanity, it is also an expression of power. In taking from or removing or limiting another, against his or her will or through deception, power is used to negative effect. It is the mobilization of and investment in reactive forces. The act of harm is an expression of power that brings about the transformation from how the victims were before that act compared to how they are after the act. Does this mean that all expressions of power are harmful? From the constitutive perspective, expressions of power that enable or empower some but do not, in the process, deny others their humanity are not harmful; rather, they are facilitative. They facilitate the potential of individuals to make a difference. Expressions of power resulting in the disempowerment of others, expressions whose own manifestations of authority, strength, or influence are enabling, are harmful and constitute crime as we have defined it.

Constitutive criminology divides crime, the expression of power that limits another's humanity, into two types: *crimes of reduction* and *crimes of repression*. Harms of reduction occur when people experience a loss of some quality relative to their present standing. They could have property stolen from them, but they could also have dignity stripped from them, as in hate crime or forms of petit apartheid (Milovanovic and Russell 2001). Harms of repression occur when people experience a limit or restriction, preventing them from achieving a desired position or standing or from realizing an accomplishment, as occurs through sexism or racism.

Considered along a continuum of deprivation, harms of reduction or repression can be based on an infinite number of constructed differences or values. In Western industrial societies, such harms cluster around familiar, socially and discursively constructed differences: economic status (class, property), gender (sexism), race and ethnicity (racism, hate), political status (power, corruption), morality, human rights, social position (status/prestige, inequality), psychological state (security, well-being), self-realization/-actualization, biological integrity, and so forth. Whatever the construction, actions are harms either because they move a human subject away from a position or state that the individual currently occupies or because they prevent a person from inhabiting a desired position or state, the achievement of which does not deny or deprive another. However, actions and processes are not considered harms of repression when they limit the undertakings of some person or group to make a difference, particularly when such individuals or collectives endeavor to thwart or restrict the attempts of others to do the same. Where attempts to achieve a desired position or standing are themselves limiting to others, then the repression of these attempts might be more accurately termed "control." Such control is, to some extent, also always a crime of repression, but the manner in which this control is achieved can be more or less harmful, and it can be more or less justified.

Accordingly, the difference between harm and simply a change rests on the following conditions (see Milovanovic and Henry 2001, 167):

(a) . . . whether the person or entity suffering the change perceives it as a loss . . . ;
(b) . . . whether the person or entity is fully free to object to the exercise of power responsible for imposing the reduction . . . ;
(c) . . . whether they are free to resist it . . . ; and
(d) . . . whether their resistance is able to prevent the reduction from occurring.

"Change," in short, "must be co-produced through a process of conscious active participation by all of those affected by it, such that those affected are able to define their own future—and particularly their own level of risk—and not have this imposed on them by others" (Milovanovic and Henry 2001, 167).

To illustrate, some forms of restorative justice are quite compatible with this understanding of change, in so much as the parties jointly reach an agreement (coproduction) rather than the settlement being unilaterally imposed downward by state power (harm). This conceptualization of harm can also be applied to other sectors. Mark Halsey (2006a, 55), for example, makes a case for applying it to environmental-damage issues, writing "What matters is not the truth or falsity [of Henry and Milovanovic's definition of harm] . . . so much as *how it might be put to work*. That is, what counts is the fact that such a definition may open up new discursive and *extra*-discursive pathways where other definitions have fallen short."[30]

Similarly, Simon Pemberton's (2004) theory of "moral indifference" argues that the expressive form is given in traditional criminal justice practices to intentional acts as opposed to "acts of indifference." In our view, in either case, if harms of reduction or repression follow, that is harm. Thus, the indifference of the International Monetary Fund, the World Bank, and the World Trade Organization to the impoverished areas of the world, while they privilege transnational corporations, constitutes harm. For Pemberton (2004, 72), in order to fall into an equivalent category of intention, "an actor or a group of actors must be shown to be capable of intervening"; if they are, then "indifference has been demonstrated to be the implicit causal factor."

At this point, we can develop a further approximation. If our constitutive theory of harm centers on "the power to deny others their ability to make a difference," and if we are to recognize innovative theorizing such as the crimes of indifference spelled out by Pemberton, we can suggest processes that generate configurations that enhance the ability of others to make a difference. In this direction, several authors are suggestive: Emmanuel Levinas (1987, 2004), writers of feminist care ethics (Gilligan 1982; Clement 1998), Zygmunt Bauman (1989), and Derrida (1991, 1995; see also Caputo 1997; Critchley 1999). Each in his or her own way dramatically demonstrates that law and justice are separate domains. Law, argues Derrida, is more akin to economics (calculation, equivalence); justice is more compatible with a duty to the other (it is not calculable and is not in the realm of economics). Derrida (1991, 1995), following Levinas, argues for the duty to the other, which is unfathomable, unconditional. It is beyond quantification. Similarly, Carol Gilligan (1982) and Grace Clement (1998) have shown that an ethics of responsibility (its central concern is to assign fault and to appropriate punishment) finds itself in a dominant role over an ethics of care (its central concern is to understand the contextual factors involved and seek reconciliation). The dominance of the former is directly connected to a phallocentric order. In short, these new directions in imaginative thinking provoke us to think about possible alternative forms for the socius. This is a form of reconceptualizing and engaging the other. This is a form in which the molecular is dominant over the molar, and the modal form of interpersonal relations privileges support for the other, recognizing the other, understanding the other, empathizing with the other, or, as Deleuze tells us, "becoming other."

This recasting of the meaning of crime/harm as an expression of power that disempowers others raises serious questions when applied to a class-based hierarchical society that is characterized by preexisting substantive inequalities, and it has serious implications for institutions within, such as prisons, that are designed both to reduce and to repress, indeed to limit, the humanity of others. In the case of an unequal society, the question becomes, is the disempowerment of those with greater power (e.g., wealth, status, prestige) through laws, such as the tax law, or other means a crime/harm under this definition? Clearly, for example, those wealthy who are disempowered by progressive taxes experience no less harm than the disempowered poor. Is this justified based on the fact that the affluent have accumulated their positions in society through the exploitation of others? To be more concrete, how would one judge the actions of Robert Mugabe's regime against white farmers in Zimbabwe according to this definition of crime/harm? Similarly, is affirmative action that privileges disempowered blacks over empowered whites a crime against whites? As numerous backlash lawsuits have shown, these disempowered whites think so. Similarly, the fining and imprisonment of Enron executives would meet all the criteria identified earlier for what counts as a crime of reduction in that these executives, as subjects of a system of control, resisted these "changes" (to which they were then subjected), which they perceived as a personal loss; nor were they fully free to resist them or to prevent the reduction from occurring; several, such as Jeffrey Skilling, Andrew Fastow, and Kenneth Lay, were fined and imprisoned while objecting. The question facing constitutive criminologists is then, was the form of reduction experienced by Enron executives due to the Justice Department's prosecution a crime based on our definition of the exercise of power over others? In each of these cases, additional harms are being created in an attempt to reempower those who have been subordinated by the dominant group's expression of power. Constitutive criminology argues that this is equally harm producing. Instead, strategies are needed to engage the powerful critically but without stigmatizing judgment, ridicule, or, indeed, injury, while simultaneously affirming and empowering those whom they have oppressed. This cannot involve additional exercises that reverse power since not only do these harm those subject to its exercise, but this also undermines their ability to make good the harms they have created. Rather, collaborative redistributions of power must occur such that those suffering from the original disempowerment are compensated and restored by those who exercised the original harm. We will develop this notion further in the context of our discussion of an alternative form of penology.

NOTES

1. COREL sets have numerous compatibilities with Deleuze and Guattari's (1987) notion of "assemblages" (see also DeLanda 2006). DeLanda (1997) earlier developed the notion of "meshwork" that resonates with COREL sets.

2. See also Arrigo, Milovanovic, and Schehr (2005) for applications in crime and justice studies.

3. We note, however, that the transformative subject can also temporarily locate identities that are potentially damaging or destructive to self and/or to others. For example, consider the narrative biographical performance the Virginia Polytechnic Institute shooter, Cho Seung-Hui, provided the media. In this instance, *becoming-a-killer* represents the considerable absence of more fully recovering one's humanity and, in fact, demonstrates how the shooter profoundly struggled to exist with others at a college campus. Instead, our version of the transforming subject recognizes that recovering human agency is a gateway to possible metamorphosis for the subject. Consider, for instance, the person who is defined as physically or psychologically disabled. The individual struggles, in discourse, to convey his or her humanity. Typically, institutional and cultural forces relegate the individual to the status of being diseased, deviant, or dangerous. However, following recovery (through self-organization, therapeutic intervention, or otherwise), the subject may indeed possess the ability to redefine his or her humanity, to transcend the boundaries of the socially imposed and alienating description. The subject may even experience some profound, life-altering clarity about his or her self-identification as disabled such that this physical or psychological condition enables the subject to comprehend what others cannot yet understand. To illustrate, the person who is blind may experience illumination beyond the abilities of those who

are sighted; the person who is deaf may experience attentiveness beyond the abilities of those who hear; the person who confronts cancer, drug addiction, AIDS, and mental illness may appreciate that human becoming occurs not despite these "afflictions" but *because* of them. This is what is meant by the transformative subject. This is a moment of self-discovery and, indeed, lucid insight.

4. The "idle chatter" to which we allude is a reference to Cartesian epistemology and Enlightenment philosophy. In this view, the subject is stable, active, centered, and in control; the subject is the locus of reason, progress, truth, and purpose. This view is contained in Descartes' (1999) maxim *cogito ergo sum* (I think therefore I am). In the realm of law, the unified self construct is found in the notion of the "juridic subject"; in criminology, it is found in the "rational person" assumption of rational choice theory (see Arrigo, Milovanovic, and Schehr 2005, 2). As we subsequently explain in our constitutive approach to human agency, insights derived from a Lacanian (1977) postmodern interpretation of the subject indicate that the individual is more decentered, divided, and unstable than in control. This is because of the intervening role that language assumes in the constitution of identity. In brief, language routinely functions as a substitute, a "stand in," for the humanity and individuality of the person who speaks. Thus, as Lacan (1977, 166) noted, "I think where I am not, therefore I am where I do not think." This Lacanian postmodern rendering of the subject helps to ground our constitutive approach to human agency, especially in relation to penology, prison life, and the identities that are constructed for, by, and about both.

5. As Stewart (1989, 139) has said, "So docile are linear equations that the classical mathematicians were willing to compromise their physics to get them. So the classical theory deals with shallow waves, low-amplitude vibrations, small temperature gradients. So ingrained became the linear habit that by the 1940s and 1950s many scientists and engineers knew little else. . . . Linearity is a trap. The behavior of linear equations . . . is far from typical. But if you decide that only linear equations are worth thinking, self-censorship sets in. Your text-books fill with the triumph of linear analysis, its failures buried so deep that the graves go unmarked and the existence of the graves goes unremarked."

6. As DeLanda (1997, 263) says, a key in analysis is identifying key parameters: "at any one moment in the system's history it is the degree of intensity of these parameters . . . that defines the attractors available to the system and, hence, the type of forms it may give rise to (that is, at critical values of these parameters, bifurcations occur which abruptly change one set of attractors into another)."

7. For instance, as Hardt and Negri (2000, 2004) demonstrate, with the coming of "empire" (a new world order of power and domination), novel forces of subversion, the "multitude," appear as the new group in opposition. In some ways, this is a response to the dialectics of Marx. Immanent within COREL sets are both stabilizing and destabilizing forces, or as Deleuze and Guattari (1987) tell us, territorializing and deterritorializing forces; where the former ascends, we may witness molar orientations, where the latter, molecular.

8. Implicated in this constitutive rendering of one's being and becoming is the reconceptualization of ontology. We suggestively revisit this matter throughout this volume. A more explicit, though provisional, review of our philosophy of ontology is undertaken in the book's conclusion.

9. In this respect, then, consistent with the phenomenological position of making one's presuppositions explicit (Husserl 1983), we situate our knowledge claims regarding constitutive penology within the transparency of our own ideological assumptions.

10. See, e.g., Duncan (1996), who indicates a symbiotic relationship between the law breaker and law abider. Each needs the other; each thrives on the other.

11. Categories are created and do begin to take on a life of their own by the ongoing unexamined assumptions that are at their base. We examine such fixed constructions and several of their presuppositions in chapter 5.

12. The experience of this separation is what Young (1999) describes in *The Exclusive Society*.

13. Consider, for example, how legally informed but not determined narratives are constructed: in Silbey (1993), and her analysis of how legal categories are integrated in storytelling before the court by victim and offender; in Matza (1964) and his treatment of how recognized excusing conditions in law are appropriated by juveniles to justify their harms committed; in Schwendinger and Schwendinger (1985) and their study of how market logic comes to dominate an instrumental rhetoric by juveniles that justifies their impending offenses.

14. For Deleuze, there are two planes: one plane (content) is the plane in which desire flows, and it is the abstract machine that invokes cuts, breaks, and ruptures on this flow; the other plane, (expression), is what gives linguistic and nonlinguistic form to these cuts, breaks, and ruptures (see Lecercle 2002, 174–201). Lecercle, too, places more value on linguistic forms than does DeLanda (2006).

15. For various applications in law and criminology, see Arrigo, Milovanovic, and Schehr 2005; Milovanovic 2002.

16. Lacan (1977, 74) believed that psychoanalysis was not an exact science; its value was in descriptive not prescriptive knowledge. In this context, psychoanalysis functions as "a discursive process in which words, phrases, extra-verbal cues, and gestures [can be] subject to constant interpretation and countless meanings in a particular domain of inquiry" (Arrigo and Schehr 1998, 632). Lacan (1977, 75) was particularly interested in deciphering the organizing parameters of meaning that "defined the language in use" (see also Lee 1990, 192–93).

17. For Lacan, the speaking (*parlant*) or speaking being (*parlêtre*).

18. Lacan (1977, 1981) demonstrated that three intersecting spheres existed in the production of subjectivity. Space limitations do not permit a more systematic analysis; however, they have been summarily described elsewhere. "The Symbolic (the sphere of the unconscious, nuanced discourse and the 'law-of-the-father'), the Imaginary (the sphere of imaginary constructions including conceptions of self and others), and the Real Order (lived experience beyond accurate symbolization). Since the Symbolic Order is phallocentric, all is tainted with the privileging of the male voice. According to Lacan (1985), women remain left out, *pas-toute*, not-all. However, they have access to an alternative *jouissance* [desire] which remains inexpressible in a male dominated order (Lacan 1985). Hence, the basis for the call for an *écriture féminine* (i.e., women's writing) to overcome [their lack or] *pas-toute*" (Arrigo, Milovanovic, and Schehr 2005, 2; see also Milovanovic 2002, 29–34 for a more detailed analysis relative to crime and justice studies.

19. DeLanda (1997, 265, 271) referred to this as an "autocatalytic loop."

20. See note 14. Two planes, relatively independent, are brought together by abstract machines, a "double articulation," providing everyday meaning.

21. They are, in Deleuze and Guattari's conceptualization (1983, 1987), "order words" and stratified regimes of signs. For Lacan (1977, 1991), they are master signifiers and the *discourses of the master* and *university*.

22. Deleuze and Guattari (1987) referred to the power to invoke bodily changes as "incorporeal transformations." J. L. Austin, too, had a similar thought with his theory of speech acts. Say, "I do" or "guilty!" in certain contexts, and it will change one dramatically. It is the intervention of expression into content. It is to place the person in a new attractor basin.

23. Consider, for example, Irving Goffman's (1961) classic study, *Asylums*, and the adaptation of some inmates who internalize the language of the therapist in order to empower themselves; ultimately, this further coproduces the very categories of confinement.

24. Commentators such as Lecercle (2002) and DeLanda (2006) differ in terms of the centrality they afford language. Lecercle devotes heavier emphasis to language proper; DeLanda, emphasizes nonlinguistic forms of expression.

25. The blurring of boundaries can be shown, for example, with a recent headline on msn.com shortly after the student mass killing at Virginia Polytechnic Institute. The lead-in story reported the following: "36 California Schools under Lockdown: Suspect Threatened to 'Make Tech Look Mild,' Sheriff's Office Says" (April 19, 2007). What is noteworthy here is how the term "lockdown" is imported from prison discourse to convey meaning about actions taken outside the correctional milieu.

26. This discourse represents a regime of signs or, following Lacan (1991), the presence of master signifiers steeped in the logic of the discourse of *the master* and *the university*.

27. Interestingly, Deleuze and Guattari (1983) note that the nuclear family has become the transmitter of the Oedipus logic, which is quite compatible with capital logic. A similar theme, though based on existentialist and phenomenological insights, is found in Laing (e.g., 1983)

28. For example, consider Hardt and Negri's (2000, 2004) work on empire and the indigenous oppositional element within, the "multitude." Their commentary indicates a very different dynamic regarding the dialectical interplay than previously reflected in the class analysis of old (bourgeoisie and proletariat). As they suggest, the emergent multitude is much more amorphous, much more in a state of internal flux, but yet sufficient in itself to form moments of clear opposition to particular elite programs.

29. Two concerns arise with respect to this definition of harm, warranting further clarification. First is the distinction between objective and subjective perceptions of harm; second is the characterization of external versus internal definitions for harm. At the outset, we return to our constitutive thesis that selecting out a part (e.g., the crime of embezzlement, the harm of neutralization from those who dwell in deviant adolescent subcultures, the violence of female circumcision as linked to tribal traditions and customs) and analyzing that part outside of its whole (its respective sociocultural underpinnings) represents a determination of harm absent an understanding of relational context. The subjective/objective,

internal/external binaries set up a matrix that begins to relocate the behavior/ practice into its appropriate context; however, much more is needed. Those who engage in embezzlement may very well find rationalization from others who similarly promote this conduct; juveniles in the delinquent subculture may very well see their behavior as justified; a cultural ethos may in fact exist perpetuating and legitimizing female circumcision in some countries. However, our response to harm here is not steeped in ethical relativism; rather, we honor the meaning that these respective groups assign to the naming of the respective acts (not as harmful), and we question the intersubjective bases on which they coproduce such definitions. Similarly, we honor the meaning that other groups assign to the naming of these respective acts (as harmful), and we question the intersubjective bases on which they coproduce such definitions. What we have, then, is not a logic of equivalence or an equal measure applied to unequal people; rather, we have an assessment of how the meaning of individual acts (embezzlement, delinquency, female circumcision) is constituted by the intersubjective appraisal of those groups who condone as well as condemn the behavior. Still further, any definition of harm that we describe as an expression of power must be connected to the wider context of expressions of power of which that identified harm is but one fragment. Thus, collective definitions of harm are themselves the outcome of differential expressions of power. In other words, these definitions themselves are expressions of greater power that become institutionalized in the wider sociocultural contexts to which they are connected. These collective definitions, then, encapsulate the parts of the wholes that they represent. Hence, crime is one form of expressing power differences; harm is the more generic form that itself is reflective of a wider expression of power difference within which it is contained.

30. As Halsey (2006a, 55) continues, "The utility of a definition of environmental crime will be the degree to which it elicits new types of existential territories, makes possible new modes of envisioning the human/earth nexus, invites a reconceptualization of the relationship between speed and damage, and, following Spinoza, asks of bodies what each can do rather than what each is (that is what manner of becomings are sustained or curtailed by particular decision to use or regulate the earth)."

2

Constitutive Penology

Critique of Modernist Philosophies of Punishment

INTRODUCTION

This chapter examines core modernist philosophies of punishment and demonstrates that rather than justify the use of prison as punishment, they add additional harm to society and, in the process, conceal their own contribution to facilitating crime. Moreover, by building on the previous discussion on human agency and social structure, this chapter lays the foundation for the conceptual facets of constitutive penology, emphasizing a semiotic analysis of penal policy. Along these lines, commentary on such notions as discourse, reality construction, and the discursive practices that inform and sustain them is similarly presented. Finally, the manner in which the theory of constitutive penology extends and deepens the prevailing and critical literature in penology also is described.

PENAL POLICY: THE SOCIAL CONSTRUCTION OF JUSTIFICATIONS FOR STATE HARM

We see penal policy as a discursive process through which aspects of existing correctional practice are selected, emphasized, refined, and formally discussed, while other facets are correspondingly ignored, subordinated, postponed, and informally dismissed. In the process of constructing this synoptic penological project, illusions of protection and justice are created by subordinating realities of pain and injustice. To illustrate, consider the modernist debate over what to do with adjudicated offenders.

Penologists differentiate among at least four philosophical approaches that underscore current correctional policy and inform routine sentencing practice: (1) incapacitation/social defense, (2) retribution/just deserts, (3) deterrence, and (4) rehabilitation/treatment (see Einstadter and Henry 2007 and Henry and Milovanovic 1996 for a critical evaluation of each). Further, several modernist perspectives, though certainly progressive, have emerged that challenge these core penological philosophies. These approaches include (1) abolitionism, (2) diversion, (3) decarceration, and (4) peacemaking/restorative justice.[1] We also note the development of the "new penology" movement, especially as linked to actuarial justice. In the ensuing section, incapacitation or containment is used to illustrate how penal philosophy is caricatured in the formation of policy, seducing the public into a false sense of protection. A subsequent section suggestively describes the ways in which all other modernist philosophies (whether traditional or radical or otherwise) similarly promote the fiction of security/safety through established courses of correctional action. For a more comprehensive critique of these penologies, readers are encouraged to review the extant literature. We conclude our assessment of penal philosophy and state harm by drawing attention to structural, poststructural, and postmodernist accounts of penality. This commentary is useful in that it informs the semiotic analysis integral to our constitutive enterprise on punishment and society.

Penal Policy and the Justification of Incapacitation

The penal policy of incapacitation argues for the removal of an offender from society in order to take the individual "out of circulation" through a variety of institutional tactics, criminal justice practices, or regulatory techniques (Zimring and Hawkins 1997). Historically, these tactics/practices/techniques have included death, segregation, and transportation; however, the most common is the use of prison confinement (Zedner and Ashworth 2003). As a mechanism of incapacitation, confinement is designed "to deny offenders the opportunity to commit additional offenses and further victimize society for the duration of their incarceration" (Hussey 1997, 120). Thus, incapacitation policy expressed through the technique of penal confinement asserts that putting adjudicated offenders in prison prohibits or *prevents* them from engaging in criminal behavior (Zimring and Hawkins 1997). Moreover, the philosophy of incapacitation implies that the "outside world" is likewise safer, that is, protected from further victimization or injury, albeit temporarily and incompletely (Hudson 2003; Zedner and Ashworth 2003).

We take the position that incapacitation is based on a set of questionable, empirically derived assumptions. Among these is the finding that 50 percent of all crimes are committed by 6 percent of the population of some cities (Wolfgang, Figlio, and Sellin 1972; Loeber and Farrington 2002) and that a five-year sentence for any felony would reduce the rate of crime by 15 percent (Greenwood 1983; Guerra 2002; Murray 1997). Some investigators see this actuarial approach as a "new penology" (Feeley and Simon 1992, 2004), one that is less interested in the lives of offenders than in risk management and case processing (Hudson 2003; Kempf-Leonard and Peterson 2000). In short, the actuarial approach utilizes "techniques of identifying, classifying and managing groups sorted by levels of dangerousness" in order to assess potential harm to the general public (Carrabine 2001, 147).[2]

From the perspective of constitutive penology, the theory of incapacitation depends, for its justificatory credibility, on the reification process. Specifically, it falsely separates what goes on internally within the prison milieu from what goes on externally throughout society at large. By strategically focusing on confining or containing the offender's physical body, incapacitation ignores and remains silent on the multiple ways that the incapacitated prisoner impacts the very society from which the transgressor is supposed to be isolated (Foucault 1977a). Missing from the logic of incapacitation is the recognition that being in prison *is* being in society. The two are inextricably bound. This is because prison is physically, sociostructurally, and symbolically integrated into our everyday experience. Thus, the conviction that there exist impermeable walls of imprisonment is a myth. Instead, there is continuity between what occurs within the prison environment and what occurs outside of it. This occurs not only through the offender's relations with other prisoners but also with his or her connections to prison workers and through the impact of confinement on the incarcerate's family and friends who are outside the prison walls. Let us explore the several ways in which prison as incapacitation fails to stop the offender's crimes or is unable to provide complete separation from and protection of the public.

First, the incarcerated are not truly "incapacitated." In far too many instances, they engage in more and worse forms of offensive behavior within their new architectural space than outside of it (Haney 2006; Owen 1999; Rhodes 2004). Admittedly, once confined, their transgressions are not necessarily directed at the *general* public but at those individuals designated to guard them and at those other offenders similarly confined. Displays of public violence in correctional settings have been well documented (e.g., Byrne, Taxman, and Hummer 2007; Edgar, O'Donnell, and Martin 2003). Additionally, the trade in weapons, drugs, alcohol, prostitution, and gambling is also noted. Not only are these prison convict economies pervasive, but they require necessary and sustained connections to the outside (Kalinich 1986; Ross and Richards 2002).

Second, the architectural space that is the prison is also a reifying medium for the generation of reactive behavior and for the amplification of previously constituted articulations of the excesses of power in street (or suite) contexts. The "kept" are not just doing worse harm to each other but are engaged in such injurious conduct against everyone. This includes those of us who work "in corrections" and those of us who falsely believe we are at a great social (and, therefore, safe) distance from the prison itself.

Consider, for example, those who work in penal settings. Correctional officers are corrupted in their pressure-filled lives to escape *their* own imprisonment through a conspiratorial dance with the incarcerated. This interaction mocks society and oppresses those who engage in such a scheme (Arrigo 2006b). Indeed, as Martha Duncan (1996) suggests, this dance extends to the waltz between the lawbreaker and the nonlawbreaker, the inmate and the noninmate. As she argues, this dialectic exhibits the seductions of imprisonment versus the regimented lifestyle of the "outside" world; the admiration and romanticization of the criminal versus the revulsion of this very thought; the excitement generated in identification with law violators versus the very repugnance of such a notion; the desire for disorder and instability represented by lawbreakers versus the desire for order and stability represented by the prison-industrial complex; the commitment to the chaotic and marginal lifestyles of the transgressor versus the displeasure with the mundane, taken-for-granted activities within a "free" world; the narratives centered on unpredictability and ambiguity versus the narratives of rational, purposeful citizens seeking meaning in their lives. In short, the *walls* of prisons are illusory, and we need to understand the significance of crime and punishment by acknowledging just how intimately connected all of us are to the various seductions of imprisonment.

Third, it is important to consider how incapacitation impacts the families and friends of those confined who remain on the outside (Arrigo and Takahashi 2007; Naser and Visher 2006). These collateral casualties of prison are impoverished in their relations with each other as well as with those with whom they interact daily (Mauer 2006; Mauer and Chesney-Lind 2003).[3]

Families and friends of the incarcerated or those released are not the only ones whose lives are impacted by the penal philosophy/policy of incapacitation. Thus, fourth, the illusion of separation from the confined offender is further revealed when we recognize that taxpayers assume the costs for society's massively expanding prison programs (1.5 million incarcerated in the late 1990s compared to less that 200,000 in the 1970s, and by 2006 we see over 2.3 million incarcerated in our state and federal prisons and jails, as well as 7.2 million in some form of supervision) instead of the costs attributed to property crime.[4] In this instance, the cost of funding prison displaces the cost of financing education in many state budgets (Jacobson 2005). This reallocation of funds is for a relatively small reduction in the actual crime rate (approximately 5 percent), which is itself only questionably attributable to the policy of incapacitation (Currie 1998; Zedner and Ashworth 2003).

Fifth, the new penology of incapacitation has accentuated the issue of race in American society. The question of race is particularly noteworthy given that one in three African American males aged twenty to twenty-nine is in prison, on probation, or on parole (Hallett 2006; Mauer 1997). This realization weighs heavily on the minority mindset of African Americans *outside* of prison, who now have readily available grounds to withdraw support from society's formal institutions, especially those reflecting the interests of government and law enforcement.

Still further, prison simultaneously corrupts the majority white population's views of minorities (specifically African Americans and Latinos), thereby contaminating the former group's routine exchanges with the latter group (Welch 2005, 25–28). Through these tainted or spoiled interactions, the organizations and structures of society are similarly perceived as polluted, reinforcing the justification for implicit and institutionalized racism (Milovanovic and Russell 2001). Thus, incapacitation has a major impact on the nonwhite population of the United States—by virtue of its meaning—regardless of the reduction of offending by those temporarily removed from society. Once moral sentiment is withdrawn, people feel ethically justified in violating all kinds of rules based on neutralizations, such as "denial of victim" (Matza 1964; see also Schwendinger and Schwendinger 1985).[5]

Sixth and finally, incapacitation produces a dialectical enabling effect. This effect is particularly salient in the false security of social order it promotes and in the "safer with them behind bars" mentality it fosters (Hudson 2003; Welch 2005). The paradox is that for each constitutive brick of incapacitation laid by society, another swirl of freedom for those "accident makers" (Bopal), "liberators" (Iran-Contra), "job creators" (GM's Jeffrey Smith), "risk takers" (Ivan Boesky, Michael Milken), and "fabricators" (Enron's Lay, Skilling, and Fastow) is released (Reiman 2006).

How then does incapacitation make for a safer and more secure society? Our perspective is that burying the physical, economic, interpersonal, and intrapsychic costs in the discourse of being "tough on crime" is nothing more than voodoo penology! This message—as an expression of state-sponsored hegemony—creates the illusion of a protected society while channeling and, indeed, amplifying the actual and manifold costs of confinement (Mauer 2006; Welch 2005).

Penal Policy and the Justifications for Other Modernist Philosophies of Punishment

A comparable form of justificatory analysis is found in each of the other contemporary penal policies. For example, the strategy of retribution/just deserts fosters among the wider population the idea that there are circumstances in which it is acceptable to harm others, thereby encouraging the search for the "seeds of neutralization" for potentially violent behavior (Matza 1964). Moreover, given other harm-producing acts, this penal philosophy endorses the view that injurious conduct will be followed. As such, the notion that cycles of violence are an acceptable part of life is legitimized.[6] However, responding to violence with state-sponsored aggression increases the overall level of societal hostility; it does not reduce it. Indeed, rather than educating the public that personal consequences will follow if socially undesirable behavior (re)occurs, it teaches, models, and endorses the view that violence begets violence (Welch 2005).

Similarly, deterrence does not instruct us on the value of refraining from committing socially unacceptable behavior. Rather, it communicates the idea that we should innovate ways to avoid making our own acts appear like those that are punishable; otherwise we, too, will be disciplined (Hudson 2003, 18–25). Thus, rather than educate the public on the importance of avoiding committing prospective offenses that actually harm others, society indoctrinates its members to disguise their crimes in order to evade detection and to disidentify with the punished and their so-called transgressive acts. This message, then, has the liberating effect of promoting a wider range of other forms of offending. Moreover, these other forms of offending are not indicative of the behavior allegedly being deterred.[7] Thus, deterrence not only legitimates harm by using it as a strategic example to create fear in others but spawns the freedom to do harm, especially since the emphasis is squarely on the consequences for the actor rather than any injury or violence to the victim.

The correctional strategy of rehabilitation/treatment is likewise flawed as a penal philosophy and policy. This strategy profoundly affects society by conveying the idea that both the harms committed and the victims who suffer are less important to the state than is the manipulation, inspection, and regulation of the offender. This view is personified in the scores of interventions that endeavor to control aspects of the incarcerate's personal or situational environment such that the lawbreaker does not choose to harm again (e.g., Crow 2001; Maruna and Immarigeon 2004; McGuire 2003). Based on the availability of such extensive programming, the offender perceives past injuries as acceptable and future transgressions as correctible. Although the latter may require alternative or more precise rehabilitative interventions, the incarcerate understands that the appropriate "treatment mix" will be sought and that a "cure" eventually will be secured (Walker 2005, 220–21).

The problem with the theory of rehabilitation is that while an assessment of what works (and why) for a given offender is undertaken (Glaser 1994), society is given a litany of prepackaged "excuses" ripe for progressive liberal and related vitriolic commentary (Hudson 2003, 62–65). This rhetoric has become so shrill that the morality of harms-about-to-be-caused collides with the tide of learned rationalizations about why the violence is not the offender's responsibility in the first place (Lynch 2000). Indeed, the logic of justification here is manifold: the incarcerate's parents failed in the rearing of their child; the lawbreaker was abandoned or neglected by the school system; the reprobate's delinquent peers were a destructive influence; the convict's therapist or counselor or probation officer was unresponsive to or not cognizant of the offender's fragile ego-identity (Palmer 2004).

Regrettably, this sad perversion of rehabilitation's original intent has produced a generation of citizens who draw on the very system designed to address their problems in order to substantiate and embellish their otherwise transparent excuses for harming others. Additional harms, even if inadvertent, arise with the inmates who do not live up to the standards set in rehabilitation programs and/or are dropped from such treatment regimens. These "double failures," unexamined in the literature, now have been provided with further grounds for continuing in a direction of investing in harm. Moreover, considerable research indicates that the rehabilitative ideal promotes a net-widening effect and generally does not select the hard cases (e.g., Cullen and Gendreau 2001, 2002). Of course, the question of "what is harm?" is taken for granted, and such issues as excusability for harm, varying as a function of socioeconomic status,[8] remain unexplored.

It might appear that some of the more progressive liberal, even radical, approaches to the philosophy of punishment would be less likely to generate the context for harm production that we have seen from those policies and practices thus far considered. For example, the abolitionist movement,[9] which seeks to place a moratorium on prison building, seems to be less harmful, especially given its emphasis on decarceration, prison diversion, community alternatives, and prison shutdowns. However, this is so only if abolitionism is considered in isolation from the background in which its penal activities would occur. In a society that has exaggerated the myth of offenders as "monsters," the likelihood of a prison abolition movement, even if it were legislatively possible, would be comparable to the outcome of closing mental hospitals (Pfeiffer 2007). The latter turned many citizens with psychiatric problems onto the streets and led many other citizens to become hostile toward this "dangerous" population (Arrigo 2002; Perlin

...s accomplished for prisons, without changing the so-
...decarcerates were released, then the likely result would be
...orms of justice, increased reliance on private police, escalation in
...ownership for personal protection, and mounting suspicion of all in-
habitants in one's neighborhood. Glimpses of this outcome are evident in
the reaction to the release of people into the community with prior sexual
offenses (Craissati 2004; Matravers 2005). Part of the problem with these
radical approaches is that they mostly fail to address the relational aspects
of the offender to the offended, let alone the wider context of power and hierarchy through which these relations unfold.

Beyond Modernist Philosophies of Punishment

A more profound mode of critical inquiry begins to find expression
among those theorists who examine the structural, poststructural, and
postmodernist dimensions of penality within the context of the prison-industrial complex. In this instance, attention to technologies of control in
the management and surveillance of prisoners is central to the analysis.
The emergence of this perspective has its roots in the attempt to break
punishment from crime and to locate it in the sociopolitical context of society.[10] In other words, there is no simple "natural" correlation (correspondence) between crime rates and imprisonment. As Deleuze (1993,
31–35) and Deleuze and Guattari (1987, 66–67) have argued, forms of expression (penal law, delinquency) and forms of content (prison) are not
necessarily in a relationship of signifier to signified; rather, they are given
a precise connection in historical and political economic conditions. In
short, they emerge so as to reside in "mutual presupposition." Let us
briefly explore this direction.

George Rusche and Otto Kirchheiner's *Punishment and Social Structure*
(1968) developed a historical, materialist perspective on how systems of
punishment develop. They suggested a version of correspondence theory
whereby systems of punishment form in relation to changing modes of
production. This separates the analysis of punishment from the behavior
of crime, or it disconnects practices of punishment, which are instead
parts of a total system. Thus, the form of industrial capitalism has given
birth to a particular regime of punishment (designed to manage social
conflict born of its contradictions) that has changed to reflect the shifting
mode of production toward advanced capitalism and beyond this into
postindustrialism. This tradition is carried on in the work of Dario
Melossi and M. Pavarini (1981). They saw prison and punishment as artifacts of the conditions of work and labor and as utilitarian responses concerning the need to punish the poor, whose situation was associated with
crime or at least the fear that the poor would commit crime.[11] Thus, there

exists a correspondence between the factory and the prison because the latter derives from the former. K. Beckett and B. Western (2001) have similarly articulated the differing results that emerge from regimes that are more inclusive or exclusive in terms of marginal groups. Inclusive regimes focus on the etiology of marginality. They strive to integrate the disenfranchised by providing them with better welfare programs and, correspondingly, a less punitive view on crime. The effects here include lower imprisonment rates. By contrast, exclusive regimes place blame on the marginalized themselves, offer fewer welfare programs, and exercise more punitive measures toward crime and transgressors. Consequently, they are more likely to promote imprisonment. Similarly, Steven Box and Chris Hale (1986) observed that sentencing and imprisonment are shaped by fear of the powerless on the part of the powerful rather than by changes in the patterns of crime. Thus, the prison is reconceived in these critical analyses as a function of systems of power.

A major break from simplistic correspondence theories that social structure shapes systems of punishment came with Foucault's (1977a) *Discipline and Punish*. He interpreted the prison as a site for the source of power through which the diverse forms of power relations were made manifest. He saw the penal system's institutions (especially its mechanisms) as embedded in their sociocultural, political, and economic conditions. Indeed, they formed just one of many disciplinary institutional sites. Schools, factories, and hospitals represented several other loci. According to Foucault, each of these disciplinary sites reflected the same patterns of power relations, whose effect was the control/manipulation of individual bodies (i.e., the corporeal soul). The mechanisms of such control materialized through microtechnologies of surveillance and regulation, producing in their wake docility, conformity, or, at the very least, accommodation. In the latter instance, only momentary resistance to the wider social order was possible (for a recent penological application, see Arrigo 2007).

Foucault's analysis indicates that prisons themselves and philosophies of punishment are interconnected with the prevailing political economy. As Foucault (1977a, 282) argued, this "mutual presupposition" is expressed in stratified circuits (police, prison, delinquency) whereby "police surveillance provides the prison with offenders, which the prison transforms into delinquents, the targets and auxiliaries of police supervisions, which regularly send back a certain number of them to prison." In this scheme, the criminal justice "system" is but one of the elements of the panoptic circuits established.

Building on Foucault's thesis, others such as David Garland, especially in *Punishment and Modern Society* (1990), situated the concern for penology in modern culture. At the same time, Adrian Howe, in *Punish and Critique* (1994), examined this "new" penality (including actuarial justice) from a feminist postmodernist perspective. She criticized dominant views of punishment as masculine, thereby excluding the role of gender in the subordination of women. She integrated feminist analysis of penality with feminist inquiry into the "disciplined" body (based on the insights of Judith Butler and Teresa DeLauretis), establishing in the process a postmodern penal politics. Howe attempted to relate the gendered control of women and the way they are penologically perceived to the form of control used over them through sentencing and prison-based practices. However promising her line of analysis might be, her original contribution "consists of ten pages, four of which are devoted to Michel Foucault" (Ferraro 1997, 787). Moreover, as Francis Heidensohn points out, "Howe does not in the end produce a major new approach to penality" (1996, 565).

Some postmodernist theorists (Henry and Milovanovic 1996) have embraced a version of anarchistic philosophy that endeavors to deal with structural power by dispersing it through noninstitutional relational contexts. These contexts seek to restore the breached social relations operating within the wider system that become manifest as crime. Thus, this postmodernist approach has found a resonance with some aspects of restitution/reparation, especially in its peacemaking and restorative forms (see Ness and Strong 2002; Sarre 2003). This version of reconciliation attempts to repair the victim's suffering or loss by having the injured party address the person(s) who allegedly caused pain, and it attempts to have the offender(s) take responsibility for the offense/harm caused.[12] Moreover, in so far as the community and control institutions have a facilitative role in this process (Sullivan and Tifft 2005), less injury is being done by this kind of mediated intervention than by the other correctional strategies/policies we have thus far considered. However, the hidden message communicated here is that the act of convening, for purposes of some dialogue, can mend or fix a problem, absent any regard for the very structural conditions (political, economic, social) that coshape the aggrieved party as well as the victimizer (Schehr and Milovanovic 1999; Arrigo, Milovanovic, and Schehr 2005; see also Annalaise Acorn's scorching critique, 2004). In other words, the "reality" of restitution is that all parties are enmeshed in material (and symbolic) forces that typically remain concealed or unspoken, despite their impact on the identities of the participants during the victim-offender mediation exchange (Arrigo and Schehr 1998). These structural (and representational) factors are very much a part of the transformational mix and, as such, warrant candid attention in the mediation dialogue and process (Arrigo 2004a; Pavlich 2005).

Unfortunately, the outcomes of restorative justice interventions rarely demonstrate that the institutions of society (e.g., the correctional, the medical, the educational, and the legal) regard themselves as contributing factors to the harm caused. However, it is in the very acknowledgement of such destabilizing effects that both dimensions of violence can be revealed for their intimate interconnectedness (Barak 2003). It is through this inexorable union that the possibility of a "transformative justice" can be made transparent (see Morris 1994, 2000; Roche 2003) and the components of a "relational justice" can be rendered accessible (Burnside and Baker 1994; see also Ness and Strong 2002, 245–49). Doing less is "compulsory compassion" (Acorn 2004).

The constitutive dialectics of penal philosophy is not restricted to correctional policy makers. The analytical discourse of penologists also contributes through their ideal-type classifications and abstractions of offenders, along with designations for their corresponding crimes (e.g., "high-risk offenders," "death row felons," "juvenile pedophiles"). This logic of categorization and risk assessment/management is at the core of the "new penology" (Feeley and Simon 2004). It is actuarial justice, whose essential aim is "waste management" (Lynch 1998, 839). These summary representations constitute order-making discursive work, inviting us to make sense of the disarray of correctional practices and to explain why disorder occurs. However, by appropriating such schemas, one inadvertently affirms and bolsters the constitutive work done by policy makers and penologists of a particular era. Omitted in such analyses is the way in which correctional strategists, practitioners, targeted agents, and theorists deemphasize some aspects of the reality of prison practice, relegating them to the status of aberrant, unofficial, informal, or atypical. These efforts at socially constructing the inmate and the offender's crimes materialize in order to make claims about the operational identity of prisons (Jones and Schmid 2005). However, by distinguishing between formally espoused penal policy goals and informal practices (including plea bargaining, discretion, prison discipline, and oppositional cultural adaptations), the discursive edifice that constitutes prison policy is further erected. A critical, constitutive penological approach examines how forms of expression have become connected in specific ways to forms of content.

Missing in much of the contemporary literature in penology is how the recursive definitions of such correctional categories, abstractions, and practices perpetuate the victimizing reality that penal policy most assuredly has become. Much of this literature is also rigidly rooted in modernist assumptions.[13] In order to avoid engaging in such constitutive prison work, while nonetheless analyzing the manifestation and maintenance of correctional strategies, it is necessary to employ a semiotic methodology. This approach permits us to deconstruct the role that language use assumes in the construction of the penal system as well as in its attendant philosophies and institutions. As such, it is to the matter of semiotics and penal policy that we now turn.

SEMIOTIC ANALYSIS AND PENAL POLICY

From the perspective of semiotics, models of penal policy can be conceptualized in terms of particular discourses. These discourses are metatheories reflecting patterns of action that are seen as constitutive of a particular ideological orientation. Words, as signifiers, are always already populated with voices. They do not reside in a neutral state awaiting instrumental use; rather, their use calls out a particular rendition of "reality." Human agents locate themselves as an "I" within certain bounded spheres of discursive practices in which appropriate terminology, rationalizations, and justifications can be found. Discursive subject-positions are always already preconstructed and provide a place from which to speak.

Moreover, human agents are not necessarily passive in this process. They invoke and recreate preexisting discourse, and they innovate, establishing new forms and novel applications. Part of the constitutive process is not only to invoke and create discourse but also to construct categories, to make distinctions, and to draw contrasts (Henry and Milovanovic 1991, 1996, 1999). One such debate within the discursive penal philosophies/policies previously described is based on the distinction between "what works" (MacKenzie 2006; Murray 1997; Sheehan, McIvor, and Trotter 2007) and "what does not work" (Andrews et al. 1990; Glaser 1994; Lab and Whitehead 1990; Martinson 1974; Palmer 1975). Neglected in these debates is any consideration of the way in which *prison*, as an entity, is being reconstituted by its liberal and radical critics who, instead of deconstructing the form, take for granted its reality and reassert its presence through their claims about different approaches to corrections. Indeed, as Lorna Rhodes (2001, 70–71) notes, "Such oppositions are enmeshed in a repetitive cycle of reform that seems to draw all who enter—whether self-consciously or not—into the strategies through which power/knowledge reconfigures and disguises itself."

Whereas traditional penologists discuss the importance of the respective models, and critical penologists discuss the failure of those models, a constitutive penological perspective suggests that we begin by suspending belief in the reality of the social constructions that are taken to underlie the model. Thus, we start by deferring or placing in abeyance the claims of the various correctional philosophies or policies that make distinctions between types of structures and their various discourses. We oppose "deductive-nomological" approaches (see DeLanda 2002, 121–26) that place a high premium on the pursuit of generating rigid axioms and the exclusive pursuit of propositions linked to them in a linear, deductive manner.[14] Instead, we analyze the discursive practices as they are employed in penological debates. This is a problematic approach (DeLanda

2002, 128–56) that seeks to understand how concepts are semiotically formulated and practiced and resists subordinating problems to given, stratified solutions that are linear in their construction (137).[15]

Moreover, by segmenting this process of naming and explicating prison philosophies through an identification of different models, penologists have merely sustained a view that neglects the active work of agents as theorists in the production of criminality and corrections (see also Gilsinan 1982). In contrast, our view situates agents who actively and discursively construct their reality and maintain these social and symbolic representations, despite the presence of contradictory background relevancies. While public as well as private rhetoric (discourse) used in constructing reality may often subtend such contradictions or inconsistencies, the constitutive task is to expose the processes employed to sustain a sense of the orderliness amid disorder as reflected in chaos theory's analysis (e.g., Milovanovic 2002; Williams and Arrigo 2002).

Consequently, we see philosophies of punishment as manifested in prison policy as one among a number of reality-claiming discursive practices whose deployment forms part of the constitutive work that sustains and reifies prison as a reality. In order to examine this constitutive work, we rely on a theory of discursive production. This theory focuses on the recursive development of relatively stable meaning constructions in which the self-referential character of particular discourses in use and the existence of linguistic mechanisms that order disorder are acknowledged. We first invoke Jacques Lacan in indicating how the subject and versions of reality construction are captured semiotically. Descriptively speaking, Lacan's focus is on how desire resides within various semiotic forms. However, following G. W. F. Hegel and Freud, Lacan interprets hegemonic desire (a master discourse) as homeostatic in form, a response to lack (in being). We then turn briefly to Deleuze and his more prescriptive approach. Desire does not emanate from lack but is inherently production, Eros, the ever-developing body, active forces seeking change, mutation, and transformation.

Jacques Lacan

Discourse analysts (Lacan 1977; Manning 1988, 1990; Milovanovic 1988, 1991) conceptualize human agents as occupying discursive subject-positions. Constructing reality in a narratively coherent manner takes place within a situated communicative system (Jackson 1988). Situated discourses (e.g., language games, regimes of signs, discursive formations, rhetoric, linguistic coordinate systems) can be viewed as bounded spheres within which words (signifiers or acoustic images) "float" (Lacan 1977; Laclau and Mouffe 2001; Manning 1988, 193–230). Speech production invariably confronts gaps in meaning such as anomalies, contradictions, and absurdities. These "un-explainables" generate a search for these objects themselves conveyed through signifiers (words or expressions). Put another way, a sense of lack mobilizes desire to overcome one's felt sense of longing and incompleteness. Signifiers can be considered but one form of objects of desire holding out the potential for overcoming lack. These signifiers "suture," or stitch over, these gaps to produce a coherent, although incomplete, picture of "what happened." Moreover, situating oneself within a particular discourse (e.g., the grammar of deterrence, rehabilitation, or incapacitation) also places the interlocutor within the purview of these readily available objects of desire (Lacan 1977).[16] Therefore, one temporarily claims ownership of available (already-constituted, filled-in) signifiers.[17] It follows from this analysis, then, that we can produce different collages of "what happened" (Arrigo 1993, 1994; Bannister and Milovanovic 1990; Milovanovic 1988; Manning 1988), especially since what is communicated is a partial representation.

Gilles Deleuze

Gilles Deleuze, often in collaboration with Felix Guattari, sees things differently. Whereas Lacan seems to have provided a tremendously important statement on how the subject is captured by the work of the unconscious paternal signifier, Deleuze and Guattari want to go beyond and release the body from the prison it finds itself in at the very moment of being inaugurated into the symbolic order. They see the cosmos in terms of forces in movement: some are active; some are reactive. Desire is an active force that makes connections. Two "levels" of movement exist. One of these is the world of the virtual in which far-from-equilibrium conditions prevail, where intensities go through various threshold states generating specific results. The other world—the actual, the more static—is the result of these dynamic states. Moreover, at one level, the "machinic," there appear cuts and breaks in the flow of matter and energy. At another level, the "collective assemblage of enunciation," signifiers and a particular form of regimes of signs emerge. The machinic is focused on content; the regimes of signs are focused on expression. The two are not necessarily connected. Connecting the two is an "abstract machine," that is, some logic. Thus, for example, panopticism (Michel Foucault), commodity fetishism (Karl Marx), the fetishism of the legal form (Evgeny Pashukanis), rationalization (Max Weber), and division of labor (Émile Durkheim) are abstract machines. They connect forms of expression to forms of content (i.e., "reciprocal presupposition").

To illustrate, consider Foucault's (1977a), Deleuze's (1993, 31–44), and Deleuze and Guattari's (1987, 66–67) discussions of the prison-form. The relationship to delinquency is not one of simple signifier to a signified.

Rather, the prison is a form of content related to others, such as hospitals, factories, schools, and military barracks. Delinquency is a form of expression: it defines harmful acts in particular ways, explains how these acts arise, and classifies their various forms of manifestation. The two are brought within reciprocal presupposition by an abstract machine presenting us with but one definition of "reality." For Foucault, it is panopticism and the exercise of power that are ubiquitous. Forms of expression (signifiers) are simultaneously composed of forces of territorialization (the tendency toward static forms) and deterritorialization (the tendency toward dissipation). Forms of expression reflect momentary thresholds that have been crossed. Thresholds determine the state in which "reality" will temporarily appear.[18] Moreover, once constituted, that is, once a signifier-signified relationship has been established, distinct effects on the body will take place ("incorporeal transformations"; see Deleuze and Guattari 1987, 81). These are "order words," having some connection with Lacan's notion of master signifiers (e.g., consider the pronouncement in court when one is found "guilty!").

The totality of order words makes up a regime of signs that, in its essence, is indirect discourse. That is, all words become populated with "voices," voices of differential power. Some regimes of signs become dominant (in Lacan's view, *the discourses of the master and university*); some remain minor (in Lacan's view, *the discourses of the hysteric and analyst*). The former tend toward homeostasis and closure; the latter tend toward mutation and transformation. Regimes of signs that are minor provide us with hope of breaking from Oedipus, capture, rigid stratification, and the dominance of reactive forces.

In short, Deleuze and Guattari offer the contrast of two main regimes of signs: the dominant forms and minor discourses. The various contemporary views on punishment (including those that are modernist and critical in orientation) can be viewed as more in line with the dominant regimes of signs. However, our constitutive penology is situated in minor discourses. Minor discourses resist the tendency toward stasis; they remain dissipative structures in form. Minor discourses constantly allow for new, emergent forms of connections, active forces, novel ways of becoming.

Let us turn briefly to how language has been incorporated in the analysis of crime and penology. Illustrative in penology is research on jailhouse lawyers (Milovanovic 1988; Thomas and Milovanovic 1999, which indicates how inmates who teach themselves law while incarcerated tend to internalize juridical language in translating the "what happened" expressed to them by fellow inmates seeking legal help into legal categories. As such, they reify the rule of law ideology and cleanse alternative forms of discursive production. In the context of juvenile offenders, Cyndi Banks (forthcoming, 138, 172, 179; see also Street et al. 1966, 185) has shown how incarcerated juveniles strategically incorporate the language of treatment in order to increase their chance of release. Staff, too, appropriate the language of treatment in their everyday activities (Banks forthcoming, 180). Thus, since both the inmates and staff tend to utilize this argot, a particular reality is being discursively constructed and cyclically renewed (reification). Hence, they are both coproducers of a "reality" of the lawbreaker and what it takes to be rehabilitated (Banks forthcoming, 181–83). Further, we note that several studies have implied a semiotic analysis. C. W. Mills[19] suggested the importance of discourse to action theory. Moreover, Donald Cressey,[20] David Matza,[21] and Herman and Julia Schwendinger[22] applied components of discourse analysis to the study of crime. Michel Foucault,[23] Dario Melossi,[24] and Martha Duncan[25] extended this analysis.[26]

Revisiting Semiotic Analysis and Constitutive Penology

Applying semiotic analysis to penological thinking helps us to gain a critical understanding of the developments in which a particular form of prison is a central feature of our capitalist structure. This is most especially the case following noncorrespondence (i.e., nonlinear) models of inquiry. Consider the issue of expanding prison populations. Under conventional analysis, this penological concern is explained in relation to growing crime rates, and these rates are then directly linked to unemployment and the business cycle. From our perspective, such simplistic causal logic fails to explain the process of how prison populations increase.

Research by Box (Box and Hale 1986; Box 1987) shows that increases in prison population have more to do with the socially constructed meaning of capitalist recession as perceived by the judiciary and with that body's discursively hypothesized connection between crime and unemployment than with actual changes in levels of crime. Box and Hale (1986) argue that during a prolonged period of economic crisis, when the "problem" population of the unemployed is growing, the state cannot maintain living standards and welfare services without adversely affecting the interests of capital. As the economic crisis deepens, the judiciary becomes increasingly anxious about the possible threat to social order posed by unemployed young males, most notably black males. As a consequence, "it responds to this perception by increasing the use of custodial sentences, particularly against property offenders, in the belief that such a response will deter, incapacitate, and thus diffuse the threat" (Box and Hale 1986, 86).

Box and Hale's statistical analysis broadly supports the view that sentences to immediate imprisonment (but not unemployment rates) positively covary with annual unemployment levels. Moreover, they conclude that little is done to solve the prison-overcrowding problem because it is a useful ideological device to legitimate an anxious state's real policy of expanding prison capacity where "social order is threatened by the current economic crisis undermining consent amongst those suffering the worst ravages" (1986, 94). In other words, prison populations are constructed by the meaning structures of the powerful members of capitalist society and serve to placate fears born of that system, rather than developing in response to real changes in levels of crime (for empirical cross-cultural support for the relationship between increased welfare expenditures and reduced imprisonment, see Downes and Hansen 2006; Beckett and Western 2001; Cavadino and Dignan 2006). The same capitalist political economy from which judges construct the meaning that frames their sentencing policy also provides a discursive resource for adjudicated lawbreakers, whose prior-to-prison experiences already have incorporated some elements of an instrumental rhetoric (in the context of class differences, see Hudson 1993, 118–21).

Further suggestive work in this direction has been done by David Garland and Zygmunt Bauman. In Garland's (2001, 193–205) view, the "reality" of crime is more a function of "a series of adaptive responses to the cultural and criminological conditions of late modernity—conditions which included new problems of crime and insecurity, and new attitudes towards the welfare state." Moreover, for U.S. and British practices, these are related to "reactionary politics." In a similar vein, Bauman (1998, 116–18) has argued that in late modernity, insecurity and uncertainty that spawned anxiety about individual safety led politicians to verbalize the cause and remedy (deviants and isolation, respectively). In late modernity, an elevated concern for order existed. During this period and its aftermath, Bauman (1998, 113) suggests, elites harvested various benefits of the prison form, such as investing in laboratories for experimentation: "The techniques of space-confinement of the rejects and the waste of globalization are tested and their limits are explored."

Prison experience itself, especially including the pains of confinement and the absurdities faced (Haney 2006; Korn 1988; Thomas and Mika 1988; Milovanovic and Thomas 1989; Rhodes 2004; Zwerman 1988), offers various discourses and, hence, explanatory constructs for use in constructing narratively coherent explanations of "what happened." The formal legalist structure (Milovanovic 1986, 1988) and the bureaucratic structure (Manning 1988; Thomas 1988; Thomas and Milovanovic 1999; Yngvesson 1993) both offer a highly rationalized discourse.[27]

Consider, too, the constitutive processes of the media during prison protests: "The coverage sets agendas, it prioritizes contrasting accounts, it legitimizes informants, it selects material and defines relevance, but most of all it reconstructs events. The media, quite literally, become the lens through which issues are brought into sharp relief" (Scraton et al. 1991, 109).[28] In other words, forms of expression are given to forms of content, the abstract machine (Deleuze and Guattari 1987) being the media and its logic. It makes connections: it includes some content; it excludes other content. Indeed, as some commentators have observed, "The media do not merely 'reflect' social reality, they increasingly help to make it" (Curran and Seaton 1981, 228).

From our perspective, this analysis can be extended in two directions. First, media coverage provides discursive elements from which protestors construct reality. This manufactured reality is further reworked by media representation in a feedback cycle producing an "understanding" that can be neither fully situated "within" prisons nor "outside" of them; rather, it must be situated between the two. Second, a counterstrategy can be suggested in response to the selective renditions offered by the media (see Henry 1994). In other words, activists may counter these often conservative constitutive constructions by becoming catalysts for the development of replacement discourses.[29] What is called for is a "minority discourse" (Deleuze and Guattari 1987) that seeks to undermine (destratify) stable forms and continuously generates new forms of expression.

We also see a constitutive process taking place with "rehab talk." Inmates registered in rehabilitation programs, such as drug programs, often begin to reconstruct their worlds around the discourse of therapy. Thus, for example, it is not unusual to visit prison drug programs in which "success cases" recount their stories. Often, we find that their discourse comprises pronouncements, in conformity with clinical rhetoric, of their past transgressions, of how they struggled and eventually hit bottom, and of how they now are in recovery. In Lacan's view, this process implicates the *discourse of the master, university, and hysteric.* For Deleuze and Guattari, these adjustments by the kept are in line with particular regimes of signs that have become stratified and offer "order words" that can be embraced in constructing "reality." These order words have corporeal transformational effects in so much as they tend to elicit certain dispositions in their usage.

However, informal (including minority) discourses also circulate within the prison. Characteristically, some inmates oppose, some acquiesce, and some become fatalistic. In each case, however, a discourse already abounds providing meaningful resources from which "reality" can be constructed, albeit with its own unique turn, which simultaneously and substantially remakes the discursive form (see also Ewick and Silbey 1998, 247). These discourses can be classified as conforming, alienated, instrumental, and oppositional.

During the imprisonment, an instrumental discourse provides a survival and self-justifying device that is well suited to preprison experiences. Subsequently, released prisoners are further constituted through their use of a discourse that, in certain contexts, assures their receptivity to further predatory behavior, which is facilitated by rendering certain potential victims as appropriate targets. In this sense, prison provides a vocabulary, structured utterances, and contextual releases of emotive-instrumental behavior, which minimizes questions concerning the moral worth of their targets. Victims are constituted as devoid of moral virtue, (Matza's denial of victim) and, in fact, are seen as a cause of their own demise: "They deserved it."

However, even where more oppositional discourses develop during the phase of imprisonment, they often are more constitutive than liberating. For example, consider Jim Thomas's (1988) insightful analysis of prisoner litigation, particularly his idea of prisoner cases by jailhouse lawyers (inmates who have taught themselves law and subsequently initiate legal suits against prison conditions) as narrative constructions. What emerges as truth behind prison practices and prisoner rebellions is problematic. The legal "reality" of "what happens" when petitions to the courts or to other tribunals are initiated by prisoner grievances is not as "oppositional" as it might at first seem. Rather, it has to do with a "gate-keeping" dynamic whereby the invisibility of the screening of legal cases submitted assures that considerable discretion and extralegal factors are used to determine decision making. Moreover, due to a multiplicity of decision-making levels and the inherent discretion that exists, a case can be denied or rerouted at numerous points (Thomas 1988, 168–69).

Additionally, underlying these decision points are the predilections, biases, and leanings of decision makers. General supporters will articulate a narrative that allows prisoners "their day in court." Contrastingly, general opponents (whether openly or not) will conjure up a narrative based more on narrower constitutional readings that limit discretion. As a result, more petitions by inmates are denied ("no standing") (Thomas 1988, 165–90).

Constitutive penology, then, enables us to see opposition in terms of various narratives in conflict. Which narrative is given priority is not without importance. This prioritization decides the prisoner's petition. Moreover, for the "outside" world, legal viewpoints are seen as what really happened, while other narrative constructions are denied their legitimacy. It is with this in mind that we might appreciate Gilda Zwerman's (1988) observation of the high-security unit at Lexington. She claims that practices there by prison officials "may be viewed as a first effort to develop a strategy which ensures that a critical analysis of political crime will have no place in the formulation of correctional policy and practices with respect to political prisoners" (1988, 41). Thus, the critical questions become reduced to a battle of discourses over truth claims. The victor is the one whose discourse explains the most pivotal of issues: "What *really* happened."

Moreover, Thomas (1988) has shown that decision making behind prisoner litigation has more to do with pragmatic, bureaucratic functioning. Indeed, as he indicates, "organizational goals [such] as fiscal restraints, control of prisoners, stable prison administration, and face-saving denial of culpability dominate the state's strategy of settling cases" (1988, 184). Thus, resolving prisoner litigation has little to do with bona fide issues. Instead, it has a great deal to do with the exigencies of the prison bureaucratic apparatus, including the prevalence of stabilized, readily available accounts; rationalizations; legitimation principles; and explanatory constructs that await appropriation and application. Given an outwardly incomprehensible event, readily available, "packaged" explanatory narrative constructions exist. As Thomas (1988, 188) poignantly states, "The actual work of acting on cases occurs not so much through rule-following as through enacting various contexts of action that justify how a particular group can attain its own ends rather than the ends of 'justice.'"

This process has its parallel at a "macrolevel" in Foucault's (1977a) extensive "excavations" of historically changing and conflicting discourses, which oftentimes are resolved by some gaining ascendancy. Ernesto Laclau and Chantal Mouffe (2001) similarly have indicated how historical upheavals by themselves remain ripe for articulation; however, otherwise "floating signifiers" must be articulated in a coherent, narrative form (see also White 1973). As Laclau and Mouffe (2001, 154) have said, "There is no relation of oppression without the presence of a discursive 'exterior' from which the discourse of subordination can be interrupted." And further, "it is only from the moment when the democratic discourse becomes available to articulate the different forms of resistance to subordination that the conditions will exist to make possible the struggle against different types of inequality" (Laclau and Mouffe 2001, 154).

Even before this process has taken place, a new notion of formal equality, an imaginary construct, must have been established. Toward this end, critical analysis has implicated the global arena. For example, Michael Hardt and Antonio Negri (2004) have argued that a new form of oppositional group has resulted from globalization. Rather than advocating class analysis, they argue that the "multitude" is the new oppositional group. Here, no inherent potential for stasis exists; rather, the multitude is characterized by its constantly evolving, mutating, and transforming nature marked by differences. Hence, only temporary alliance can be the basis of new forms of struggle. The World Wide Web is a key ingredient in its communicative makeup; thus, network struggles have replaced Marxist notions of the struggle between the proletariat and bourgeoisie. The multitude, in short, is a dissipative structure without a persevering identity. Its nature is that of permanent change and only temporary stasis. Within this dynamic, regimes of signs would be more inclusive and less stratified; they would tend toward minority discourses.

Alternative Programs and Constitutive Penology

Alternative programs to prison, those that ostensibly list as their manifest goals reintegration or reconciliation (i.e., those proposed under the rubric of "restorative justice"), can also be conceptualized as arenas where opposing discourses compete for dominance. Reality is constituted by everyday discursive practices in which ideologically laden dominant signifiers are given sustenance. Conventional criminology, as well as much of critical/radical criminology, has overlooked the effects of the clash of divergent discourses. This occurs even as the same person/agent uses two or more discourses to explain his or her actions: one at the private level, one at the public level. So, for example, even though an interviewed inmate may be asked for his or her personal beliefs, the inmate's response may operate at a different level than the discourse that lies behind actual behavior itself (Muir 1977; see also Gilsinan 1982, 1989; Manning 1988). Asking guards to explain their actions after the fact may even crystallize a rendition of reality in accord with conventionally understood practices. Prevailing dominant discursive practices may act as explanatory constructs of otherwise perceived disorderly, unexplainable events.

Moreover, community mediation, as Deborah Baskin (1988, 105–10) has pointed out in the tradition of Mills (1959), attempts to neutralize conflict by reducing social problems to a discourse of individual problems. Interpersonal disputes are reduced to a discourse of hedonistic individualism and a failure of communication, whether the problem is sexism, racism, poverty, or the like. Additionally, motivational patterns associated with commodity production and consumption are given articulate and preferential form (idealized expression). But again, we see human agents maneuvering various discourses for ascendancy and dominance.

Baskin's insightful article on community mediation can be conceptualized as a statement concerning how a specific discourse, conveying a particular ideology, encroaches on other narrative constructions of social problems (see also the critique by Schehr and Milovanovic 1999). Establishing the "what happened" is situated in a psychological, mental health discourse rather than in a political discourse, thereby shifting attention away from critical examination of the social structure. As such, community-based corrections, including their attendant, particular narrative constructions, become increasingly pervasive (Baskin 1988, 106) and permeate every detail of private life.

Constitutive penology focuses on how human agents embrace specialized discourses (rather than on others in constituting reality) such that they create order out of disorder. Agents do not merely participate in nominalistic exercises; rather, they cocreate structure because its attribution is a discursive undertaking. Indeed, this discursive project is the construction of the object itself. Given this, a fundamental instability exists; hence, potential alternative articulations can take place (Zizek 1989, 89–92).

Academic penologists as well as policy makers often make use of a metatheory divergent from the actual world experienced by the lawbreaker and law enforcer. In other words, academic discourse is not necessarily in correspondence with the minor discourses of the subaltern. On the other hand, some inmates do in fact internalize a conforming or traditional discourse, even to the point that it comes to replace previously internalized linguistic structures (e.g., local, familial). These "rehabilitated" subjects are often paraded as success "stories." After experiencing additional setbacks at "rehabilitation" (double failures), or after interpreting the formal court and prison structures as nothing more than an extension of the street scene, human agents may incorporate an alienated discourse replete with fatalistic views of life. Under the same conditions, others may reinforce their preprison instrumental discourse and become more dangerous, yet more elusive, as criminals. A smaller group, those who espouse an oppositional discourse with elements of a replacement discourse, may develop. Theirs is a contradictory state, both opposing and, even in so doing, reifying structures of domination (Henry and Milovanovic 1991, 1996; Milovanovic and Thomas 1989; Bannister and Milovanovic 1990). For Thomas (1988, 242–43), although jailhouse lawyers may demonstrate rudiments of an oppositional (political) discourse, they do not typically pursue abstract political agendas (see also Milovanovic and Thomas 1989; Thomas and Milovanovic 1999), and neither do "freeworld" activists substantially aid jailhouse lawyers in developing their incipient political agendas. Needed is the development of minority discourses that, when provided semiotic forms, can hinder and undermine repetition. Potentially, this can lead to a stable oppositional discourse within which rebels can take up oppositional stances in producing coherent, persuasive narrative forms.[30]

In sum, neglected in the penological literature is an analysis of the cognitive structurations that work at the level of discursive practices. Absent this, theorists are left to constitute renditions of "what happened." These renditions define and give meaning to prison uprisings, street disturbances, or outright political acts of rebellion. However, as the previous sections have disclosed, these characterizations are only partial accounts of the totality of these richly textured experiences.

Diagrams of Power and Constitutive Penology

David Rothman's (1971) classic investigation of the "discovery of the asylum" indicated that architectural designs are often the reflection of changes in ideological positions that are in turn connected with the industrializing order. But once constructed, the ideology connected with the architectural space becomes the operating background, a linguistic structure, within which discussion, resolution, and policy are formulated. Foucault (1977a), too, has indicated that the rise of panopticism is connected with materialistically grounded, changing needs of a political economy. Discourses that are generated from these sources can then appear relatively autonomous, being continuously reaffirmed in their use (see also Manning 1988, 207; Milovanovic 1988). These discourses, too, can permeate various domains, otherwise unconnected with the original source.

As Deleuze (1988) and Foucault (1977a) have indicated, power relations permeate all relations. Power, too, can only be defined operationally (Deleuze 1988, 27). Power finds its expression in particular forms, in "diagrams of power" (Deleuze 1988, 34–44, 72–73). The diagram "is the map of relations between forces, a map of destiny or intensity, which proceeds by primary non-localizable relations and at every moment passes through every point" (Deleuze 1988, 36). Diagrams of power are embedded within discursive practices. Thus, various linguistic coordinate systems provide alternative crystallizations of power relations. Agents either finding themselves in or inserting themselves within these power relations reproduce its essential themes. Consider James Gilsinan's (1982, 84) point as to the functions of punishment:

> It is an attempt to convince people that the decisions made about others are not only rational, logical, and coherent, but are in fact the only decisions that can be made given the "reality" of the situation. . . . Punishment is the ultimate means of confirming the accounts of particular groups in society.

Penologists, academic theoreticians, policy makers, and operatives (e.g., guards, counselors) on the one hand and clients (inmates) on the other take up residence in various discourses in their daily activities.[31] Constitutive penology examines these changing, as well as always already stabilized/crystallized discursive, subject-positions (see also Smith 1988; Deleuze 1988, 55; Pecheux 1982). Criminologists, policy makers, and administrators on one level and operatives (guards) on the second are catalysts.[32] They sustain and stabilize systems of linguistic relevancies, and these in turn become the background linguistic relevancies to which inmates must adjust. Inmates invoke both with those they have imported while generating others anew. Thus, news coverage of protests or of "riots" may provide explanatory frames that are elements from which protestors can select in their construction of the protest. For Gilsinan (1982, 236), "Within the arena [of criminal justice], different social worlds struggle for recognition and legitimation, so that the process of justice results in a number of decisions about whose worldview will prevail." Thus, some prisoners incorporate consent (conventional discourse), some oppose (oppositional discourse), some become estranged (alienated discourse), and some receive reassurance for their preprison, utilitarian, and self-justifying frame/attitude (instrumental discourse). The latter discourse, ironically, contributes to the "virulent" subject (Athens 1989, 72–79): one who frequently and strongly espouses the instrumental rhetoric at a private level, which makes future criminal activity replete with rationalizations and neutralizations that much easier.

Transpraxis and Constitutive Penology

Constitutive penology asks us to rethink the discursive structures within which we situate our research on the penal question.[33] We concur with the idea that struggle is dialectical and often nonlinear and that conformity, struggle, and change come in package deals. Much of this literature can be reconceptualized as practices and strategies that "subvert repetition" (Butler 1990, 145–49). For example, news-making criminology (Barak 1988; Henry 1994) disrupts repetition and provides a reconstructive tactic to generate alternative, more reflective narratives. To illustrate, consider some of the early critical literature on media coverage of prison protests and riots (Scraton et al. 1991). Much of it argued for a unilateral construction of what happened led by media representatives. However, postmodernist-informed criticism showed how this could be reconceptualized with the interventionist tactics of news-making criminology (e.g., Henry 1994). Thus, we suggest that repetition could be subverted and new understandings could be generated, which then could become the basis for alternative, relatively stabilized stories. In this reconstruction, oppressed subjects could generate important signifying elements for narrative constructions rather than relying on the interjection of these semiotic forms from the "outside." That is, alternative forms of content could be engendered (cuts in flow of desire) along with connectedness to alternative forms of expression, contributing to minor discourses that remain dynamic and in constant states of mutation. Previously, we reviewed Foucault's and Duncan's respective suggestions about providing opportunities for inmates to speak for themselves such that they gained a more acute understanding because of it. Here, we extend this (they did not go far enough) by arguing that a critical catalyst (i.e., an activist applying the tactics of news-making criminology) is a key component, much like Paulo Freire's (1973) work on dialogical pedagogy suggests.

Constitutive penology, then, would take as its first priority the development of a social formation that (1) minimizes harms of reduction and repression, and (2) contributes to forms of expression and active forces that are in constant states of mutation and transformation. To be sure, conflicts will always exist. However, it is in their very resolution that we need creative initiatives. These initiatives must transform the process whereby the dispute does nothing more than reproduce harm that sets in place new conflict. This cycle of conflict production must end. Two million plus Americans imprisoned is, by any standard, an ultimate harm of reduction and repression!

Some theorists have already begun to advocate a multifaceted approach to "criminal" justice policy (Henry and Milovanovic 1996, 189; Einstadter and Henry 1995, 4). In particular, a "radical accusatory" policy has been proposed. It implicates the entire society for its contributions to harm. Moreover, a "reformist remedial" policy has been suggested. It is in accord considerably with Roberto Unger's superliberalism. The latter supports an empowered democracy. A social justice approach would implicate, simultaneously, the individual, community, and societal levels as is consistent with "transformative justice" (Morris 1994, 2000; Burnside and Baker 1994; Ness and Strong 2002, 245–49).[34] It would privilege responses to harm that are concurrently reintegrative and transformative, even while communicating disapproval for harms done. Where shaming (Braithwaite 1989) was deemed necessary, it would always be in relation to both of these components.

What we propose is not a form of linguistic determinism. On the contrary, we argue that discourses are recursively generated, their boundaries are often blurred, and they can be seen as providing alternative signifiers in constructing reality and in making truth claims about reality. Subjects, whether physically situated behind bars or psychologically confined by their manufactured renditions of imprisonment, construct mind patterns of their daily lives and develop believable (logical) narrative "accounts." Agents locate themselves within a discursive frame, taking up temporary residence within discursive subject-positions as an "I" who speaks. These subject-positions provide a system of linguistic relevancies for orientation and for narratively constructing projects/goals. Different decision makers within prisoner litigation suites may make use of various narrative constructions justifying their already assumed decisions. Operatives engage in "cognitive mapping"; they construct believable "accounts"; they develop narratively coherent stories of "what happened." Of course, the production and rendering of various dominant discourses has not been fully addressed here; however, we have hinted that these are connected to such phenomena as capital logic, bureaucratic imperatives, technological advances, architectural design, phallocentricism, and those, with their particular professional interests in mind, who give these often amorphous and contradictory forms idealized expression. We posit that once a discourse is "in place," by which we mean that it is repetitiously and routinely reproduced (e.g., it becomes a statistical regularity), it provides a framework in the production of particular renditions of reality. From these accounts, an object reality is implied and is constituted through the rendition of that discourse. Accounts are only generated within bounded spheres of floating signifiers always already populated with a voice. The creative capacity of human agency is such that in generating accounts, it remakes the voice *as well as* adds to it, extends it, and attenuates it. It is this recursive account making that constitutes prison policy and prison life.

An adequate penological analysis must begin by examining "the how" of that constitutive process rather than becoming just another builder of the prison edifice. Alternative discourses, replacement discourses, may only arise as different accounts are given hearing at every level of crime-control proceedings (Gilsinan 1982, 236). However, we also recognize that traditionally alternative programs to corrections, like alternatives in other spheres of social life, often duplicate dominant forms of expression. Genuinely alternative discourse would capture "the fluid nature of criminal violations and the legal processing of such infractions" (Gilsinan 1982, 243). This replacement grammar would envelop not just the declarations of policy but the ways its practitioners and decision makers distinguish their reality from the totality on which their unique rendition is constructed. At a more macrosociological level, it would specify the conditions whereby signifiers are anchored to particular signifieds (Zizek 1989; Lacan 1991; Deleuze and Guattari 1987) within specific, differentiated, and sedimented discursive regions (Milovanovic 1986). Moreover, where oppositional movements are articulated, replacement discourse would indicate where and how they emerge more often than not in system-preserving forms (Laclau and Mouffe 2001). The notion of alternative systems of communication would require a "bringing back in" of the underemphasized, informal, unofficial, marginalized practices (the unspoken) that are part of the totality of prison business. Thus, in principle,

(a) [replacement discourse] includes almost every conceivable reaction to an event—individual, collective, structural, material, or immaterial. (b) It implies that response is mandatory, without pre-defining the event as a crime, an illness, or anything else. (c) It invites analysis of the event before deciding or choosing a proper response. [And] (d) . . . it invokes the consideration of historical and anthropological forms of dispute settlement and conflict resolution for possible cues to rational forms of response. (de Haan 1990, 158)

De Haan's suggestion is worthy of further examination. It speaks to providing various (repressed, marginalized) discursive practices a forum for authentic consideration. Only with such a comprehension of the totality and the contribution of these excluded parts to the reality-making process is it possible to provide an alternative understanding of the phenomena of crime and crime control in our society. Only from such an understanding of the total constitutive process is it possible to generate replacement discourses that begin the deconstruction of penology, the reconstruction of corrections, and the ultimate penal policy that is its own demise.

NOTES

1. We recognize the logic and language of peacemaking as a necessary step in the direction of reframing the debate in penal philosophy and policy (e.g., Braswell, Fuller, and Lozoff 2000; Fuller 1997; Pepinsky and Quinney, 1991). However, even this approach reifies prisons and correctional practice. Thus, penal abolition, despite its efforts to promote social justice (MacLean 1993), essentializes the discourse of penology that constitutive theory rejects.
2. The issue of false positives remains always present.
3. If two million members of the U.S. population are confined in prison, we can assume conservatively an additional four million family members (two per inmate) are affected and a further eight million friends. So, approximately twelve million people connected to prisoners—although living outside the prison—are affected by imprisonment. Moreover, where offenders are drawn from concentrated areas (such as inner cities), the impact on the population of these cities is more concentrated. These numbers expand enormously when those who are released into reentry are considered. Indeed, Nasar and Visher (2006) show that the impact and significant hardships experienced by family members during the incarceration and reentry process include financial strain and increased anxiety.
4. See Bureau of Justice Statistics, www.ojp.usdoj.gov/bjs/correct.htm; Austin 2007.
5. To illustrate, the "victim of crime" designation for whites may not resonate with nonwhites, especially when the latters' perception/experience of racism against people of color can (and does) locate the majority in the position of the aggressor. Thus, minorities may very well believe that they are merely taking back what was taken from them, including dignity, property, and even life itself. A variant in the latter could be seen, in the extreme, in Katz's (1988) notion of "righteous slaughter."
6. Eventually, the notion of a "cycle of violence" becomes normalized. This normalization is sustained through penal philosophies/practices in which the kept,

their keepers (prison workers/officials), and the general public legitimize such harm. The philosophical dimensions of this cyclical and repetitive normalized violence is examined in chapter 4 and understood as the "pains of imprisonment."

7. Consider, for example, white-collar crime, such as the Enron fiasco, in which vast numbers of employees lost their pension funds. This is described by business as "shenanigans" or as "unethical," rather than as crime that devastates the lives of people more extensively than many classic street offenses, such as theft or burglary (Reiman 2006).

8. For example, the literature indicates that as we move upward in the stratification system, more latitude is given in which to provide a reason for one's harm; hence, understanding and excusability are extended. Conversely, as we move downward in the system, latitude becomes narrower and responsibility is asserted (see Black 1976, 1989; Kelman 1981).

9. More recently, a "minimalist" position has been developed: "Abolitionism, in its purified form, is not an attainable position. We cannot abolish the penal institution totally" (Christie 2004, 85).

10. Perhaps one of the clearest and earliest expressions that separated crime from punishment was Mark Kennedy's (1970) analysis. Utilizing legal principles, he logically argued that the prime differentia of crime is politicality, that is, who defines it.

11. See also the correspondence established between imprisonment rates and welfare spending by Downes and Hansen (2006). Their cross-cultural, historically driven, empirical investigation indicates that "countries that spend a greater proportion of [gross domestic product or] GDP on welfare have lower imprisonment rates." See also Beckett and Western (2001). The latter show this relationship even holding constant crime rates.

12. The question of "shaming," integral to reintegration as Braithwaite (1989) suggests, is problematic. To the extent that it reduces overall injury by way of remediation and the transformation it engenders at various levels of the socius, it can contribute to a less harmful, more integrative, more humane society. However, it does imply that some moral party will exert a particular understanding of correctness in the mediation exchange; hence, shaming contributes to hierarchy and further invests in harm.

13. Modernists all too often locate their "science" in linear logic, in dualisms (free will versus determinism), in static notions of truth, homeostatic models, outdated notions of the subject (the individual), instrumental language analysis, and deductive, axiomatic-driven thinking (axioms once established become rigid "givens" in further deductive logic). Our notion of COREL sets and Deleuze's notion of assemblages takes us in a much different direction in recognizing orderly disorder, nonlinearity, many truths, dissipative systems, singularities, bifurcations, attractor states, thresholds and intensities, nonstatic problem-solving approaches, alternative constructions of the subject, recognizing human beings' potentials and imprisonments, and so forth. It is with concepts such as these that a constitutive approach can be further articulated and advanced.

14. At first glance it may seem that the constitutive approach falls victim to the same tendency. However, the constitutive approach is akin to a dissipative structure. Constitutive theory beckons the reader to temporarily suspend "normal sci-

ence" and the axioms, postulates, deductive logic, and conclusions to follow. However, this imaginative leap to a new set of axioms from which alternative postulates, principles, and deductive logic may take place is not static; instead, it is subject to revision, qualification, death. Elements within constitutive theory (such as the notion of nonlinearity, singularities, intensive states, attractors, catastrophe, and the like) necessarily imply that the perspective will remain dynamic and mutational in form.

15. As DeLanda (2002, 141) argues, following Deleuze, "Matter under nonlinear and non-equilibrium conditions is, on the other hand, intensive and problematic, capable of spontaneously giving rise to form drawing on its inherent tendencies (defined by singularities) as well as its complex capacities to affect and be affected."

16. Lacan's (1991) presentation of the four structured discourses brings this into sharp relief. On the one hand, the *discourses of the master and the university* assure repetition; that is, a core set of master signifiers is constantly reinvested, which sustains static, conventional versions of reality. On the other hand, the discourses of the *hysteric and analyst* tend toward disequilibrium and transformation. They generate alternative master signifiers that are more dynamic in form.

17. Signifiers for Lacan privilege the paternal (i.e., the phallocentric symbolic order). Much like Sigmund Freud, the person is subject to the oedipal complex whereby gender roles are created: the male's voice, his subjectivity, and masculine ways of knowing are all privileged over that of the female's.

18. Heat water to the boiling point, and it changes to a gaseous state; decrease the temperature, and it eventually becomes a solid form. Liquid, gaseous, and solid states are all the results of certain thresholds having been reached.

19. See C. W. Mills's (1940) pioneering discussion of language use as the motives for action.

20. In discussing the verbalizations of convicted embezzlers, Cressey (1953, 94) sees a direct link between the human agent's selected use of discourse and action with his notion that "the rationalization is his motivation" and "the words that the potential embezzler uses in his conversations with himself are actually the most important elements in the process that gets him into trouble" (Cressey 1970, 111). A crucial issue here is the timing of the use of signifiers. For Cressey, the work environment is critical where signifiers exist that rationalize/justify a line of otherwise illegal action. Thus, according to Cressey, given the presence of nonshareable financial problems, skills and opportunities to commit delinquency, and a discourse prevalent that rationalizes illegal conduct, the expected result will be embezzlement. If believable accounts are prevalent, the act will be committed. If they are prevalent in the work culture, the words and phrases will provide a key element in the motivation for the offender. More recent work has suggested that the "context" issue must consider how signifiers are constituted within the larger political economy.

21. For Matza (1964), signifiers based in formal law are invoked in particular contexts by juveniles, albeit distorted and extended in the process: "The criminal law, more than any other system of norms, acknowledges and states the principled grounds under which an actor can claim exception" (Matza 1964, 61). The implication of this analysis is that language use and the invocation of particular

signifieds (and not necessarily by the actor but as an inadvertent and unwitting extension of existing beliefs) are enough to render an action morally acceptable *prior* to its contemplation and execution. Matza's theory (1964, 1969) has been applied by Athens (1989), who argues that becoming a committed lawbreaker entails stages of development. In his explanation of becoming a "dangerous violent criminal," Athens sees four stages. In the brutalization stage, an actor directly experiences violent behavior. In the belligerent stage, a "state of emotional turmoil and confusion" is experienced, leading to the neutralization of the otherwise moral bind of norms. A third stage is the violent performance, which involves the actual carrying out of a volatile act. Finally, there is the stage of virulency, which is a feeling of omnipotence and a subsequent willingness to act out violently, even in situations of minor provocation (Athens 1989). At every stage, a narrative construction is developed, each in turn preparing the actor for a more fully developed response pattern, replete with self-justifying moral principles. Being sentenced to prison provides a cultural milieu where each of these stages can be further reinforced. In other words, moral rhetoric within brutalizing prison environments enhances the process, providing further support for investment in violent criminal activity.

22. The Schwendingers (1985, 128) argue that different cultures can be characterized by their different styles of "moral rhetoric." This moral rhetoric can change with different contexts and may even be conceptualized in terms of smooth transitions between public and private rhetoric. They further identify an "egoistic rhetoric" (133) and an "instrumental rhetoric" (136). The former, the dominant form in a capitalist mode of production, expresses market thinking: individualism, utilitarianism, and hedonism. The latter, as a variant of the former, "seems to apply egoistic operating principles to a particular set of conditions, but it disregards egoistic standards of fairness" (136). More specifically, this

> guiding principle . . . assumes people to be engaged in a vast power struggle, with the weak and the powerless as legitimate victims. In this view of reality, the images of humans are virtually stripped of meaningful moral qualities, and individuals are seen primarily as instruments for egoistic ends. Often, moral qualities are not even present in the consciousness of the criminal or in the criminal's selection or definition of the victim. (137)

The delinquent has learned the appropriate vocabulary that justifies the infliction of pain or suffering on the victim (Schwendinger and Schwendinger 1985, 147–48; see also Katz 1988; Athens 1989). This discourse is often incorporated in "pragmatic experience[s] in market relationships" (Schwendinger and Schwendinger 1985, 275–76). Constitutive penology seeks to extend this kind of semiotic analysis to the prison context.

23. Foucault's classic work, *Discipline and Punish*, indicates how various technological discourses emerge in political economy situated in historical conditions, which become the logic of various institutions: schools, hospitals, asylums, factories, army barracks, and prisons. All of these regimes attempt to produce "docile bodies" and "bodies of utility" (1977a, 25, 136–39, 218). These "disciplinary mechanisms" are discursive constructions that map the forces of the body and the vagaries of the soul through their usage in various contexts.

24. Melossi (1985) provides additional insights for the development of a constitutive penology. He implicates the interconnectedness of the "macro/micro" in devising an alternative approach to investigation by focusing on "a 'discursive chain' between, on the one hand, the ways in which the social conflicts around the business cycle are rationalized . . . and, on the other hand, the vocabularies of motives which are available to the agencies of penal control as they account for their actions" (Melossi 1985, 178). His key variable is "moral climate" (1985, 1989). Punitive verbalizations/discourses used by social-control apparatuses and their operatives are more dependant on economic conditions and the articulations that arise. Hard times generate a war-on-crime ideology; good times, less so (1989, 320). Thus, "moral climate" is an intervening variable between the economic and penal ideologies. This direction is in accord with constitutive penology in so far as it does not prioritize the economic by itself (although acknowledging its contributing energy) but prioritizes the generation of discursive structures, which in turn become the basis of action by various law enforcement officials.

25. In *Romantic Outlaws, Beloved Prisons* (1996, 165), Martha Duncan argues that a "narrative model" is critical to understanding prisons in so far as it is directly implicated in how people construct various stories that give meaning to their lives. Accordingly, she shows how discourses of the nonlawbreaker regarding the lawbreaker connect the two in intimate ways. As she tells us, "criminals are far from being an unequivocal evil; they are, in fact, necessary for us to be what we are" (Duncan 1996, 117). Duncan's analysis suggests that prisoners and nonprisoners alike constitute meaning structures in a more hidden form that belies often verbalized, manifest, overt public statements and policies about prisons. Constitutive penology seeks to understand these interconnected aspects, particularly the latent and manifest functions of prisons.

26. For a discourse-oriented analysis of the criminal process, see Solan and Tiersma (2005); for the originations of legal discourse, see Tiersma (1999); for how judges' discourse reflects ideologies, see Philips (1998), Brunner (2000), and Kennedy (1997, 2001).

27. They also offer various behavioral patterns that await subjects for inauguration (see Quinney 1970, 20–21). That is to say, discursive subject-positions are created, stabilized, and reinforced that provide those most likely to be under the purview of state control a place in which an "I" can take up residence.

28. Ray Surette (1998, 223, 235) has argued that the relation between media and crime is "reciprocal" and "multidirectional," not linear. The media can be seen as a "steering mechanism." But its workings are more "bidirectional" and "cyclical" (235). "The media are both reflections of the culture and engines in the cultural production process" (237).

29. On the danger of conservative constructions of replacement discourse, see especially Kappeler and Kraska (1999). Foucault also has argued that the role of the intellectual should be to try and create a space from which the subaltern can speak, rather than speaking for them. This is consistent with one-perspective, standpoint epistemology. However, Foucault's position—as well as standpoint epistemology—is not sufficiently sensitive to the semiotic forms that the subaltern often use to frame their "realities." Consequently, the semiotic forms embraced "imprison" logic, rationality, time frames, and notions of linear causality.

30. For a suggestive direction that draws on Lacan's four discourses, Paulo Freire's work on critical pedagogy, and chaos theory as applied to the development of potentially oppositional forms of discourse (minority discourses) in law practices, see Milovanovic (2005).

31. For example, Banks (forthcoming, 181) has argued that "for staff [and incarcerated juveniles], the language of treatment frames and shapes the problems and issues of the residents and through this language, residents are described, assessed, labeled, and classified."

32. Their control discourse is tantamount to an abstract machine (Deleuze and Guattari 1987) that connects forms of expression to forms of content.

33. Duncan's findings seem to be in accord with (1) Foucault's call for intellectual activists to provide conditions that could allow prisoners to speak for themselves and to "appreciate the fact that only those directly concerned can speak in a practical way on their own behalf" (Foucault 1977b, 206–209; see also Howe's favorable nod, 1994, 170, 209), and (2) much of "standpoint epistemology." However, left unexamined is how stabilized discourses, dominant discourses, become the framework within which the subaltern situate themselves and from which they borrow given signifiers to construct reality. This is repetition. These very forms need subversion.

34. Milovanovic has also indicated how replacement discourses might develop in the interaction between client and lawyer (1996, 2002) and in conflict resolutions between parties in situations of escalating hostilities (1999, 203–23; 2001, 409–28).

3

The Phenomenology
of Penal Harm

*On the Criminology of the
"Shadow" and the "Stranger"*

INTRODUCTION

An agency/structure duality implicated in the coproduction of penal philosophy and practice has profound implications for the reification of harm. Our constitutive approach in penology, however, recognizes multiple "levels" consisting of COREL sets/assemblages that transcend a rigid dualistic model. These embedded levels are recursively constituted (repetition), are influential on the whole of which they are ultimately a part, and are dissipative structures in composition. Moreover, our constitutive approach addresses nonlinear change and modes of resistance rather than privileging reciprocal production, a "seamless hole," and stasis.[1]

Chapter 1 drew attention to the relational context in which expressions of power that specify harm or injury emerge from within historically mediated sociocultural conditions. These conditions give rise to certain phenomenal forms (e.g., the prison-form). Its parts (e.g., penal practices such as solitary confinement, the administration of lethal injection for death row incarcerates, child visitation policies for criminally confined mothers and fathers), along with the form itself, are constitutive of the whole society that stands above both. Moreover, this form and its parts reciprocally and simultaneously sustain the whole. Thus, parts and whole exist in a dynamic, mutually interdependent coproductive relationship. Even though repetition reconstitutes the whole, indigenous forces assure ongoing change. Accordingly, constitutive penology integrates notions of nonlinear, disproportional effects; emergents and spontaneities; the outcomes of dialectical struggle and inadvertent, serendipitous actions; oppositional discourses undermining dominant discursive representations; and the ongoing under-lying effects of molecular intensive forces (deterritorialization).

Additionally, chapter 2 critiqued the limits of various penal philoso-phies and policies. Although each one of them offers a unique view on the strategy or goals of incarceration, collectively they legitimize and are rei-fied by a discourse that essentializes prisons. Constitutively speaking, then, the language and logic of these justificatory schemes imprison us all. Once again, we are drawn to the implications of penal harm. Human agency, social structure, and intermediary "structures" in the form of as-semblages are held captive by recursive activities that reduce and repress human flourishing and becoming.

However, what is absent from consideration within the reification ac-tivities of contemporary penology is any critical regard for how the re-cursive definitions of its correctional categories, abstractions, and prac-tices perpetuate the victimizing reality that penal policy most assuredly has become. Missing thus far in our assessment of constitutive penology is any alternative vision for responding to harm without simultaneously reproducing the prison-form or its constitutive parts. In order to avoid en-gaging in such constitutive prison work, while nonetheless specifying how such injury or violence can be addressed, we examine two facets of our constitutive penological theory. In short, these include the *criminology of the shadow* and the *criminology of the stranger*.

The criminology of the shadow specifies the depth and breadth of the structural (molar) problems penal harm has come to embody. These harms are traceable to the psychoanalytic contours of penology's cultural identity and the capture of multiplicities in nominal, static forms that sub-sequently undergo reification. The criminology of the stranger examines how the activities of the recovering subject (being) and the transformative subject (becoming) recast the character of human agency as constituents of a replacement discourse and logic. This is a discourse that derealizes the notion of harm while humanizing (rather than objectifying) the of-fender. This is a logic that identifies injury through the expression of one's power that denies another's difference, yet reterritorializes knowledge about harm, always and already in provisional, positional, and relational ways. Of course, as Patton (2000) has warned, we must also be vigilant against the emergence of a replacement discourse that rediscovers hierar-chy anew.

ON THE CRIMINOLOGY OF THE SHADOW

The genesis of a criminological shadow originates in the application of psychoanalytic and nomadological[2] principles and concepts to cultural analysis.[3] This includes the trajectory of thought linked to the mechanistic and biologically driven insights of Sigmund Freud (1989, 2002), the Marxist-Freudian integrationist efforts of Frankfurt School critic Erich Fromm (1994, 2005), the deconstructionist sensibilities of the poststructuralist Jacques Derrida (1977, 1978), the semiotic formulations of Freudian revisionist Jacques Lacan (1977, 1981), and the dynamic, system theory–informed schizoanalytic approach of Deleuze and Guattari (1987). Contemporary examples demonstrating a steady reliance on psychoanalytic and emerging nomadological concepts as a basis to critique the cultural reality of criminal justice and criminology are considerable.[4] Indeed, some scholars have gone so far as to suggest that "there is something of a psychoanalytic comeback" relative to these concerns (Maruna, Matravers, and King 2004, 282), and they have even, ironically, been encouraged by way of critique to decenter and challenge several of its core premises. Interestingly, much of what appears to be a psychoanalytic resurgence addresses questions linked to punishment and penal punitiveness (e.g., Arrigo 2002; Duncan 1996; Evans 2003; Valier 2000; Veruz 2004). Deleuze and Guattari's work has also been applied to postconfinement adjustment concerns as specified in desistance theory (Halsey 2006b, 2006c).

The potential linkages among the criminological shadow, penology proper, and further articulations of the phenomenology of penal harm are worth noting.[5] To be clear, the criminology of the shadow is a deliberately introspective analytical lens consisting of a number of intersecting psychoanalytic, nomadological, and related philosophical components. Thus, in what follows, specific insights derived from the work of Fromm, Derrida, Lacan, and Deleuze and Guattari can only be tentatively enumerated. Collectively, however, these observations demonstrate how the recursive activities of existing correctional abstractions, categories, and practices work to coproduce and reify the prison-form, its constitutive parts, and the whole of society that legitimizes and essentializes the discourse of penology.

Fromm and the Criminology of the Shadow

Following Fromm (1994, 256) and his critique of capitalism and materialist culture, at issue is the extent to which the character of our personal freedom is both "spontaneous and positive." This is a condition in which "*the right to express our own thoughts [is meaningful] only if we are able to have thoughts of our own*" (Fromm 1994, 240, emphasis in the original). For Fromm, the pervasive absence of such a state of affairs was linked to a profound and often unspoken sensibility about our personal "insignificance and powerlessness" (1994, 108). He attributed these negative dimensions of our existences to the rapacious activity of accumulating (of having) for its own sake. Indeed, as Fromm (1994, 110) observed,

> It becomes [the individual's] fate to contribute to the growth of the economic system, to amass capital, not for purposes of [one's] own happiness or salvation, but as an end in itself. [The individual therefore becomes] a cog in the vast economic machine—an important one if he [or she] has capital, an insignificant one if he [or she] has none—but always a cog to serve a purpose outside of the [self].

Elsewhere, drawing attention to the quality of our freedom, given this persistent climate of fear, isolation, impotence, and desperation spawned by prevailing materialist cultural arrangements, Fromm (2005, 2) noted that

> the dream of being independent masters of our lives ended when we began awakening to the fact that we ha[d] all become cogs in the bureaucratic machine, with our thoughts, feelings, and tastes manipulated by government and industry and the mass communication that they control.

In response to these socially and psychologically debilitating circumstances, Fromm (1994, 239–54) suggested that individuality was an illusion and that identity was a pretense. In other words, notwithstanding the unmistakable advances of capitalism, negative freedom reigned supreme. As he further explained it,

> By making the individual free politically and economically, by teaching [the person] to think for [self] and freeing [the person] from . . . authoritarian [state] pressure[s], one hoped to enable [the person] to feel "I" in the sense that he [or she] was the center and [the] active subject of his [or her] powers and experienced himself [or herself] as such. [However,] for the majority, individualism was not much more than a façade behind which was hidden the failure to acquire an individual sense of identity. (2003, 62)

Fromm's concern for the possibility of positive freedom, of independent thought and affect absent sustained intrusion from or regulation by the state, led him to explore the methods people employed in order to cope with the consequences of their psychic discontent and social discord (Arrigo 2008).[6] Fromm termed these strategies "mechanisms of escape." In brief, they included authoritarianism,[7] destructiveness,[8] and automaton conformity (Fromm 1994, 140–204). For purposes of understanding the criminology of the shadow, the most significant of these is automaton conformity.

According to Fromm, this mechanism represented the panacea pursued by most citizens, given the lack of true individuality and authentic identity they experience in their lives. As Fromm (1994, 184) succinctly explained it,

> The individual ceases to be [a self and] adopts entirely the kind of personality offered to him [or her] by the cultural patterns; and [the person] therefore becomes exactly as all others are and as they expect [the person] to be. The discrepancy between "I" and the world disappears and with it the conscious fear of aloneness and powerlessness. . . . The person who gives up his [or her] individual self becomes an automaton, identical with millions of other automatons . . . [and] need not feel alone and anxious any more. But the price [the person] pays, however, is high; it is the loss of the self.

The significance of Fromm's (1994, 2003, 2005) commentary on capitalism, freedom, and automaton conformity, specifically as key insights that contribute to the criminology of the shadow, resonates with the phenomenology of penal harm and the coproduction of correctional abstractions, categories, and practices that perpetuate and reify the prison-form and its constitutive features.[9] At issue is the degree to which the message embedded within the discourse and logic of penology proper "legitimate[s] existing social structures" (Anderson 2000, 101), including the prevailing economic and political order (e.g., Christie 2000, 2004). This matter considers the *systemic pathology* of the principals and practices themselves that represent the extant correctional philosophies and that, knowingly or not, recursively reproduce the malaise of automaton conformity.

Equally importantly, at issue is the extent to which support is provided to the prison-form and its constitutive parts (e.g., death row executions, solitary confinement, child visitation policy for criminally confined fathers and mothers) through the mostly unreflective will of the public (Arrigo 2006b). As Fromm observed, this "additional factor" constitutes "the psychic readiness of the great majority to adjust to the existing society and to subordinate themselves to the ruling powers" (cited in Anderson and Quinney 2000, 125). This concern implicates the *social pathology* that is the collective conscience of the general public and indicates how their habitually uncritical regard for penal harm, whether from correctional philosophy to actual practices, may unwittingly be symptomatic of their own seemingly comatose-like and anesthetized tendencies: a strategy of escape seeded in the public's deep sense of personal insignificance and abject powerlessness, a mechanism of retreat that insulates the masses from the freedom that they lack, a technique of withdrawal whose effect merely guarantees the façade of individuality and the pretense of identity (Fromm 1994, 151–56).[10]

Mindful of these concerns in relation to psychoanalytically specifying the cultural identity of penology in which harm is both sustained and legitimized, a shadow criminology would deconstruct how the state ensures collective consent and docility (e.g., reliance upon the metaphors/practices of fear and terror; official statements/routine decisions that affirm the state as paternalistic guardian) and investigate why the public unreflectively reifies such insidious governmental authority in their lives (e.g., fear stemming from anxiety, insecurity over social responsibility, gratification of sadomasochistic impulses in which the state is perceived as "master"). In both instances, the Frommian lens would seek to expose the *unconscious mind* of penological reality as expressed through its discursive abstractions, categories, and practices. Additionally, this more introspective undertaking would entail some consideration of the nature and quality of penal harm, endeavoring to determine how it could be reconfigured to be consistent with the interests of positive freedom, individual thought, and personal identity (see "Toward a Criminology of the Stranger" below).

Jacques Derrida and the Criminology of the Shadow

The insights of Erich Fromm in relation to the criminology of the shadow help to clarify the breadth of the (Freudian-Marxist) psychoanalytic problem that penology proper confronts. Missing, however, are constructive intervention techniques that make more explicit the unspoken logic embedded within the field's principles and practices but, nonetheless, remain dormant. This is an effort to reveal the *unconscious intent*, embedded in diagrams of power, communicated through correctional categories and practices themselves. Accessing the unstated narrative and configurations (abstract machines, assemblages, molar and molecular forces) that lie beneath or deep within penology endeavors to make what is absent present or what is obscure apparent. Thus, this exercise specifies the *latent content* lodged within the text of penology. In part, the contributions of Jacques Derrida are instructive for this purpose. We will later turn to Lacan and Deleuze and Guattari for additional insights furthering a constitutive penology.

Derrida offers a considerable critique of Western philosophy and thought, which he termed the "metaphysics of presence" (Arrigo 2002, 156; Balkin 1987, 746–51).[11] The metaphysics of presence is a deconstructive or decentering strategy that reveals the "hierarchical oppositions" situated within words or phrases that result in the conveyance of restricted meaning (Balkin 1987, 746–51; Forrester 1991). Several routine instances of hierarchical oppositions are discernible in the written and spoken word. Representative examples include the following: the term "positive" conceals the value "negative," the term "objective" obscures the value "subjective," the term "straight" diminishes the value "gay," the term "white" defers the value "black," the term "man" distorts the value "women." The first term in each binary is esteemed or privileged (i.e., made present or apparent); the corresponding second term for each binary is postponed or discounted (i.e., relegated as absent or obscure). What makes these respective value positions troubling is that they communicate certain unstated, shared, and even commonsense beliefs in the dominance of the first term *over and against* the second one (Balkin 1987, 747–48; Derrida 1977, 3).

Admittedly, following a preliminary reading, these binaries as hierarchical oppositions may seem altogether harmless. After all, they are just words whether written or spoken. However, the potential difficulty lies in their contextual use, particularly if, for example, penological discourse and logic unknowingly promote as appropriate or acceptable, foundational or true, certain modes of sense making, particular ways of being/becoming, specific forms of social interaction (Arrigo 2002, 156; Milovanovic 2003, 133–34). Indeed, in the extreme, Derrida (1978) warns that the metaphysics of presence can result in the "privileging of certain *ideas* over others" (Balkin 1987, 746–51).

The significance of deconstruction, then, in relation to the metaphysics of presence and hierarchical oppositions is in its ability to make manifest the hidden biases or undisclosed preferences located within and behind language (e.g., the prison-form; correctional abstractions, principles, categories, and practices (Arrigo 2003, 61–63).[12] This is not to suggest that it is a totalizing recommendation for social change; rather, deconstruction functions to reveal and to decenter, albeit incompletely and provisionally, how the logic of various points of view, whether in principle or in practice, often disguises ideological positions (Milovanovic 2003, 133).[13] Consequently, deconstruction not only directs attention to the hidden and covert meanings embedded in what is written or spoken but functions as a discursive strategy for making that which is latent manifest, revealing the contested terrain over which (privileged) meaning operates. In order to demonstrate the utility of deconstruction for purposes of explaining the criminology of the shadow and its potential contribution to furthering our understanding of the phenomenology of penal harm, the related Derridean concept of reversing hierarchies is explored.[14]

Reversal of Hierarchies

The purpose of reversing hierarchies (e.g., "white over black" becomes "black over white"; "man over woman" becomes "woman over man") is to consider whether something more or something other might be learned about the two terms in the binary (as well as their newly constituted relationship) than had been ascertained before the terms were inverted (Arrigo 2002, 157; Balkin 1987, 746–51). For example, by switching the hierarchical oppositions "objective over subjective" to "subjective over objective," what replacement interpretations, if any, might be made about science, truth, progress, and reason? If we invert "straight over gay" to "gay over straight," what alternative claims might be made about sexuality, the body, intimacy, and identity?

Following Derrida (1977), the point is not to establish new power relationships or privileged standpoints that are solidified; rather, the reversal of hierarchies is intended to demonstrate how the "implied centrality of the first or dominant term masks and conceals the interdependence of both values" (Arrigo, Milovanovic, and Schehr 2005, 25). In other words, the activity of inverting terms in opposition decenters our favored ways of interpreting phenomena and invites us to consider other, potentially transformative configurations in which *both* terms are valued (Arrigo 2003, 62; Milovanovic 2003, 133–34). This is noteworthy because the articulation of correctional principles and practices operates on the basis of a "hidden premise that what is most apparent to our consciousness (i.e., what is most simple, basic, or immediate) is most real, true, foundational, or important" (Balkin 1987, 748). Decentering this unconscious intent, especially as delineated in penology proper, reveals this academic field's shadow that awaits articulation.[15]

Through the strategy of inverting contested terms in hierarchical opposition, deconstruction helps to make what is absent present. Moreover, by getting at the latent content (i.e., what is covert, postponed, or discounted), the possibility for demonstrating how both terms are *interdependent* is made all the more explicit (Forrester 1991). This line of reasoning is particularly significant because it suggests that once the obscure value is made apparent, given what is already privileged, "neither term is foundational [and] both mutually rely on each other to express thought and action" (Arrigo 2002, 157). This is the point at which the criminology of the shadow potentially leads to a novel understanding of penology proper, indeed, to one that can reconstitute the discourse and logic of penal harm.[16]

Bearing in mind the previous comments outlining Derrida's observations on the metaphysics of presence, hierarchical oppositions, and reversal of hierarchies, let us now consider as an example the construct of "punishment." The principles on which this term is founded (i.e., its prescriptive ideals or official conceptions) are traceable to such source materials as federal, state, and statutory law; Department of Corrections policy statements; and legal, behavioral, and social science research. In each instance, various issues related to punishment are addressed (e.g., the death penalty and competency to be executed, visitation for incarcerated mothers, solitary confinement, intermediate sanctions). The everyday operation of punishment (i.e., its descriptive reality) is situated in those routine correctional practices and decisions pertaining to the above-stated issues.

These practices and decisions may or may not be aligned with their official conceptions.

However, following Derrida and deconstruction, the criminal justice system's focus on "punishment" conceals, postpones, and/or dismisses its oppositional term, namely, "reward."[17] In other words, in its prescriptive ideals and descriptive reality, criminal justice makes overt and apparent the notion of punishment; it renders covert and absent the notion of reward. This is the metaphysics of presence at work. Further, the binary relationship between punishment and reward is as a hierarchical opposition. In corrections, the value of the first term, "punishment," is privileged; the value of the second term, "reward," is diminished. Troubling about this hierarchical opposition is that circumscribed meanings are conveyed in criminal justice (e.g., specific appellate court interpretations on solitary confinement, particular institutional decisions related to visitation for incarcerated mothers) in which the idea of punishment displaces (dismisses and undoes?) the idea of reward. Indeed, the dominance of the first term (i.e., "punishment") makes the presence of the second term (i.e., "reward") absent.

The bias or preference for punishment in corrections over reward leads to one deconstructive query: what additional or alternative insights might be gained if the two contested terms were reversed? By privileging "reward" over "punishment"—whether through official criminal justice sources, actual practices of the same, or both—would a different set of questions (and responses to them) emerge? Admittedly, rewards are gifts, incentives, or even prizes that are bestowed upon an individual. Thus, how might the prescriptive ideal and descriptive reality of corrections *as reward* get reconfigured under these circumstances? What sort of appellate court decisions might surface regarding solitary confinement or competency restoration for persons with mental illness on death row following the proposed inversion? What kind of institutional decision making might occur with respect to visitation for incarcerated mothers or the use of intermediate sanctions if the oppositional terms were switched? In what ways would the mutual interdependence of reward and punishment be alternatively enacted in corrections, given the reversal? How might the Frommian notions of positive freedom, individual thought, personal identity, and automaton conformity be recast on the books and in practice by placing the term "reward" over and against "punishment" in the realm of corrections?

The point of this deconstructionist exercise is not to insist on rigid and fixed categories of interpretation. Instead, by relying on several insights derived from Derrida, the aim is to suggest that a focused reading of the unconscious intent of the official source material on punishment as well as its expressed decision-making practices helps to deconstruct the unconscious mind of penology. More specifically, the activity of decentering, as an aspect of the criminological shadow, draws attention to the depth of the psychoanalytic challenge that exists, especially with respect to decoding reified notions for, by, and about penology proper. Undertaking such an excursion, although most assuredly difficult, begins to reorient the field to what it could be about both in principle and in practice. This may very well signal the birth of a new direction: one that helps to establish a different discourse and logic of the phenomenology of penal harm in which the subject's being is retrieved and the subject's becoming is transformed. The criminology of the shadow can be further developed in the works of Lacan and Deleuze and Guattari. We first turn to Lacan.

Jacques Lacan and the Criminology of the Shadow

Derrida's (1977, 1978) deconstructionist strategies make more explicit the latent content or the unconscious intent situated within words, expressions, codes, decisions, and practices. However, this psychoanalytic approach is insufficient for purposes of interpreting the penological principles, categories, and practices that recursively victimize the subject and perpetually reify the discourse of penal harm. Missing is some assessment of the *unconscious desire* of the field itself, whether in the ontological form of lack (Lacan) or production (Deleuze and Guattari). This desire discloses the relationship between language (whether written or spoken) and the person who speaks (e.g., correctional workers, researchers, policy analysts, victims, offenders).[18] Examining the inner workings of this discourse-subject relationship tells us a great deal about the meanings assigned to the absent or obscure terms in hierarchical opposition once made present or apparent. Selected contributions from the Freudian revisionist Jacques Lacan (e.g., 1977, 1981, and 1991) are integral to this enterprise. We shall then turn to Deleuze and Guattari for additional insights toward developing a constitutive penology.

In part, chapter 1 drew attention to the relationship between discourse and subjectivity, specifying the importance of unconscious desire in the process (Lacan 1977). Moreover, in describing the nature and manifestation of this desire, commentary on two planes of subjectivity (i.e., *the subject of speech* and *the speaking subject*) was supplied (Lacan 1981). As we explained, the speaking subject is the voice and narrative of the "Other." Psychoanalytically, this "Other" conveys only scripted meanings and is not directly or immediately accessible. However, for purposes of describing the unconscious desire of penology, revisiting the insights of Lacan (1991) is warranted. Indeed, the question Lacan (1977, 1981, and 1991) explored throughout the course of his considerable career was one of identifying the voice (language) and way of knowing (desire) that spoke the subject.

Lacan's (1991) seminar on the four discourses is particularly instructive. Lacan's attention to discourse and subjectivity included a dynamic understanding of speech production and its psychic mobilization (Arrigo 2002, 135–40; Milovanovic 2002, 47–51). Interested in both the communication that took place between people (the intersubjective plane) and the communication that occurred within the self (intrapsychic plane), Lacan (1991) graphically depicted these discourse-subject relationships in what he termed the four discourses.[19] Of these four schematizations, the *discourse of the master* and the *discourse of the hysteric* are most relevant to our focus on the phenomenology of penal harm.[20]

Before describing the operation of these discourses, it is important to remember that this section endeavors to examine more deliberately and descriptively the meaning-making process. In particular, as a feature of the criminological shadow, at issue is the character of speech production (e.g., what it signifies and from whose perspective), *especially* for absent terms made present. As the discourse of the master suggests, even in the moment of their articulation, a unique form of desire (of self and language) is embodied; however, is it responsive to different voices and replacement ways of knowing? In the context of understanding penology proper in which the field's principles and practices, as well as its abstractions and categories, are made psychoanalytically explicit, accessing this desire tells us something about the quality of what could be for the subject of penal harm. In other words, even when what is dismissed or deferred is retrieved and spoken, on whose terms do we comprehend it and in what way do we speak of it? Additionally, answering these sorts of questions discloses something quite profound about the type and extent of constitutive recovery and transformation that is presently possible, given the discourse of the master and the discourse of the hysteric.

Each of the four discourses includes four main terms and four corresponding locations. These terms include the following: *S1*, or master signifiers (privileged expressions or values); *S2*, or knowledge; *$*, or the slashed subject or the desiring subject; and *a*, or the *objet petit a*. This latter term is understood by Lacan (1991) as *le plus de jouir*,[21] or that excess in enjoyment left out (*pas tout/e*) or lacking in the discursive arrangement of the particular discourse (e.g., *university, master*) in operation.

Master signifiers are primordial; they originate through our childhood experiences and form the basis for how speech production customarily unfolds.[22] To illustrate, principles in criminal justice like "fairness," "due process," "just deserts," and "reasonableness" operate as master signifiers. The meanings assigned to these words or phrases are anchored in ideologically based contents, consistent with a materialistic political economy,[23] established during one's formative development. For Lacan (1991), the knowledge term, *S2*, is a part of a chain of self-referential signifiers where a specialized meaning (e.g., legalese) insists. Consider, for example, the master signifier "competency to stand trial." It is linked to other signifiers, such as "mental health treatment refusal," "knowing," "voluntary consent," and "reasonableness," and these signifiers form the basis of or become the subject for yet other key values in the administration of courtroom justice. The divided or slashed subject is depicted by the $ term. The subject is divided because his or her interiorized identity (as well as individuality and humanity) is not fully embodied in the words or phrases used to convey speech or invite action. All systems of communication (e.g., criminal justice, computers, engineering, basketball) are specialized discourses where communicating effectively means that one must insert oneself and/or be positioned within the parameters that give that language system narrative coherence. However, displaced or discounted in this process is the subject's being; this is the interiorized self (Lacan's lack, *pas tout/e*, or *a*) that remains silent. In Derrida's (1977, 1978) deconstructive terminology, this is the absent or obscure term not yet made present or apparent. The *a* is repressed because its utterance, although a more authentic representation of one's desire, would not be consistent with the operative mode of communicating.

In addition to his four terms, Lacan also identified four structural positions or pivotal locations. These four locations correspond to the terms and include the following:

AGENT	OTHER
TRUTH	PRODUCTION

On the left side of the equation (*agent/truth*) is the person or agency who/that speaks or conveys some message. On the right side of the equation (*other/production*) is the recipient of what is spoken or the receiver of some message. The upper left-hand structural position (the *agent*) is the author of the message or of what is conveyed. The upper right-hand structural position (the *other*) is the recipient of the message or is the reader/listener of the text. The relationship between *agent* and *other* takes place above the bar; thus, communication here is more active, overt, or conscious. The lower left-hand corner location (*truth*) represents what is unique to the person who sends the message to the recipient. The lower right-hand corner location (*production*) signifies the unconscious effects following the dissemination of information from sender to receiver. The relationship between *truth* and *production* occurs below the bar; thus, communication here is more passive, covert, and latent.

Bearing in mind the four terms and their matching four locations, we can now specify the operation of Lacan's discourse of the master (see table 3.1).

Table 3.1. The Discourse of the Master

$S1$	$\rightarrow$	$S2$	The message sent to the other is based on master signifiers that are
$\$$	$\leftarrow$	a	limited and constrained, yielding circumscribed knowledge. These

constrained signifiers stem from what is implicit in the sender (partial truths). The product of the exchange leaves something out; namely, incomplete understanding. This incomplete understanding experienced by the recipient of the message cannot be embodied in the truths that originate from the sender of the message.

Given the Lacanian conceptual work outlined above, particularly as an element of the criminological shadow, we briefly consider an example relevant to the phenomenology of penal harm, remaining mindful of penology's principles and practices.

The notion of penal harm (e.g., who is punished?, by what methods?, for how long?) emerges from within a commitment to the value of science. The emergence and importance of evidence-based practice in crime and justice studies (including penology) aptly conveys the significance of and esteem afforded this particular value (e.g., Burnett and Roberts 2004; Sherman 2002). Science, then, is a master signifier, occupying the position of *agent* in the discourse of the master. It is informed by a chain of master signifiers (related terms) and includes such notions as objectivism, logical positivism, theory testing, and quantification and measurement (Popper 1959, 1963, 1972).[24] These related terms are more concealed or covert; they inform what message is conveyed about the principles and practices of penology. As such, these additional values occupy the position of *truth* in the discourse of the master.

However, the scientific knowledge that is received by all conveys circumscribed information about the correctional apparatus and its various principles/philosophies, the penal system's institutional practices, and those subjected to its discursive mechanisms of control. This information/data—steeped in the logic of reductionism, absolutism, linear cause-effect relationships, equilibrium conditions, the logic of capital, and status quo dynamics—occupies the position of *other* in the discourse of the master. Moreover, the tension between penological science and various correctional principles/practices—expressed best, perhaps, in the manifestation of the burgeoning prison-industrial complex—indicates that something else is missing. In other words, the insights that are conveyed to us remain incomplete. Thus, the question is, what is absent in the communicated message

Table 3.2. Penology as the Discourse of the Master

SCIENCE_(e.g., evidence-based research)	$\rightarrow$	PENOLOGY (principles/practices)
POSITIVISM	$\leftarrow$	CRIMINOLOGY OF THE STRANGER

between (penological) science and correctional principles/practices? The answer is a *philosophy of the subject*! Stated differently, criminology lacks a *theory of the stranger*.[25] Thus, we take the position that the Lacanian (1991) *pas tout/e* in the discourse of penology seeks the embodiment of a replacement grammar steeped in the logic of constitutive theory. Penology has an underdeveloped philosophy of the subject. Consequently, its manifold applications of penal harm—from its correctional abstractions to its instruments of surveillance, from its institutional categories to its technologies of control—operate in the absence of a fully articulated criminology of the stranger. This lack is the Lacanian (1981) *speaking subject* at work, yielding nothing more than scripted meanings that undermine what could be for all those who undergo penal harm.

The recursive production of reality becomes more apparent in the discourse of the hysteric.

The philosophy of the subject as the lack in penology (Lacan's 1981 *subject in speech* as unspoken and obscured subtext) cannot be fully retrieved, and it cannot experience its potential becoming within the master signifier of science or the truths that support it. Something more is needed. Following Derrida (1977, 1978), a criminology of the stranger is the absent term awaiting expression, signifying, as Deleuze (1983) would say, a "people yet to come." It is concealed, postponed, and deferred through the principles and practices of penology. However, the stranger's relationship to science is one of mutual interdependence. Thus, the unexamined philosophy of the subject supports, although mostly unconsciously, the incomplete scientific knowledge claims that are communicated. In this respect, then, the criminology of the stranger, as the lack or the not-all, is the source of what is needed to further reveal the coproductive nature of human agency in penology. Moreover, its absent but felt repression is the result of what is communicated from sender to receiver of the constrained penological message. In the Lacanian (1991) schema, then, the criminol-

Table 3.3. The Discourse of the Hysteric

$\$$	→	$\underline{S1}$
a	←	S2

Here, the "hysteric," more broadly defined as a person in struggle (including both the clinical as well as the alienated, oppositional, and revolutionary subject) communicates her or his suffering to the other, who only offers master signifiers (slogans, ideology, dogma, truths, rhetoric) from which a body of knowledge may be constructed. The person in struggle, $\$$, has only a limited range of master signifiers from which to construct a narrative of her or his plight. A constitutive penology witnesses this daily in the various routine interactions between those imprisoned and those operatives offering key master signifiers, often bureaucratically informed.[1]

1. For a suggestive direction in law practices identifying dynamics that may generate alternative master signifiers that are more open, more reflective of unique desires, and the basis of replacement narrative constructions, see Milovanovic's (2005) integration of Lacan's four discourses, Paulo Friere's critical dialogical pedagogy, and dynamic systems theory.

ogy of the stranger assumes the position of *production* in the discourse of the master.

Gilles Deleuze and Felix Guattari and the Criminology of the Shadow

Deleuze and Guattari set out to overthrow "Oedipus," a complex, they argued, that was born during the transition to the nuclear family[26] and the emergence of the capitalist socius. Both inherently converged to privilege the phallic signifier and desire as lack. Deleuze and Guattari perceived much that was insightful in the Lacanian schema. Specifically, Lacanian theory, seen as descriptive, is in accord with Deleuze and Guattari's notion of how desire is captured in one form rather than being allowed to run its own imminent course. They maintained that Freud's notion of libido was a great discovery; however, it lost its productive force in the logic of the Oedipus and capital logic. In response, Lacan's "linguistification of Oedipus," a strategic move away from the imaginary to the symbolic order, liberated Freudian analysis from its many (masculine) limitations.

This consensus notwithstanding, Deleuze and Guattari's fundamental disagreement with Lacan was with the nature of the unconscious and desire. The unconscious, they argued, is not theater; desire does not ontologically emerge from lack; rather, it is a factory rife with production.[27] That is, the unconscious is a machine that only knows cuts of flows, is driven only by desire that makes connections—some of which attain stasis (molar forms)—but is constantly subject to decoding/deterritorializing processes that undo what has been done (molecular). Hence, the molar stands for closure, stasis, statistical regularities, repetition of the same, reactive forces, resistance to change. In contrast, the molecular stands for active forces, for nonlinear developments (rhizomes), and for ever-dynamic, open, fluid, and transforming change.

In their view, the plane of immanence, the virtual realm, lies at the very ontological basis of being human and the endless process of becoming (Deleuze and Guattari 1987). It is an intensive plane with differential speeds, extremes, depths, and threshold levels. This is a realm in which bifurcations transform otherwise relatively stable systems into ever-new phase spaces (Milovanovic 2002; Williams and Arrigo 2002). These phase spaces, identified by the number of degrees of freedom they embody, are replete with new attractor states that can be subjected to genealogical analysis whereby these states can be discovered and articulated. Admittedly, while strata do emerge, they are molar formations (e.g., class statuses, gender identities, bureaucracies, political parties, nuclear families). However, in the Deleuzian ontology (1983), they are constantly exposed to deterritorialization, to mutation, and to transformation.

For Deleuze and Guattari (1987), the molecular lives in the plane of immanence, where only multiplicities are to be found. But these multiplicities take on form in the real, in the form of assemblages or, in our view, COREL sets. These pervade the socius. They *are* the socius. It is in a particular socius that we find statistical regularities. Historically, Deleuze and Guattari (1983) identified the savage, despotic, and capitalist forms. It is only in the capitalist form that human beings are drastically separated from the fixed public codes of the former two. But it is also where "capturing mechanisms" mold desire into system needs, where subjects often "willingly" (and unknowingly) reconstitute this organized and scripted desire into their everyday practices. At the core of assemblages are abstract machines, a logic that is overdetermining in connecting content to expression.[28] Abstract machines include "regimes of signs."[29] These relatively stable discursive assemblages are stratifications of signifiers and connected signifieds. They limit which narratives can be constructed.

For Deleuze and Guattari (1983), a regime of signs is the particular way expression has been connected with content.[30] The guide here is not Saussure but instead Louis Hjelmslev. Equally central is the literature on the performative and illocutionary functions of language, indirect speech, and even linguistic relativity theory. "Order words" are fundamental forms.

Order words have certain affinities with master signifiers by way of Lacan (1977). They are commanding words. They are performative and illocutionary. Their expression produces incorporeal transformation. To illustrate, say "I do" in a wedding ceremony, "Guilty!" in a court of law, "Hey, you" by a policeman, and these utterances produce material responses. Order words are invested with expectations and presuppositions. They reflect power. Order words reflect the voices of the many, even as expressed by the one. Indirect speech is replete with order words, the voices of the many incorporated in the subject of the statement. A dominant discourse, or regime of signs, is a major discourse, more akin to molar assemblages; minor discourses are more dynamic and subversive, less static and fixed—they denote the language of the "people yet to come."

In accord with Lacan, Deleuze and Guattari decenter identity. The speaker always is spoken. Identity comes after the fact.[31] Discourse speaks the subject, and not the other way around. It is the regime of signs with its key order words that limits what can be articulated in speech. The "I" is but a marker in discourse; the producer of the narrative remains elsewhere. Accordingly, various working ideologies of "corrections" are expressive forms, regimes of signs, that are recursively constituted: by the operatives who are the relays of their primacy and intent, by the receivers (incarcerates, released inmates) who continuously find themselves in situations that demand homage to the language of corrections (i.e., in the form of probation and parole agreements, in rehabilitation programs, in restorative justice programs, and the like).

Desistance Theory, Deleuze and Guattari, and Constitutive Penology

Let us now be more precise in explaining how the previous framework may apply in specifying a constitutive penology as well as a criminology of the shadow. Desistance theory (see Farrall and Calverley 2006; Maruna and Immarigeon 2004) is exemplary for this demonstration. Desistance theory focuses on the process over time, not the final termination of recidivism (see particularly Maruna, Matravers, and King 2004, 17–19).

Following Giddens (1984), with qualifications to his primarily linear thesis, Stephen Farrall and Adam Calverley (2006, 173–81) provide a clear beginning. For them, the departing point is "critical situations," initially analyzed by Giddens (1984) but later to disappear in his structuration theory. Giddens indicated how these critical situations disrupt normal expectations. Even though they may initially produce fear and anxiety, they also represent the basis of "positive opportunities" for change (Farrall and Calverley 2006, 175). They are a source of epiphanies.[32] However, according to Farrall and Calverley's review of the literature, the issue of the subject's motivation was lacking in Giddens' analysis. More specifically, the critical literature on Giddens' thesis indicates that even though individuals may devote considerable energy in responding to the need for security, which tends to reconstitute dominant understandings and actions, they also can be seen as investing in "deliberate departures from routines" (see Johnson as cited in Farrall and Calverley 2006, 177). The constitutive theory of Giddens (1984) is more concerned with reconstituting forces, not disruptive forces,[33] or how new forms may materialize, or the various motivations by which subjects experience transformation. Thus, the constitutive theory of Giddens addresses the subject of being, not becoming.[34]

Applying structuration theory to that of desistance theory, Farrall and Calverley (2006) focus on desire during the life course. They identify how prison, contrary to stated manifest functions, has "the major impact . . . to disrupt the journey of 'going straight'" (2006, 181). They argue that "prison rules place people under an institutionalized routine that virtually suspends their power" (2006, 181). Ultimately, in their view, it is informal control, the provision of employment, expressions of hope, and the presence of support for noncriminal activities that offer more opportunities for bonding and a greater likelihood of desistance from crime.

Few reformists would find this direction unfruitful. However, the difficulty with their approach is in its inadvertent bolstering of dominant forms: work, family, normative aspirations, and faith in the "English dream" and/or the "American dream." Empirical investigation might very well indicate that the premises of desistance theory for the confined and postconfined indeed produce greater desistance (e.g., Farrington et al. 1986; Piquero, Farrington, and Blumstein 2007; Laub and Sampson 2001; Sampson and Laub 1993). What is being inadvertently reconstituted, however, are the molar forms. Thus, we have come full circle in indicating how, after all qualifications, constitutive theory shows that the socius is fundamentally both recursively and continuously reconstituted by various forces, even those designed for reform beyond the limitations of traditional prison literature, such as deterrence, rehabilitation, and so forth. In short, on the one hand, desistance theory can be easily interpreted as a direction that may reduce crime; on the other hand, it reconstitutes dominant, molar forms.[35] For example, the capitalist socius remains beyond incrimination: alternative forms of employment, family structure, and hope are not adequately contemplated, let alone voiced. Consistently with the preceding analysis on Fromm, Derrida, and Lacan, the insights of Deleuze and Guattari, especially as applied to desistance theory, demonstrate that, to a considerable extent, contemporary penology lacks a fully developed theory of the subject, of the "stranger."

TOWARD A CRIMINOLOGY OF THE STRANGER

One recent Deleuzian strategy (Halsey 2006a, 2006b, 2006c) offers a direction that moves our understanding of the prison-form beyond the critique of the criminological shadow. This novel orientation resists emphasis on being and, instead, considers possibilities for the subject's transformation, flux, and becoming. We see this direction as contributing to a *transdesistance* approach. This approach begins to specify constitutive penology's theory of the transforming subject or the criminology of the stranger.

Halsey (2006b) notes that the postreleased are often caught in the tension of a hope-despair dynamic. Specifically, he indicates that the family structure is often nonexistent for the former incarcerate, and where it exists, it is replete with forces that reinforce despair. The "pains of release," then, must be counterposed to the "pains of imprisonment." Accordingly, for Halsey (2006b, 2006c), we must look at the body and its mobilization of active and reactive forces, its flows and its affects, which is consistent with the work of Deleuze, Guattari, and Nietzsche.

Halsey (2006c) argues that Deleuze and Guattari's (1987) notion of desire as flow can be applied to criminality. It is a flow, much like recidivism is a flow.[36] As he tells us, "Recidivism . . . has most often been dealt with as if it were an administrative event to be managed as opposed to a lived and therefore inherently unpredictable process" (2006c, 162). Desire, in short, has been captured by administrative categories, not the realities of those entering and leaving prison.[37] Thus, we must look at the body, its mobilization, and what it is capable of doing.

To illustrate, consider the ex-offender's "release plan." It is cast in a rigid discourse of responsibilities, schedules, prohibitions, and time frames. Typically, it has very little to do with the desires of the newly released custodial subject: "Young men on conditional release desire to be young men—to be able to drink, relax, have a good time, sit around with friends, stay up late, and to choose whether they will participate in this or that programme" (Halsey 2006c, 164). In addition, "young men released from custody continue to offend because that is what works best for them relative to the milieus they inhabit" (Halsey 2006c, 166). The contemporary "deficit model"[38] of prison focuses primarily on monitoring potential failures, not on dynamics that may lead to desistance (Halsey 2006c, 167).

The postcustodial subject, faced with the pains of release, must be situated in a broader framework of assemblages, of historically contingent configurations of interconnecting iterative loops (CORELS), where active and reactive forces prevail. It is the mobilization of these COREL sets that must be studied for contributions to desistance. Each subject, then, in accord with Deleuze and Guattari, must be seen as a multiplicity, not a subject that lives only within the narrow diagrams of the release plan.

Halsey's (2006c) perceptive insight is that not only must the custodial and postcustodial subject be reenvisioned but the various correctional workers and policy makers must also be reconceptualized. Each of them must be "linked to processes, contexts, and events occurring beyond yet contiguous with each person" (Halsey 2006c, 172). "Factors" (e.g., gender, race, class) identified in contemporary penological literature must be deconstructed along the lines that Derrida (1977, 1978) proposes, rather than being taken for granted (i.e., static, fixed, and rigid categories). They must be seen as concepts (molar forms) rooted in assemblages in the socius. Moreover, what needs to be sought are the imminent forces of deterritorialization, of desires captured in one set of assemblages rather than another, of the body and its multiple forms of expression, only some aspects of which are allowed materialization. They remain as the "Other," the lack, and the stranger, awaiting expressive form.

Radicalized Desistance Theory and the Criminology of the Stranger

Given Halsey's perceptive analysis and extension of the desistance literature (guided especially by Deleuze and Guattari's conceptual framework), what needs to be theorized is a radicalized version of desistance theory, a transdesistance theory that gets us beyond often unintended, overall-system-sustaining logic. That is, we need to create directions away from energizing or further investing in the axiomatics[39] of capital and oedipal logic. For a good part of desistance theory, it is employment, family structure, and reinforcing hope, along the direction already given in capital and oedipal logic, that is ultimately being advocated, often in the form of bond theory (Hirschi 1969; Laub and Sampson 2001; Bazemore and Erbe 2004, 46). Furthermore, polarizing exercises or reinforcing dualities—"deviant or conforming citizen" (Uggen, Manza, and Behrens 2004, 287)—does a disservice to issues of understanding process, contradiction, nonlinearity, the nature of choice, and the postcustodial subject faced with both hope and despair. In other words, without more, it is the molar structure that is being reconstituted. It is being (or the molar), not becoming (or the molecular), that is privileged.

Constitutive penology asserts that desistance theory, without more, fundamentally reinforces flows that are molar in form. The postcustodial subject finds her- or himself constrained in molar structures with promises of molecular forces to come, *but only in the forms prescribed by capital and oedipal logic.* Constitutive penology, however, argues that desire must be allowed its most diverse forms of expression; it should not be limited to the axiomatics of capital and oedipal logic. Employment, hope, and nuclear family structures must each be deconstructed, or in Deleuze and Guattari's words, subject to schizoanalytical/nomadological examination.

Prison and postcustodial release plans[40] not only focus on creating the bodies of docility and utility (Foucault 1977a) but tend toward the stabilization of reactive forces—the separation of the body from what it can potentially do (see also Halsey 2006b, 16). The custodial subjects "are taught to react rather than act. They are taught to respond rather than initiate" (Halsey 2006b, 16). It is but one sense of subjectivity that finds reinforcement within the prison apparatus (Halsey 2006b, 17). Thus, as Halsey suggests, we must look for strategies whereby the body's active forces are more completely brought to center stage during the "pains of imprisonment" and the "pains of release." Admittedly, to some extent, this already happens, given the various networks in which the postcustodial subject finds him- or herself.

To illustrate, consider "mateship." It is a form of social capital that provides support for the struggling subject. The "critical situation" of Giddens (1984)—here, postrelease—provides a profound opportunity to interrupt repetition. However, the limited available assemblages in which mateship is constructed, legitimized, and experienced weigh heavily against the emergence of alternative directions. Mateships, or significant peers, represent a mesolevel of analysis that, according to DeLanda (2006), is vital to the pragmatically lived interactions of human beings. Following a review of the extant literature, Farrall and Calverley (2006, 188) assert that "certain meso-level social or community structures influence individuals' desires, motivations, and abilities to engage in, or refrain from, offending." This literature, however, often lacks a well-theorized notion of a subject and the nature of these mesolevel organizations.

DeLanda (2006, 47–67) has provided some refreshingly new insights as to the nature of these mesolevel forms as assemblages. One form is networks. This is where particular identities can find support; networks are a source of social capital.[41] They can be specified in terms of two key dimensions. One dimension includes their forms of content (differentials in time, energy, movement in speed, at rest, and across space, and commitments), and forms of expression (linguistic and nonlinguistic). The other dimension consists of territorialization (forces that keep the networks together, such as solidarity, often based on conflict between "us" and "them") and deterritorialization (e.g., forces that tend to the dismantling of a network—mobility, forced separation, and evasion of law or predators collecting debts).

A component of networks is the space within which they operate and the events they may generate. As such, certain mesolevels "influence individuals' desires, motivations, and abilities to engage in, or refrain from, offending" (Farrall and Calverley 2006, 188; see also Hagan 1997; Bottoms and Wiles 1992; Meisendhelder 1977). These networks, encounters, and spaces fundamentally provide opportunities for active or reactive forces to take form. Thus, according to Halsey (2006b, 21), "the question to be asked with regard to mateship and responsibility for crime is one which inquires into the conditions which produce and require that groups of young men engage in crime as a means of acquiring those things to which most others aspire—security, recognition, and respect." Thus, for Halsey (2006b, 31) "repeat incarceration . . . is an event constituted not by the choices this or that individual makes or does not make, but by particular configurations of the social—configurations which permit only a limited supply of pathways and contexts." It is not just structure or just the individual that is overdetermining. Differentials exist in the ability to structure and to be structured, and it is to the various interlocking assemblages/COREL sets that we must look for insights on recidivism (see also Halsey 2006b, 31–34, 39).

What necessarily must change in these recursively constructed thoughts and actions, in the repetition that is the reality of prisons, are opportunities for disruption (Halsey 2006b, 34). Indeed, what must change are the critical situations themselves. The penal assemblage must be creatively and pragmatically challenged in order that molecular lines of flight become dominant over molar ones, already and always in provisional, positional, and relational ways. As Halsey (2006b, 35) suggests, indigenous or minor narratives do make their emergence but need to be "plugged in." In other words, they warrant serious (correctional) policy-making consideration. However, the problem is that the very narratives constructed by those in struggle to desist are constituted within existing regimes of signs consistent with the *discourses of the master* or *hysteric* (Lacan). To resurrect a key activist question, "From where do the subaltern speak?" (Spivak 1988).

For constitutive penology, a pivotal factor in response is the development of an alternative discourse, an alternative regime of signs in combination with outright radical changes of molar strata throughout the socius. One cannot be done without the other. Consistent with this position, Halsey (2006b, 41) suggests in his concluding recommendation that "shared responsibility" be explored. In short, he recognizes that a number of interlocking assemblages (both formal and informal), operating at various "levels" of the socius, must be reconfigured to provide the very milieu within which alternative forms and expressions of desire may be given wider latitude for materialization. This shared responsibility would also necessarily implicate the various administrative entities and their expressive forms that currently are part of the control apparatus (see also Bazemore and Erbe's call for a partnership, although it does not extend to transformative components, 2004, 36). This means that strategies to reduce recidivism cannot be directed only to a person; rather, its more complete understanding extends to the historically contingent configurations of assemblages—their content, their forms of expression—to territorialization tending toward molar structures, and to deterritorialization, which tends toward the molecular.

We add to this recommendation that desistance theory must also find a wider framework within which to incorporate strategic challenges to the various molar structures throughout the socius. Recognizing the positive influence of family, employment, and hope begins a line of flight, a flow. However, these very concepts must be deconstructed and situated within a historically contingent socius. Alternative configurations or mutations of the same must be articulated, enacted, and endorsed if the stranger's transformative becoming is to be more completely realizable in nonrecursive ways.

By undertaking these genealogical activities, we begin to understand how desire (mostly unwittingly) becomes captured within the nuclear family[42] via Oedipus and under capitalism via its various embedded abstract machines. Lacan (1977, 1981, 1985, and 1991) certainly explicates how manufactured lack and consequent limited forms of desire materialize, as well as how the *discourse of the master* and *hysteric* further confine the expression of desire. His schematizations here significantly contribute to our understanding of the criminological shadow in penology. However, the material side of this process is absent. Deleuze and Guattari's work is particularly well suited to respond to the interconnection of social and libidinal production and to explore how, via schizoanalysis, avenues may be found in which active forces and molecular structures may become dominant over molar forms.[43] In this respect, then, Deleuze and Guattari offer a potent transition from the silencing of the subject's being to the emergence of the subject's becoming. We will return to these notions in greater detail in this book's concluding chapter. Before doing so, however, we first explore two protean areas where constitutive penology provides insightful direction for the reform of penal harm and for the advancement of transformative justice.

NOTES

1. The latter is a shortcoming recognized in Anthony Giddens' (1984) constitutive approach and the structuration of society. For a cogent analysis on this point, see DeLanda (2006).

2. The notion of nomadology is drawn from Deleuze and Guattari (1987) and is a perspective that is directed at understanding how molar (stratified, statistical regularities) and molecular (destratified, more unconscious) forces are arranged in assemblage format that are continuously subject to deterritorialization (the "war machine").

3. The use of the term "shadow" in psychoanalytic circles is metaphorical in its account of one's unconscious personality. It implicates Freud's psychic system of the id, ego, and superego, reconceptualized by subsequent analysts, such as Jung (1964) and Klein (1985). However, the phrase "the criminology of the shadow" is a relatively recent expression used to account for punitive public attitudes (Maruna, Matravers, and King 2004) and, to a lesser extent, the underlying psychoanalytic dimensions of Garland's (2001) thesis on the culture of control and penal policy (Matravers and Maruna 2004). However, as appropriated in this book, the phrase is associated more with elucidating the absent but felt dimensions of penal harm more generally. In this respect, then, the notion of a shadow refers to a "radical reading of the psychoanalytic literature" (Maruna, Matravers, and King 2004, 294) in which penology proper comes to terms with and owns its *unconscious mind* (for applications in crime and justice studies, see Arrigo 2002, 175–90; Arrigo 2008).

4. A very brief, though representative, list of such studies would include the following: for applications relative to Freud, see Groves (1987), Groves and Galaty (1986), and Stein (2006); for applications relative to Fromm, see Anderson (1998) and Anderson and Quinney (2000); for applications relative to Derrida, see Arrigo (2003) and Borradori (2003); for applications relative to Lacan, see Arrigo and Schehr (1998) and Milovanovic (2002). For applications of nomadology, see Halsey, 2006a, 2006b, 2006c; Milovanovic 2007; Murray 2006; see also the 2007 special issue of the *International Journal for the Semiotics of Law* 20(1).

5. At the outset, we note that this psychoanalytic (and nomadological) excursion is not without its own set of restrictions. For example, Maruna, Matravers, and King (2004, 281) aptly summarize a number of the main apprehensions with appropriating the psychoanalytic lens when investigating crime and justice issues.

Among other concerns, they note the framework's "failure to meet Popperian standards for falsification; lack of conceptual limits; [and] masculine bias." Notwithstanding these observations, the purpose of the foregoing theoretical exercise is not to "prove" the legitimacy of psychoanalytic inquiry as much as to demonstrate how several of its conceptualizations (1) invite us to rethink the penological domain and (2) encourage us to undertake a reformulation of the field, consistent with deconstructing the cultural embeddedness of penal harm. For more on the contemporary relevance of psychoanalysis to cultural studies, see Forrester (1991); in crime and justice, see Arrigo, Milovanovic, and Schehr (2005); Milovanovic (2002).

6. As Fromm (1994, 240) observed, "Freedom from external authority is a lasting gain only if the inner psychological conditions are such that we are able to establish our own individuality."

7. Authoritarianism enables a person to escape unbearable feelings of aloneness and powerlessness. For Fromm (1994, 162–63), "Authority is not a quality one person 'has,' in the sense that [one] has property or physical qualities. Authority refers to an interpersonal relation in which one person looks upon another as somebody superior to him[- or herself]." It is the tendency on the part of the subject to rely on sadistic and/or masochistic activities that are rationalized. Outwardly, these rationalizations are expressions of wanting to dominate others and wanting to be dominated by others, respectively. However, the more covert explanation for these inclinations is that the person is *terrified* by the freedom that he or she lacks. In this context, then, sadistic and/or masochistic strivings reflect the subject's "inability to bear the isolation and weakness of one's own self." In other words, these proclivities symbolize one's desire *"to get rid of the burden of [negative] freedom"* (Fromm 1994, 151–56).

8. Destructiveness is a technique of escape as described by Fromm (1994, 177–83). It is closely aligned with authoritarianism, expressed through sadistic and/or masochistic inclinations. "Sadomasochistic strivings [can be] differentiated from destructiveness, although they are mostly blended with each other. Destructiveness is different [however] since it aims not at active or passive symbiosis but at the elimination of an object" (178).

9. We note that the early Fromm developed three articles expressly addressing criminal justice concerns. The first of these, "Oedipus in Innsbruck," considered the psychology of the individual offender in the high-profile case of Phillip Halsmann; the second, "The State as Educator: On the Psychology of Criminal Justice," reviewed the application of psychoanalytic approaches to the an understanding of crime and criminals; and the third, "On the Psychology of the Criminal and the Punitive Society," examined a wide range of criminological theories, integrating them with Fromm's own brand of Freudian Marxism. For more on these articles and their relevance to critical criminology, see Anderson (2000, 97–106); for a translation of the latter two from the original German, see Anderson and Quinney (2000, 120–56).

10. Michel Foucault (1977a, 192–96) offered a similar critique, arguing that the state relies on mechanisms of surveillance or techniques of control that function as forms of power/knowledge and that discipline the subject's corporeal "soul." As he explained, institutional strategies (penal, medical, or legal codes, practices, and

apparatuses) that discipline are omnipresent. Their deployment renders human subjects nothing more than "'docile bodies,' 'bodies of abject utility,' and mere 'functionaries of the state'" (210).

11. According to Derrida (1978, 3), the metaphysics of presence advances logocentrism. Logocentrism "assumes the centrality in thought (and action) of the first term in a binary association. The dominance of this value (i.e., its imagery, logic, and meaning[s]) conceals the interdependence of both terms" in relation to one another (see also Arrigo, Milovanovic, and Schehr 2005, 25).

12. The application of deconstruction proposed here is not a complete destabilization of meaning ad infinitum. What is contested, however, is the legitimacy and authority given to established penological meanings as located within the field's identified principles and practices. To the extent that these values, assumptions, cultural commitments, and the like represent dominant interpretations, they potentially render, unwittingly or otherwise, alternative values and relationships unacceptable or unimportant. However, it is this latent content (the shadow of what is) that may very well be the basis for articulating replacement values, assumptions, and cultural commitments that could significantly help penology chart a new direction in which penal harm was not recursively reified.

13. This point has been made by Balkin (1987, 786): "Deconstruction by its very nature is an analytic tool and not a synthetic one. It can displace a hierarchy momentarily, it can shed light on otherwise hidden dependencies of concepts, but it cannot propose new hierarchies of thought or substitute new foundations. These are by definition logocentric projects, which deconstruction defines itself against."

14. In order to have a more fully developed deconstructionist psychoanalytic reading, Derrida's notion of *différance* (with an *a*), the trace, the logic of the supplement, and arguments that undo or unground themselves would all warrant consideration. For a discussion of these notions and their relevance to crime and justice studies, see Arrigo (2002, 157–58, 165–70) and Arrigo, Milovanovic, and Schehr (2005, 25–27).

15. This point is particularly salient in penology, where the object of inquiry is overwhelmingly thought to be the study of punishment and penal practices, including the instruments of penal surveillance and harm. The reversal of hierarchies would debunk this logic by questioning what the concealed or dismissed terms are that reside underneath, behind, or through the valued position of "punishment," particularly as expressed through its corresponding philosophies, categories, and principles. What we discover may very well be the basis for reimagining the prison-form and its constitutive parts such that the subject exposed to penal harm can experience recovery and transformation.

16. For example, the application of Derrida's deconstructionist logic would be particularly salient for decentering the Frommian-based notion of systemic pathology that fosters automaton conformity and the Frommian-based notion of social pathology that displaces positive freedom. As previously discussed, both conditions are symptomatic of the malaise that presently underpins the culture of penology in which a psychoanalytic remedy is proposed. The suggestion here is that deconstruction is one facet of the "cure."

17. The oppositional terms "punishment" and "reward" are significant given the related terms to which they are connected, namely, "crime" and "justice." As

Hoffman (2001, 227) notes, "Whereas criminal justice seeks a correlation between punishment and crime, distributive justice seeks a correlation between rewards and some measure of deservingness." Here, too, we see the potential relevance of deconstructive praxis.

18. In Lacanian (1977) psychoanalysis, desire is embodied in the relationship of discourse and subjectivity. It is "a reference to all the longings, aspirations, fears, passions, and joys residing in the unconscious [that] await . . . articulation" (Arrigo and Schehr 1998, 633; Milovanovic 2002).

19. The four discourses, as distinct mechanisms for understanding speech production and its psychic configuration, explain how desire finds or fails to find expression (and legitimacy) in the written or spoken word. They also explain what sort of knowledge is privileged (or dismissed) when one of these specific speech mechanisms is in use.

20. The other two mechanisms employed by Lacan (1991) for understanding speech production and its psychic configuration include the *discourse of the university* (a variation of the *discourse of the master* traceable to institutional practices, indoctrination techniques, and education models) and the *discourse of the analyst* (a strategy for overcoming the lack in discourse and subjectivity experienced by the *hysteric* (see Arrigo et al. 2005, 3–5; Milovanovic 2002, 47–51, Milovanovic 2003, 237–42). Interestingly, a fifth Lacanian formulation, the *discourse of capitalism*, "was briefly developed [by Lacan] but remains to this day unanalyzed" (Milovanovic 2002, 48)

21. Lacan often instructed the reader to interpret his *objet petit a* in context rather than giving it a rigid meaning. Here he implies that it connotes the left out.

22. At a more primordial level, master signifiers find their originations in the Oedipus complex. Lacan was to give the Freudian imaginary Oedipus dynamic a linguistic form: the unconscious is structured like a language. Thus, Lacan stipulated that within the nuclear family, what functioned as the coordinator of the unconscious was the identification with the phallus (the master signifier of domination). This identification provided stability and was the source of investments in various forms of hierarchy via displacement.

23. Following Marx, two spheres can be delineated: the sphere of linguistic production is the locus (i.e., higher-court decision-making based on balancing of interest tests) where particular signifiers are connected with particular signifieds; the sphere of linguistic circulation is the domain where these signs circulate, where, through a homologous process to commodity fetishism, they undergo more universal meanings, devoid of nuanced accentuations. They become master signifiers within the control apparatus. Subjects entering the various linguistic regions (courts, police, probation, prison) also enter a sphere where signs are already preconstituted, are populated with voices.

24. As discussed in chapter 2, most recently actuarial models have been employed to forecast dangerousness and to recommend incapacitation as a function of government's concern for risk management (e.g., Feeley and Simon 1992, 2004).

25. The work of philosophy, in relation to establishing theory (in penology or otherwise), is to assess the kind of ontological, epistemological, ethical, and/or aesthetical commitments that inform that which is proposed. In this respect, then, philosophy is the necessary antecedent to theory (Williams and Arrigo 2006). It is

the "underlaborer" (Benton and Craib 2001, 93). Moreover, as an aspect of the criminological shadow, philosophy considers how any theory of the stranger promotes or fails to promote positive freedom, individual thought, and personal identity, ensuring where it can that automaton conformity is avoided, indeed, resisted. Constitutively speaking, then, a philosophy of the subject in relation to penal harm examines how the flourishing (being) and the transformation (becoming) of the stranger occur, provisionally, positionally, and relationally.

26. Deleuze and Guattari (1983) argued that under savagery and despotism, family and kinship relations were extended, identification with significant others was more diverse, and generally social organization was more of the alliance and filiative nature. The place for Oedipus in nonnuclear family structures did not have extensive support. We see the nuclear family as the core unit of social organization and as a limited space where Oedipus can arise only under capitalism. This is a locus of support where primary identifications have been greatly restricted to dualisms.

27. Deleuze and Guattari (1983) identify three processes, or syntheses, that coordinate production in the unconscious. The *connective synthesis* knows only connection. Desire makes connections of various free-floating parts. It connects various "part-objects" (sources of energies) into partial unities. For example, hand movement is connected with eye movement; they become synchronized as a basis of action. They become the basis of a distinct flow of energy. In more stable form, they become "organs" of the body. The *disjunctive synthesis* stands for recording on the body. It also stands for antiproduction, a revised death instinct by which what is done is continuously undone to allow new recordings. Antiproduction undermines fixity; it allows new connections and recordings to take place. Unlike the coding specified by Lacan in the form of metaphor and metonymy and a displacement of desire, Deleuze and Guattari see the disjunctive synthesis as more of an indeterminate flow of connections among signs. Hence, the disjunctive synthesis stands for production and antiproduction, connections and disconnections, recording and unrecording. The *conjunctive synthesis* stands for the consummation of the products of connection and disjunction. It is also a moment where the subject recognizes itself as the consumer of desire: "So, that's me!" The subject emerges as an aftereffect. It is provided the illusory notion of mastery in the form of an "I" privileged in modernist thought. It is subject to capturing mechanisms in a particular socius.

28. Consider some abstract machines: capital logic and the fetishism of the commodity and legal form; rationalization in Max Weber; division of labor in Emile Durkheim; panopticism in Michel Foucault.

29. These could include legal, religious, scientific, oppositional forms, but also rehabilitation-talk, deterrence-talk, restorative-justice talk, and so forth.

30. Some regimes of signs include rehabilitation rhetoric, actuarial justice, restorative justice talk, and so forth.

31. This is so for both Lacan (see his four discourses, 1991, and also his graphs of desire, 1977, that is, "a signifier represents a subject for another signifier") and Deleuze and Guattari (1983), most clearly identified at the "conjunction synthesis" ("that's me!") (see note 27 for additional commentary).

32. One study (Edin et al. 2001) investigating the life narratives of some three hundred fathers indicated that imprisonment offered space for reflecting on the

life course. Although this may be true, the question of significance is to what degree is the subaltern able to frame narratives within dominant regimes of signs that genuinely reflects his or her struggle? Is it ultimately a *discourse of the hysteric* (Lacan) within which they find meaning? If this is so, accepting their life histories on their face, without something more, may reconstitute dominant forms, albeit inadvertently.

33. Only recently, however, does he (2000) contribute to a thesis of the emerging risk society and its disruptions.

34. Ironic, but to the point, is Uggen, Manza, and Behrens, (2004) enthusiasm for their version of desistance theory. "People seek stable and coherent identities," they tell us. They further advocate offenders "trying on the roles of productive citizen, responsible citizen, and active citizen" as "an imaginative rehearsal for their assumption upon release" (265–66).

35. In this sense, much of contemporary desistance theory, even though going well beyond the dismal failures of traditional penology, has much to be criticized for, consistent with the limitations of the restorative justice model (see Arrigo, Milovanovic, and Schehr 2005). They both share a topological space; hence, many of the assumptions and premises are equally substitutable. On the one hand, the core issue deals with the often inadvertent support of dominant conceptions; on the other hand, it lacks a transformative component.

36. A "flow" of energy along a particular pathway and not another can be seen as a "line of flight." One form of this is repetition of the same, following what fixed axioms dictate. Another flow of energy consists of lines of opposition, mutation, and transformation. Recidivism is a flow; it follows the presuppositions built into the various abstract machines that are the core of its multilevel and intersecting assemblages. Becoming is a flow; it is a continuous process of change and transformation. It is not rooted in fixed axiomatics. The disjunctive synthesis organizes energy-matter flows on the body and the socius. Savagery, despotism, and capitalism each encourage a particular flow of energy-matter. For example, commodity-fetishism as an abstract machine produces exchange-value. This is the transformation of energy-matter from use-value to an abstraction that takes a life of its own and becomes a core manufacturer in the axiomatics of capital logic. On the other hand, schizoanalysis/nomadology suggests flows that are becoming in form: indeterminate, fluid, and mutating.

37. Reading the various chapters in Shadd Maruna and Russ Immarigeon's *After Crime and Punishment* (2004) would have Michel Foucault (1977a) applauding the support for his thesis concerning panopticism, disciplinary mechanisms, the creation of docile bodies, and bodies of utility.

38. This is conceptualized by Bazemore and Erbe (2004, 45) as: offender (deficits and dysfunctions) → remedial or therapeutic intervention → offender adjustment (desistance from crime).

39 According to Deleuze and Guattari (1983), the capitalist socius, unlike the previous two regimes, overcodes in the form of key axioms. We see this in the homology of commodity and legal fetishism. We also see this in the rationalization process spelled out by Max Weber. According to Unger (1986, 1987), we see a general subjection worldwide to the "rationalizing legal analysis" whereby formal rationality prevails over continuously changing everyday pragmatic encounters.

This is a "repressive formalism" that subjects all to the axiomatic and the syllogisms that follow.

40. Consider the perspective of the potential custodial subject whose release is contemplated and the reentry hurdles that follow: "During structured re-entry, offenders sign behavioral contracts that set priorities, specify supervision requirements and service participation and detail sanctions for not complying with the contract" (Taxman, Young, and Byrne 2004, 244). Is it any wonder that Halsey (2006c) found that custodial subjects sometimes refuse conditional release and create their own "risk-management plans?" In other words, they may opt for serving their full time in prison rather than being "messed around."

41. The notion of social capital is traced to Bourdieu (1986) and Coleman (1988, 1990) and has been insightfully applied by Hagan (1997) in criminology. However, its more expansive definition, especially as to scope, has often been reduced to employment and good family relationships (e.g., see Farrall 2004, 61).

42. To illustrate, consider Drucilla Cornell's (1998, 111–30) suggestion for an alternative nuclear-family structure that deprivileges the molar forms. Underlying her argument is a call for a molecular structure of the nuclear family (even extending it to a team concept) where custodial responsibility is separated from the sexuate being but in combination with state support of essential services. In her view, "there would be no normal family" (128).

43. Roberto Unger (1987), in the "remedial accusatory" style, still remains exemplary as to his blueprint for a "superliberalism" and an "empowered democracy." Many of his ideas can be accommodated to Deleuze and Guattari. "Role jumbling" is in the direction of becoming-other, becoming imperceptible; "rotating capital funds" provides social capital across the socius to teams of workers; new forms of rights provide a framework within which molecular structures may take on form (i.e., "destabilization rights" assure that all molar structures can be subject to criticism and revision; "market rights" assure ready access to capital by teams of workers; "immunity rights" protect those who challenge contemporary molar structures and assure active participation by the many; "solidarity rights" go beyond the legal tendency toward the further rationalization in law [see also Unger, 1996] and reinforce trust and reliance on the other). The superliberal socius envisioned by Unger would certainly have more occasions for conflict; however, these would be opportunities to know the other, to challenge ossified molar structures, to further invest in molecular structures.

II

DEVELOPMENTS IN CONSTITUTIVE PRACTICE AND PENOLOGY

4

Constitutive Penology and the "Pains of Imprisonment"

INTRODUCTION

In this chapter, we specify how constitutive penology more fully accounts for the *pains of imprisonment*. This is a specific reference to the construction of penal harm, maintained, legitimized, and reified by the recursive activities of those human agents and structural/organizational forces that appropriate its totalizing logic. These activities encompass the discursive work of prisoners, correctional officers, government officials or other administrators, and the general public. Each functions as an excessive investor that sustains the prison-industrial complex (i.e., the prison-form). This complex, an artifact of historically mediated social-cultural conditions, reciprocally and simultaneously reproduces its parts (e.g., philosophies of punishment, penal practices, and offender reentry strategies). As such, the agency/structure duality implicated in essentializing the prison edifice is steeped in a mundane discourse that draws support from the prison-form that stands above this duality. This is what is meant by the coproduction of penological reality. Accordingly, the recursive activities examined in this chapter explain how human flourishing and becoming for *all* concerned is reduced and repressed. This is what is meant by the pains of imprisonment. To address these concerns, we return to our assessment of the criminological shadow. Insights derived from Michel Foucault on panoptic power, Jean Baudrillard on technologized culture, and Erich Fromm on negative freedom figure prominently in the analysis. Deleuze and Guattari's notion of the constitution of the subject and assemblages is also especially relevant.

In addition, this chapter suggests how the molar forces that manufacture the reality of penal harm can be deterritorialized. In other words, even though repetition reconstitutes the whole, a totality that signifies the pains of imprisonment, indigenous forces, minor narratives, and subaltern voices can displace homeostasis and equilibrium conditions. These strategies of resistance represent struggles for transformative justice without reconstituting hierarchies. Accordingly, we draw on the selected insights of Jacques Lacan, Jacques Derrida, and Gilles Deleuze, as well as on key observations from complex systems science, to suggest how the stranger in penology can experience molecular intensities (over molar) and a becoming (rather than a being). However, before addressing these matters, the prevailing research that accounts for the problems of imprisonment is summarily reviewed. At issue here is how penology proper endeavors to explain the expanse of violence that is imprisonment.

RESEARCH ON IMPRISONMENT: EXPLAINING VIOLENCE

A review of the classic (modernist) research on penology indicates that four actors are connected to the violence that permeates imprisonment (Clemmer 1958; Jacobs 1978; Sykes 1958). These include the behavior of prisoners, correctional officers, public officials (as agents of the prison-industrial complex), and the general public. This time-honored research demonstrates that each group significantly contributes to the nature of harm that pervades the culture of prisons and represents the basis for research in correctional philosophy and practice. Consistent with Erving Goffman's (1961) thesis, the confinement setting, in this approach, functions as a total institution and as a generative milieu for the exercise of power and the administration of control.[1]

Contemporary social scientists have continued the tradition of exploring the manifestation and maintenance of violence through imprisonment practices for each of these groups. For example, the work of Todd Clear (2007), Nils Christie (2000, 2004), Michael Hallett (2006), Craig Haney (2006), Jeffrey Reiman (2006), John Irwin and Barbara Owen (2007), Lorna Rhodes (2004), and Michael Welch (2005) echoes the debilitating, corrosive, and inhumane conditions in which the "kept" are indeed confined.[2] To be clear, what they document suggests both the breadth and depth of society's punitiveness. Prisoners act violently (e.g., riots, underground pariah economy), correctional workers act violently (e.g., beatings, sexual abuse), administrators act violently (e.g., increased inmate restrictions; reduced inmate privileges), and the general public acts violently (e.g., endorsement of mandatory-minimum sentences, 3-Strikes legislation, juvenile waiver, and capital punishment). Thus, the question is raised, how can such penal harm be explained? Three models are discernible in the extant modernist literature.

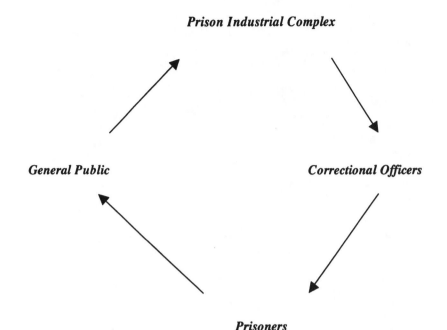

Diagram 4.1. The Cause(s) of Violence as Linear

The first of these explanations focuses on the violence of confinement, whether originating from the prison-industrial complex (i.e., officials), inmates, correctional workers, or the general public. In this model, a linear trajectory of thought accounts for the manifestation and maintenance of punitiveness. Thus, for example, the decision making (or harm) at the institutional level (onerous restrictions of child visitation for incarcerated mothers, demeaning body and cavity searches, noncontact visits, reduced vocational and educational programs, increased confinement to cells, the use of soft shackle restraints, death row executions, and solitary confinement) contribute to reactive behaviors among inmates or fosters a certain mindset among correctional workers that is, itself, violent, inhumane, and unjust. Other linear relationships also are apparent. The classic penological studies, both ethnographic and often historical, convey this approach to the problem of violence that saturates the logic of penal confinement (e.g., Clemmer 1958; Goffman 1961; Sykes 1958).

With the onset of actuarial science in criminology and penology, especially as a basis to predict behavior (dangerousness), develop programming around deterrence through incapacitation, and serve as a platform for public policy, social scientists are promoting a "systems analysis approach" (e.g., Piquero, Farrington, and Blumstein 2007; Welsh and Farrington 2006). This risk-management strategy to penal harm is designed to predict and prevent violence based on statistical forecasting and

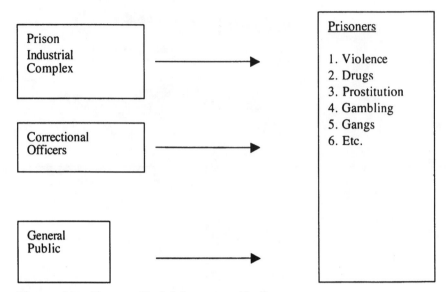

Diagram 4.2. The cause(s) of violence as multicolinear.

evidence-based research. Mona Lynch (1998, 839) distressingly and un-
easily identifies this orientation as the "waste-management" approach to
corrections. This "new penology," so coined by Malcom Feeley and
Jonathan Simon (1992, 2004), seeks to expose the multicausal bases of violence, to predict their onset, and to contain them through criminal justice
practices, programs, and policies. In this model, the violence enacted by
inmates is linked to the punitive behavior of the system itself (especially
those actions extolled by correctional and other governmental authori-
ties), to prison workers, and to the general public, notwithstanding bio-
genetic and/or neuropsychological correlates.[3]

The more conservative efforts of the new penology movement represent the current (and increasingly popular) counterpoint to the established investigations of the last quarter of the twentieth century (e.g.,
Clear 1994; Cullen and Gilbert 1982; Irwin 1992). These progressive liberal
inquiries emphasized the absence of correctional treatment and offender
rehabilitation, the need for political-economic analyses, and the presence
of social inequalities (e.g., limited access to health care, problems with il-
literacy/education, the lack of decent affordable housing, race/gender
discrimination) as the structural determinants underpinning the problems of penal harm (i.e., violence). Several contemporary works in penology have made similar arguments (e.g., Christie 2004; Clear 2007; Irwin
and Owen 2007; Rhodes 2004).

The more progressive liberal agenda situates the debate concerning the
problems of imprisonment (from prisoners to correctional workers, from

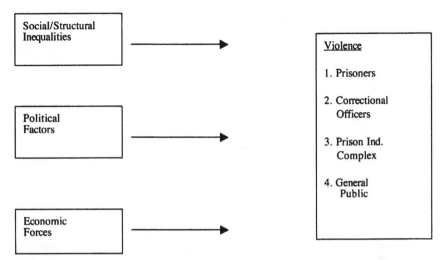

Diagram 4.3. Violence as effects not causes.

the prison-industrial complex to the general public) within a framework that stresses violence as an artifact of social disorganization, that is, as an effect rather than a cause. Perhaps, to this extent, the progressive liberal prescription, unlike its more conservative counterpart, recognizes that harm, whatever its manifestation, does not simply reside within or through the individual. To the contrary, something more is needed to account for such violence, especially given its pervasive and pernicious nature. Mindful of our discussion in chapter 3 on the criminology of the shadow, we contend that the insights of constitutive penology extend and deepen the existing penological research. Accordingly, in the ensuing section, we demonstrate how our approach more completely accounts for the manifestation of penal harm and the agency/structure repetition that signifies the pains of imprisonment.

PENAL HARM AND THE PAINS OF IMPRISONMENT: A CONSTITUTIVE CRITIQUE

In our assessment of the criminological shadow, we drew attention to the insights of several key figures. Fromm's (1994, 2003, and 2005) Marxist-Freudian thesis on negative freedom, mechanisms of escape, and the illusion/pretense of individual/identity was considered. Derrida's (1977, 1978) poststructural methodology involving deconstruction, the metaphysics of presence, and the reversal of hierarchies was delineated. Lacan's (1977, 1981, 1985, and 1991) psychosemiotic formulations on subjectivity, desire, and the "lack" in discourse were reviewed. Deleuze and

Guattari's (1987) nomadological and schizoanalytic approach to Oedipus, capital logic, and molar territorialization was briefly explained. In this section, we invoke the conceptualizations of Michel Foucault and Jean Baudrillard for further guidance. Deleuze and Guattari offer some additional concepts.

Cognizant of our previous discussion on the criminology of the shadow, the theorizing of Foucault, Deleuze and Guattari, and Baudrillard amplifies our constitutive penology and clarifies the recursive forces that reify penal harm, essentialize prison, and legitimize the pains of imprisonment. In effect, our efforts here are intended to more deliberatively access the psychoanalytic and philosophic roots in which the culture of violence is coproduced. This more probing examination, then, seeks to uncover the covert forces, perhaps somewhat symbolic in form but certainly real in consequence, that underscore the problems of imprisonment in an ultra-modern society. This is a society in which the dynamics of power and culture are inexorably bound.

Foucault on Power, Knowledge/Truth, and the Body

According to Foucault (1977a), power is ubiquitous; it resides or is lodged in many sources. In the modern age, power's sources are inventive, technical, efficient, and productive. Intermediate sanctions such as electronic home monitoring, intensive probation/parole supervision, boot camps for juveniles, secure housing units (the SHUs), surveillance/security equipment stationed throughout the prison confines, the administration of the death penalty (now, by lethal injection), and functional magnetic resonance imaging (fMRI) protocols (increasingly used as aggravating/mitigating evidence during the penalty phase of a case) all represent mechanisms of surveillance (Arrigo 2007). They send the message that forms of technology monitor, regulate, and police our activities and our thoughts. Following Jeremy Bentham and his notion of panopticism, Foucault termed this *le regard* (i.e., the gaze or the panoptic gaze).

More problematic for Foucault (1977a), these instruments of surveillance (called abstract machines in the Deleuzean-Guattarian model), these techniques of power that inspect, order, and define our thoughts/behaviors, represent a constellation of disciplinary practices that are discursive; that is, they are omnipresent, omnipotent, and, presumably, omniscient. In the realm of penology, these disciplinary practices (as the manifestation of the panoptic gaze) constitute a "text" about incarcerates, correctional officers, the prison-industrial complex, and the general public. All participants become a part of the text or script that they reproduce, a text that (mostly unreflectively) is taken to be de facto legitimate. This legitimacy endorses knowledge about imprisonment through its mechanisms of surveillance.[4] For Foucault, this understanding about the self, about others, and about the social world constituted a regime of truth, of knowledge/truth, as power. Indeed, alternative interpretations for imprisonment that fall outside the panoptic gaze are vanquished, individuals who resist such disciplining are pathologized and normalized, and our very existential identities—whether as the kept, their keepers, or the public at large—are mostly made compatible with the economic and political interests of the state. Thus, in Foucault's sense, we are that which government (methodically, technologically, panoptically) insists that we do!

Moreover, according to Foucault, the disciplinary text of imprisonment and the discursive mechanisms of surveillance that sustain it are so pervasive that the regime of knowledge/truth that power constitutes saturates and regulates the body (those confined, correctional workers/administrators, and the general public). This is what Foucault means by biopower or the biophysics of power. So all-consuming is biopower when assessing the problems of imprisonment that all those exposed to its panoptic gaze are rendered, in Foucault's words, docile bodies, bodies of utility, mere functionaries of the state or the internal logic of political economy (i.e., capital logic). This is the point at which the soul is territorialized and vanquished. For Foucault, this is the moment in which we are all *prisoners* (casualties) of the discursive practices, disciplinary text, and knowledge/truths of violence that signify imprisonment.

Foucault's position on power, knowledge, and the body forms the basis of an arresting and disturbing critique concerning the problem of confinement, a condition in which we are all punished by this disciplinary, discursive, and potent narrative. However, Foucault's critique is incomplete. Missing from his analysis is any sustained commentary on the mechanisms by which the message of imprisonment is not simply rapaciously communicated but conspicuously consumed. Missing, too, is any extensive analysis of resistance, even though Foucault was quite active in prison movements.[5] We shall return to (the dialectics of) struggle in chapter 5. However, we first turn to Deleuze and Guattari and then to Baudrillard for guidance.

Deleuze and Guattari: Control Society and Points of Subjectification

Mindful of Foucault's observations regarding the disciplinary society, Deleuze (1995, 174), however, argues that we have entered into a different form of control.[6] This "control society" goes beyond the notion of surveillance mechanisms as operative in enclosed locales such as prisons, factories, schools, army barracks, and hospitals. Instead, such panoptic inspection is now dispersed throughout our habitus. The emerging informational age relies more on "continuous control and instant communication."[7] We see this in camera and electronic monitoring both inside and outside prison. It is no longer one's signature but codes on which the disciplinary society relies. Indeed, according to Deleuze (1995, 180), they are "passwords" providing or denying access to key resources, to key information. In the prison system, electronic "tagging" for continuous control is the exemplary practice.[8]

Additionally, Deleuze and Guattari (1987, 129–37) delineate the process of subjectification as a product of late modernist (postmodernist) society. Within the regimes of signs of capitalism, this process represents a moment in the time-space energy-matter flow of communicating in which the self is reconstituted (i.e., reduced/repressed). The subject of the statement, the person who has taken up a position as an "I" in discourse (e.g., a prisoner responding to a correctional officer's accusations), "recoils" into the subject of enunciation, the producer of the narrative. This process remains mostly unconscious to the speaker-inmate.[9] The recoiling of the latter into the former produces identities ("faciality") that tend toward molar reinforcement. External power is not so much the driving force for this dynamic; rather, it is the "willing" subject who identifies with the language that speaks him or her.[10] Once indoctrinated, the person not only situates her- or himself in particular molar regimes of signs in order to communicate but becomes *imprisoned* in extant lexical and syntactical structures.[11] The person who makes a statement (e.g., the responding incarcerate) "recoils" into the subject of enunciation only to recognize that she or he is a particular molar entity: "That's me."[12]

In short, those who invoke a particular regime of signs that are most dominant in the prison-industrial assemblage will find many points of subjectification from which this recoiling activity will unfold. In the end, what is reconstituted (built, named) is the spoken subject. Even in one's opposition, the subaltern will often make use of dominant signifiers in constructing speech (see, e.g., the case of the transcarcerated mentally ill, Arrigo 2002; and the jailhouse lawyer, Thomas and Milovanovic 1999).

More recently, the movement to the supermax prison is reorienting the mission of imprisonment. In Bauman's (1998, 113) analysis, prisons in the emerging global socius typified by the prison at Pelican Bay[13] are not so much focused on creating docile bodies of utility (Foucault)—there is no work, there is no training, there is no pretense of rehabilitation, no isomorphism with a factory in these supermaxes—they are more about exclusion and immobility. In Bauman's (1998, 113) words,

> If the concentration camps served as laboratories of a totalitarian society, where the limits of human submission and serfdom were explored, and if the panopticon-style workhouses served as the laboratories of industrial society, where the limits of routinization of human action were experimented with—

the Pelican Bay prison is a laboratory of the "globalized" . . . society, where the techniques of space-confinement of the rejects and the waste of globalization are tested and their limits are explored.

Moreover, as he suggests, "it was designed as a factory of exclusion and of people habituated to their status of the excluded" (1998, 113). Put in the Deleuzian-Guattarian framework, the supermaxes offer points of subjectification whereby identities are rendered singular in the most profound ways. It is a marriage of hi-tech resources in drastically confined spaces; it assures the "outside" socius that the stranger will be kept away (Bauman 1998, 122). The hi-tech culture in postmodern society merges with the anxieties of the many and produces the machinery for singular identities, a recursive process assuring order (Bauman 1998, 122).

Baudrillard on Simulations, Hyperreality, and Simulacra

The theorizing of Jean Baudrillard (1972, 1976, 1983a, 1983b) complements and extends the insights of Foucault, as well as of Deleuze and Guattari. Given our constitutive inquiry in this section thus far, the principal question is as follows: what product or commodity is voraciously consumed by society through the violence or harm that is imprisonment? In order to more completely respond to this query and to more appropriately position Baudrillard within this canon of thought, two additional perspectives warrant some mention. The first is offered by Marx (1964, 1984), the second by the Situationists (Debord 1983; Lucaks 1971). Marx emphasized political-economic analysis; the Situationists stressed a cultural critique of technology (for applications in criminology, see Arrigo 2006c).

For Marx, the answer resided in the political economy of capitalism in which status quo dynamics prevailed. This is the realm of violence proper. Rusche and Kirchheiner make this very point in their classic text, *Punishment and Social Structure* (1968). This logic is exemplified in the notion that "the rich get richer and the poor get prison" (Reiman 2006).[14]

For the Situationists, the response was situated in the technorationality of advanced state-regulated capitalism and consumer class consciousness. This is the point at which stylized and mass-marketed images of the real, communicated through various print and electronic outlets (e.g., TV, film, radio, newspapers, sophisticated advertisement campaigns) and devoured by an insatiable public, outpace and undo the commodity form (i.e., violence). This is the realm of the spectacle: prison privatization as marketed industry; politically charged commercials that insist on 3-Strikes legislation, mandatory minimum sentences, or "get tough on crime" policies; sexually violent predator (SVP) and sexually dangerous person (SDP) statutes; continuous discussion of serial offenders or psychotic killers on

CNN, C-SPAN, FOX, or other outlets that presumably represent the news division; "reality" TV shows that depict prison life for the kept, for their keepers, and for their managers; Nintendo, PlayStation, or Game Cube games that create a violent world in which the participant is the executioner, the punisher. With the spectacle, the imitation/illusion of life is bigger, larger, and more real than life itself.

However, for Baudrillard, the response was located in the evolving "message" that the images themselves conveyed. This message, communicated through the information superhighway (especially the Internet), is nothing more than mundane language, or what he termed "simulacra." As an effusive text or code, the prisonization message inundates and engulfs society. What we experience is a hyperreality. This is the point at which models or replicas of the real are relentlessly and instantaneously disseminated through various media-based outlets. Repeated exposure to films, news/entertainment videos, DVDs, sound bytes, games, songs, representational images, or iconic symbols about prisons, incarcerates, correctional workers, prison facilities, and punitive public attitudes becomes a "stand in" for deliberative thought and reflection. Rapaciously devoured by an insatiable society hungry for more sights and sounds, the various messages these hyperreal images convey leave no room for distinguishing between what is real and what is illusion, between what is authentic and what is representational. Thus, reality implodes. Foundations disappear and with them, the grounding of truth, the factual, the real, and, more troubling, the self and the social. All that remains are the messages themselves that give us choices about what imprisonment is, options regarding the meaning of violence, but choices and options that only these "illusionists" allow us. These assorted viewpoints displace the image/object (the Situationists' position) and the object-commodity on which the image itself is based (Marx's position). For Baudrillard (1983a, 1983b), this is what we conspicuously devour in our ultramodern society.[15]

Constitutively speaking, Foucault's position on power, knowledge, and the panoptic gaze demonstrates the pervasive nature of the state's disciplining of the body for incarcerates, correctional workers, prison officials, and, indeed, the general public as personified in the prison-industrial complex. We are all victimized or punished, that is, rendered docile bodies of utility. Deleuze's extension on the disciplinary society in the form of a control society highlights a socius in historical movement. Baudrillard's thesis on simulated image, hyperreality, and the conspicuous consumption of simulacra specifies the pernicious dimensions of control ultramodern society wields over and against the subject through the mass media. This, too, is in accord with aspects of cyber-Marxism (postmodern Marxism; see Dyer-Witheford 1999). We are anesthetized by the vapid, nonreal, and illusory conditions that define our very existences. Authentic experience, real relationships, and genuine understanding pass through the prism of representation and replica and, correspondingly, what we say about them. The status of imprisonment qua violence, as an artifact of materialist culture, is no different.

However, in need of further analysis is the understanding of *why* the disciplining of the corporeal soul and the undoing of the self and the social occur. In other words, why do we allow this to happen? And, in the context of the problems of imprisonment, why is the reproduction of violence the communicated hyperreal message to which we steadfastly adhere? Baudrillard, even with his noteworthy contributions about the hyperreal and simulacra, can also be critiqued for his pessimism, his unilateral renditions, and, without more, his resignation—how does simulacra get challenged and subverted? To address the first set of questions, we revisit the work of Erich Fromm. We will return more specifically to struggle and resistance in chapter 5.

Penal Harm, the Pains of Imprisonment, and the Criminological Shadow

Fromm's (1994, 2003, and 2005) Marxist-Freudian integrationist perspective specifies that the subject's essential conflict is waged over freedom. This is the ability to express one's own thoughts, to have one's own thoughts, and *to be* one's own thoughts undone in an altogether alienating materialist culture. So profound was this existential crisis that, for Fromm (1994), it produced mechanisms of escape (e.g., sadomasochistic authoritarian tendencies, human/societal destructiveness, and automaton conformity).

These strategies are our response to the burden of negative freedom. Negative freedom is the profound *terror* each of us faces given the lack of spontaneous interaction and genuine expression in thought, reason, and action. Of these mechanisms, automaton conformity is most germane to our constitutive assessment of penal harm and the pains of imprisonment.

As described in chapter 3, automaton conformity represents uncritical, unreflective thought and action about one's self and about society at large. Thus, consider the following: sustained punitive public attitudes (e.g., increasing and more intense restrictions on prisoner rights, increasing and tougher penalties while confined); dramatically increased sensory deprivation in new, supermax prisons; intensified violence enacted by guards against incarcerates (e.g., the use of cattle prods, collective beatings, the use of Taser guns, strip searches, sustained exposure to solitary confinement, torture); dramatic reductions in vocational and educational programs; massive cover-ups perpetrated by prison officials (e.g., prison mismanagement, falsification of incident reports, authorizing the use of unnecessary force); and cultural adaptations employed by the kept (e.g., the underground economy, rationalizing discourses, prostitution, drugs, gambling, gangs).[16] Each of these actions *demonstrates conformity to the will of the state!* The character of this conformity (the nature of this docility) emerges principally from a new form of Foucaultian panopticism, a novel form of biopower. In ultramodern society the instruments of surveillance are the omnipresent messages themselves communicated to us all through assorted media outlets that *simulate and replicate the normalization of violence.* This is violence enacted by prison workers, extolled by correctional officials, and endorsed through the silent consumption of a mostly politically uninvolved, though psychologically enthralled, public. This is violence that makes the thug or gangsta' lifestyle popularized as chic in contemporary culture the new rite of passage for adolescents, glamorized in some forms of hip-hop and rap music, dramatized in television and film, lionized on Internet blogs and YouTube sites.

Thus, following Fromm (1994, 2003, and 2005), in order not to experience the increasing aloneness, or insignificance, or emptiness of our lives stemming from the consumption of a virtual and illusory reality that mediates our thoughts, feelings, and decisions and disciplines our corporeal soul, we acquiesce. We sacrifice our selves (and our humanness) at the alter of automaton conformity.[17] This forfeiture is the price that we pay for displacing the burden of negative freedom, a quality of freedom borne out of our relentless commitment to have rather than to be, to conspicuously consume rather than to authentically become.

We take this view on the normalization of violence to be consistent with Hannah Arendt's (2006) notion of the banality of evil. This evil—traceable to the absence of positive freedom that incarcerates, correctional workers, prison administrators, and the public profoundly embody—reminds us how the consumption of technologized culture territorializes knowledge, reontologizes the subject, and promotes automaton conformity.[18] Thus, in order to more fully comprehend the pains of imprisonment and the reification of prisonization discourse, it is not enough to utilize progressive liberal models of analysis. Instead, the development and deployment of a constitutive penological strategy warrants consideration.

Theoretical Integration: Constitutive Penology and the Normalization of Violence

Our first three diagrams represented modernists' views on imprisonment and violence. We now turn to a constitutive penological view of the normalization of violence. Diagram 4.4 depicts a first approximation of a constitutive rendering. Of particular interest is the interplay among human agency (the Body-without-Organs [BwO]) and social structure (molar

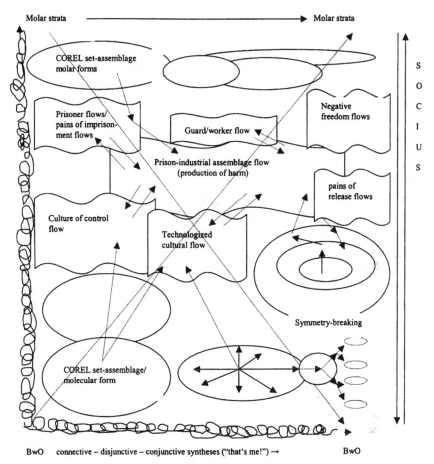

Diagram 4.4. Constitutive penology and the normalization of violence.

strata) in which the pains of imprisonment are recursively produced by way of panoptic power (Foucault), the control society (Deleuze), technologized culture (Baudrillard), and negative freedom (Fromm). Stated differently, the subject is disciplined, reality is manufactured via replicas of the same, and automaton conformity (i.e., the normalization of violence) prevails. Negative freedom implicates the criminological shadow. Contributing to this condition in which prison discourse is essentialized is Derrida's position on the metaphysics of presence, Lacan's thesis on the *discourse of the master/hysteric*, and Deleuze and Guattari's position on the socius and molar lines of flight.

As previously specified in chapter 3, Giddens' (1984) structuration theory has been diagrammatically presented by Farrall and Calverley, who depicted the mutually constituting relationship between structure and agency over time (2006, 178). However, we want to re-present this schema by integrating key concepts from Deleuze and Guattari, dynamic systems theory, and relevant insights from contemporary, postmodernist penology. The purpose of this reorganization is to undo the recursive "incarceration-release-reincarceration machine" (Halsey 2006c, 35). Instead, the formulation that follows is more consistent with the Foucaultian/Nietzschean notion of genealogy and Deleuze and Guattari's notion of noology[19] and nomadology.

In diagram 4.4[20] we note that a given socius is constituted by various COREL sets/assemblages: some overlapping, some intertwining, some embedded within other assemblages, some emerging, some dissipating.[21] At the "structural" level, we have molar strata distinguished by statistical regularities, stasis, linearity, closure, repetition, and reactionary forces. At the agency level, we have the Body-without-Organs, a concept borrowed from Antonin Artaud (1988), which sees the body as a field of intensities, of flows, of differing speeds, of various threshold levels where perturbations produce bifurcations, symmetry breaking, an interruption of repetition (e.g., lower right-hand side of diagram 4.4). We have previously reviewed how three "passive syntheses" produce a subject of enunciation. The final one, conjunction, represents a particular molarized subject in political economy ("that's me"!). We see this depicted (diagram 4.4) in the squiggly lines from the BwO to the molar strata and similarly from the BwO at one time versus another. This represents the recoiling of the subject or the point of conjunction where subjects are given static form, molar identities of being, rather than molecular identities of becoming.

Flows are interconnected with the BwO in recursive constructions. Not only do they provide "points of subjectivation" (Deleuze and Guattari 1987) or *master discourses/university discourses* (Lacan 1991), but they can also be envisioned in terms of what Deleuze called the "fold."[22] "The world must be placed in the subject in order that the subject can be for the world. This is the torsion [read Möbius band] that constitutes the fold of the world and of the soul" (Deleuze 1993, 26). The "outside" (flows) and the "inside" (which includes the soul, according to Deleuze) may be seen as interconnected by a Möbius band. The outside is folded back onto the inside creating a "doubling," which "allow[s] a relation to oneself to emerge" (Deleuze 1988, 100)[23]—a "subjectivation is created by folding" (1998, 104)—a self that has further determinants in the logic of points of subjectification and of the third synthesis (conjunctive synthesis): "That's me!" This is a topological space, not Euclidean, marked by intersecting and twisting surfaces.[24] Folds assure a multiplicity of connecting points that are not tied to linear logic or to spatial restrictions. Hence, the "inside" is always already connected to the "outside" at a multitude of points ("every inside-space is topologically in contact with the outside-space" [Deleuze 1988, 118–19]). Various strata, or COREL set assemblages, become "intermediary" (Deleuze 1988, 119) in the completion of the circuit from the outside to the inside to the outside. In short, a constitutive penology draws from the dynamics of folding and the Möbius band that is its constitutive logic.[25]

We identify several flows[26] without being exhaustive: technologized cultural flows (see Baudrillard 1983a, 1983b), culture-of-control flows (see Garland 2001), prisoner flows, correctional officer/guard flows, negative-freedom flows (Fromm), pains-of-imprisonment flows, pains-of-release flows, prison-industrial assemblage flow. We can also posit recidivism and violence as a flow.[27] We further depict how some flows converge with the prison-industrial COREL set/assemblage flow[28] in producing a static, recursively constituted social reality of imprisonment and violence.[29] This flow specifies how harm is both manufactured (linguistically and unconsciously) and amplified (materially and culturally). We also note the various COREL set/assemblages, each uniquely constituted by an abstract machine (i.e., capital logic, panoptic logic, control logic, rationalization, and so forth), which tend to produce lines of flight (indicated by the dotted lines). Some escape the immediacy of the particular generating COREL set/assemblage to have an influence on others. Others can be likened to a soliton (a vibration, a wave that cuts across the socius) producing significant resonances (e.g., entrainment or couplings) that change (perturb) the extant threshold levels, which in turn produce bifurcations, new basins of attractions, and new attractors. Some of these nonlinear dynamical effects are more permanent; others are more temporary. In this process, flows and BwO dance the waltz of sameness and difference, reconstituting in recursive form dominant emergents, yet harboring the seeds of deterritorialization, on the one hand producing the docile molar subject, on the other, the potential for permanent revolution and the becoming subject.

We also note the presence of territorializing forces tending toward stasis, that is, toward molar regularity. Thus, prisoners, guards, and the general public find themselves in fields of "capture"; their flows[30] are inclined to be molded by the various abstract machines that can only be fully historically understood by a genealogical and noological examination.

Moreover, regimes of signs are assemblages: they give expression to various flows (consider, too, Lacan's *discourse of the master* and *hysteric*); they produce static signifiers that are apt to become master signifiers and order words from which narratives and subjects are constructed. Embedded are preconstructed discursive subject-positions within which a person can take up temporary residence as an "I" in narrative production. Subjects in the socius make use of these in producing narratives (subject of the statement) but undergo the recoiling process into subjects of enunciations. The point of subjectification can be located within the flows, within abstract machines that both constitute subjects and are reconstituted by "willing" subjects in their very discourse.[31] The Möbius folding assures that a circuit exists between the outside and the inside and back to the outside.

We also contend (with more to be said in the final chapter) that molecular assemblages are predisposed to deterritorializing the socius; that is, they release lines of flight that mobilize active forces, mutation, and transformation. Even though Giddens' (1984) structuration theory posited two elements of motivation (desire for security, autonomy), he privileged the first of these, which consequently amounts to a heavy emphasis on reconstituting forces. For others, such as Doyle Paul Johnson (1990, 118), the latter (i.e., autonomy) may produce "deliberate departure from routines."[32] Thus, in diagram 4.4 we show in the lower left-hand corner a COREL set/assemblage, more molecular in form, typified by opposition, revolt, civil disobedience, and the like.[33] This COREL set/assemblage's lines of flight may also extend into the socius with effects.

The lower right-hand portion of diagram 4.4 depicts this in more detail. A line of flight moving to the right perturbs a neighboring COREL set/assemblage that had been resting at some equilibrium with a characteristic defining attractor (i.e., point, periodic, toris, and strange attractor). With this, a "symmetry-breaking transition" (DeLanda 2002, 18–19) emerges; that is, at critical values or thresholds, the COREL set/assemblage undergoes a phase transition in which new possible outcome basins result, characterized by their own unique attractors.[34] These critical values are sensitive to frequency, duration, intensity, and the tactical timing of a particular line of flight. In our example, a bifurcation has produced four distinct COREL sets/assemblages (periodicity of four). With further perturbations and symmetry breaking, we could also witness the emergences of a torus or strange attractor.[35]

Consider the newly incarcerated person. With the various, often abrupt, and mostly rational-defying perturbations in criminal justice processing culminating in the individual's assignment to a particular cell, we hypothesize that symmetry-breaking transitions may take place. This symmetry breaking will emerge, given the appropriate frequency, duration, intensity, and critical timing of various converging lines of flight. A set of attractor basins will emerge, each with its own distinct character. Consider, for example, Robert Johnson's (2002) explanation of various adjustments to prison life. The "yard," for example, provides various niches, including the basis for violent "state-raised convicts."[36] It would be difficult to forecast in advance in which of these attractor basins the inmate will ultimately take up residence.

This inability to predict with precision the incarcerate's final "confinement destination" is a function of contextual/pragmatic factors as well as motivational inputs. In other words, the basin of attraction that becomes the most relevant one within which the inmate operates rests, in part, on pragmatic/contextual considerations and the workings of desire in motivation. If we take Giddens' (1984) view on motivation (desire for security, desire for autonomy) and extend it by incorporating Johnson's (2002) critique concerning the privileging of the former, we then need to address the question of how inmates (and postincarcerates) create change in their lives, that is, how they desist from investing in harm (Farrall and Calverley 2006, 179).

Constitutive penology would reply in terms of the Deleuzian-Guattarian notion of desire as production and the dynamics of intersecting COREL sets/assemblages. The prison-industrial COREL set/assemblage flow certainly provides constraints in marshalling active forces. In fact, this COREL set/assemblage is primarily concerned with reactive forces. Indeed, as Farrall and Calverley (2006, 181–82) asserted, "the major impact of prisons on the desistance process, is, arguably, to disrupt the journey of 'going straight.' . . . Incarceration completely transforms the potency of an individual's agency, leaving them with few resources at their disposal. . . . Prison rules place people under an institutionalized routine that virtually suspends their power." Notwithstanding Farrall and Calverley's otherwise insightful perspective, their conception of the subject is wanting; hence, their suggestions fall short of a fully developed notion of desistance.[37]

The question of how choice is invoked in "deciding" one basin rather than another is a key problem in constitutive penology. In furtherance of this understanding, some[38] have argued that differentials exist in capacities of structuring or of being structured. As Halsey (2006c) notes, "One gets to choose between and within a complex field of constraints." Thus, either privileging agency or structure is illusory. At any moment, either agency or structure is in movement (nonstatic) and stating precisely the intersections of the two at any given time and their effects is problematic.[39] To this end, some investigators (LeBel et al. 2008) have offered a "subjective-social" model that explains desistance from crime in terms of a simultaneous focus on the subject and the social. To this insight Halsey (2006a, 33) adds, "Repeat incarceration needs to be read as an event whose precursors are lodged as much in the systems of administration, rules, and requirements levied upon those released from custody, as it resides within the 'good' or 'bad,' or 'right' or 'wrong' choices made by offenders." He continues by arguing that recursivity exists because there are insufficient forces to interrupt repetition. In short, reactive forces are dominant, producing resistance to symmetry breaking. Moreover, where symmetry breaking does occur, the "choices" available are stacked in favor of further investment in reactive forces and molar forms.

Consider, too, a newly released inmate now subject to the pains-of-release flow. This perturbation, at some level (frequency, duration, intensity, critical timing) may produce compliance; at other levels, it may produce wilding, adaptations to lawbreaking networks, and escape into excessive alcohol and drug usage; at still other levels, it may produce transmutation (politicalization of one's past being and prelude to a future becoming; consider Malcolm X's much cited journey).

Thus, in our example from diagram 4.4 (lower right-hand side), we note that four distinct attractor basins have emerged. Each of them deals with affect. In other words, following Deleuze and Guattari (1983, 1987), each attractor basin deals with what bodies are capable of doing and feeling (see particularly Halsey 2006c, 163–64). Some basins will privilege being and reactive forces (Foucault's "docile bodies"); some will tend toward becoming and active forces. For instance, we might see three of the attractor basins privileging being whose effects produce security. Consequently, their attractiveness and motivation (via investments in conventional jobs, family, American/British "dream") might even positively impact desistance. Perhaps here we could hypothesize that the point attractor becomes more dominant, resulting in less investment of (self/other/societal) harm. Sustained, too, are molar forms (e.g., given stratifications). However, we could also posit a basin of attraction where autonomy and becoming are privileged,[40] where active forces predominate, and where molecular intensities prevail over molar regularities.[41] In this instance, torus and strange attractors would merge, providing both molecular and molar emphases, but with the privileging of the former over the latter. The question, then, is raised, how do we promote molecular forms of (strange) attractor basins? In other words, how do we resuscitate the stranger?

CONSTITUTIVE PENOLOGY AND THE EMERGENCE OF THE STRANGER

Constitutive penology argues that the reincarceration COREL set/assemblage, the so-called prison-industrial complex, works quite well. Prisons do a remarkably successful job of maintaining, even amplifying, harm. Any institution that systematically produces adult recidivism rates of 66 percent or more after three years and customarily witnesses upwards of 90 percent of its incarcerated juveniles progressing to the adult system would certainly receive high marks for its "accomplishments."[42] If we add to these figures the sustained injury/pain experienced by victims and the offenders' and victims' close relationships ("reflex stroke"), then the composite picture is of monumental proportions, particularly in the perpetuation and even amplification of harm (Mauer and Chesney-Lind 2003). The progression from pains of imprisonment to pains of release and then back in cyclical fashion to pains of imprisonment says a great deal about molar formations and the mobilization of reactive forces (see, e.g., Maruna and Immagerion 2004; Petersilia 2003; Travis and Visher 2005). It tells us more about how the whole and the parts of society have reached an equilibrium in which continuous harm is a given. We need creative visions and strategies to resurrect molecular forms, active forces, and, in the process, to provide space for the resuscitation of the stranger. Three postrelease models in contemporary discussion address the response to harm: the first two are more modernist; the third is postmodernist.

The contemporary "deficit model" in corrections focuses on failures, on punishing transgressors, on "going straight," on the singularity of the event, on unilaterally constructed plans (operative while incarcerated and in release plans), on the behavioral surface of bodies, and on creating docile bodies—"geared toward recognizing and responding to failure" (Halsey 2006c, 167). Indeed, as Halsey (2006c,16) argues, "young men in custody generally are not permitted, let alone expected, to show initiative or take anything approaching a meaningful degree of responsibility for their daily lives. Instead, things are done to them and for them and only very rarely with them (and/or with their consent). In this sense, inmates are taught to react rather than act. They are taught to respond rather than initiate. They are taught what to think rather than how to (un)reason." In short, for Halsey, they are products of *learned helplessness*. This logic is consistent with Deleuze and Guattari's subjectification framework (1987). Everyday connective-disjunctive-conjunctive syntheses foster a recoiling of the individual. The subject of the statement reverts into the subject of enunciation. This reconstituted person is compatible with the noological image that is generated by conventional "law and order" decision making and its agents, who recursively reify the control society.[43]

Contrary to the deficit model, the desistance model (see especially Maruna and Immarigeon 2004; Farrall and Calverley 2006) is a paradigm shift in understanding the reintegration of the postcustodial subject. It builds on already existing forms of intervention. Contrary to the deficit model, the desistance approach recognizes that a dynamic process, not necessarily linear,[44] is involved whereby a person gradually abstains from investing in harm to another. This model balances the "good lives" philosophy against the normative strategy of reducing/avoiding risk (Ward and Maruna 2007). For many of its adherents, the ultimate aim is to increase "social capital" (Farrall 2004). This includes a commitment to work, the presence of a stable family structure, the promotion of hope (American/British "dream"), and the initiation of "reentry community justice" (Taxman, Young, and Byrne 2004). This approach resonates with restorative justice theorizing/programming (Braithwaite 1989). The conviction is that reintegration strategies such as those just enumerated will enhance desistance and "restore" the ex-offender within civil society (Strang and Braithwaite 2005). In this model, it is not the imagery of "going straight" but of "going crooked" (more rhizomatic) that pervades the social consciousness (Maruna 2001).

A third model builds on the desistance approach, but with a considerably more radical (postmodern) direction. This constitutive approach is equally concerned with prison and postprison connectivity. It questions the core categories advocated by desistance theory: the nature of employment under capitalism; the nature of the nuclear family; the political economic bases on which hope, dreams, and collective aspirations are generated. These activities merely assure being. As we have argued, pathways to becoming are indeed needed. Accordingly, a paradigm shift to a *transdesistance theory* is advocated. In the subsequent chapter of this book, the revitalization of the stranger will be showcased through one protean illustration. This application work will focus on techniques of transformation given the correctional technologies of created (molar) but illusory categories of race, gender, and class[45] control. For now, however, we identify the salient features of our transdesistance theory in diagrammatic form. (See page 125 for meaning of symbols.)

Diagram 4.6 depicts that process by which the stranger is resuscitated in nonhierarchical (i.e., contingent, relational, positional) fashion. This activity, more in keeping with a vision of change rather than a blueprint for reform, implicates the person confined, those who serve as keepers of the kept, the general public, and all others who reconstitute and legitimize the recursive cycle of the pains of imprisonment, the pains of release, and the pains of imprisonment. In effect, then, diagram 4.6 proposes a conceptualization in which the subject is liberated from the agency/structure duality that repetitively fosters penal harm, essentializes prison discourse, and reifies the correctional edifice that stands above both.

In this schema a replacement socius is envisioned.[46] The molecular strata convey nonstatic movement, the presence of spontaneity and fluidity, openness to change, randomness, and active forces.[47] The dotted line situated from the upper left-hand to the upper right-hand sides of the diagram depicts this movement. At the agency level is the Body-without-Organs. In the transdesistance formulation, the person is a subject-in-process (Kristeva 1984): transparent, in flux, mutating, and experiencing various flows, speeds, and threshold levels. This is depicted by the dotted circles and their differing sizes.

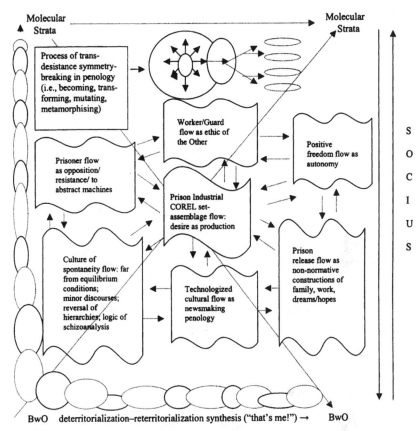

Diagram 4.6. Constitutive penology and the symmetry-breaking transdesistance model.

Further, we note that unlike a Deleuzian-Guattarian conjunctive synthesis in which the person recoils (is the subject of enunciation), the transforming subject experiences fleeting epiphanies (Giddens), a "flash of light" (Deleuze 1988, 116), a "poetic spark" (Lacan 1977), contingent universalities, (Butler 1992), and experimental/pragmatic insights (Rorty 1989; Unger 1987) that provide the basis of an emerging, temporary, though incomplete, sense of one's identity: an evolving self. These transitory, though lucid, instances entail the strategic use of deterritorialization and reterritorialization. These techniques resist and decenter molar, axiomatic categories of sense making (passive syntheses; subjectification), while simultaneously embracing, extolling, and celebrating molecular intensities (active lines of flights, minor literatures, schizoanalysis). We term this engaged reworking of the self, of both continuously displacing and redefining one's authorship, a "coupling moment." These moments emerge from the subject-in-process in which the activities of deterritorialization and reterritorialization occur. In diagram 4.6, they are depicted by the solid circles that further specify our constitutive view of human agency as becoming. Their differing shapes convey the variable impact each has on one's evolution. Thus, as a dimension of our transdesistance theory, the subject's mutating identity (i.e., as correctional worker, prison administrator, the public at large, and incarcerate), depends on the activities of deconstruction/reconstruction, of disassembling and reassembling the self. This representation of human agency (as a subject-in-process in which coupling moments materialize) extends from the molecular strata to the BwO as well as from the BwO at one time versus another.

The dynamic process of symmetry breaking is prominently featured in diagram 4.6 (top of diagram). As conceptualized in the schema, a COREL set/assemblage flow begins with molar rigidities. Statistical regularities, organizational closure, order words, and reactionary forces dominate. This is depicted by the embedded COREL set/assemblage in which various static lines of flight are featured where point and cyclical attractors are ubiquitous. The pains of imprisonment, the pains of release, and the normalization of violence prevail in cyclical, crystallized fashion, reenacted and reified by all those who essentialize the prison-form.

However, as the socius experiences molecular intensities, a symmetry-breaking cascade begins to to take form, contributing to human agents undergoing transformations as subjects-in-process prone to coupling moments. This cascade represents a transition from what is (being) to what could be (becoming). It surfaces from the intersection of various COREL set/assemblages in which dynamic flows, varying intensities, differential speeds, and fluctuating threshold levels are both mobilized and activated. In diagram 4.6 (top center), this is depicted by an active line of flight moving to the right that perturbs a neighboring COREL set/assemblage otherwise resting at some equilibrium state with its characteristic point or limit attractor. In penology, examples of equilibrium or status quo conditions that result in delimited outcomes are manifold (e.g., routine drills/inspections by correctional staff, standard release plans for probationers/parolees, maintenance of sentencing guidelines by judges, sustained public support for capital punishment). However, the perturbation to the "system" that the symmetry-breaking cascade represents is a function of the ever-reconstituted agency-structure, molecular-molar tensions. As we conceptualize it, novel and emergent outcome basins can be discerned, characterized by distinct attractors. In our schema, four such possibilities are depicted, and each functions to resuscitate the stranger, given their sensitivity to the critical timing, frequency, intensity, and duration of an active line of flight.

How does the revitalization of the stranger as a molecular Body-without-Organs materialize? The four COREL set/assemblage flows presented in diagram 4.6 help to address this concern. With further perturbations and symmetry-breaking intensities, additional lines of flight would follow. Indeed, the amplification of this transdesistance process is more completely illustrated in the remaining portions of the schema and is summarily discussed below.

Several active COREL set/assemblage flows are depicted in diagram 4.6. These include the prisoner flow as challenging/resisting/opposing abstract machines (molar investments such as panopticism and docility, the logic of capital, bureaucracy, and formal rationality); the correctional worker flow as facilitator/healer (generating a care ethic for the Other; embracing the Lacanian *discourse of the hysteric* and *analyst* in a dialogical fashion); the positive freedom flow (libidinal investments in autonomy rather than security, authenticity rather than anxiety/fear/terror); the prison release flow as disruption in the repetition of "going straight" (nonnormative constructions of family, work, hope, and aspirations); the technologized cultural flow as the conspicuous consumption of replacement images, sound bytes, iconic symbols, and simulated themes/messages for, by, and about incarcerates and the logic/discourse of "corrections" (the activities of news-making penology)[48]; and the culture of spontaneity (rather than control) flow (including the presence of far-from-equilibrium conditions; minor discourses; the nonhierarchical reversal of dominant values; and the logic of schizoanalysis).

Central to these COREL set/assemblage flows, their intersectionalities, and the active lines of flight that foster molecular intensities is the prison-industrial assemblage flow. As we depict it, this assemblage is saturated in desire as production. By desire as production we refer to "overcoming," in the Nietzschean (1968) sense, the constraints of the shadow in criminology, and, for our purposes, penology proper. This is the emergence of a will to power (Nietzsche; see also Deleuze 1983): a primal and creative force that mobilizes and activates (Nietzsche 1966). This overcoming, as active movement, is not an ontological representation of the self (i.e., being); rather, it is the embodiment of those energy flows (in our model, intersecting and active COREL set/assemblages) that reside within the process of becoming itself.[49] This will to power, as a fundamental drive, impulse, or motivation, is what makes metamorphosis possible. This overcoming is the desire to exert one's will, one's potentiality, in transcending the social, material, linguistic, and symbolic forces that unconsciously or otherwise reduce and repress the self's actualizations and transformations.

The various and intersecting COREL set/assemblages featured in diagram 4.6 converge on the prison-industrial flow, and simultaneously and correspondingly, the latter extends to all other assemblages found in our schema. This active and ongoing movement, consisting of diverse molecular intensities, differing speeds, and various threshold levels, signifies the mobilization of lines of flight agitating for change, mutation, and transformation. These energy flows—as the nexus for becoming Other and for disassembling and reassembling the agency/structure duality that sustains penal harm, that normalizes violence, and that essentializes prison discourse—displace and transcend molar forces. These reactive forces represent nothing more than the criminology of the shadow whereby incarcerates, their jailers, correctional officials, and administrators, as well as the general public, are all situated and insert themselves within the circumscribed logic and grammar of its abstract machines (e.g., the *discourse of the master*, the disciplinary society, status quo and equilibrium conditions, the logic of capital, the metaphysics of presence, risk-avoidance and governmentality, the iron cage of bureaucracy, simulated hyperreality; and formal rationality).

However, in our view, the stranger will only be resuscitated with the emergence of a new socius, a "permanent revolution" (Holland 1999), which assures continuous transformation and the benefits of active molecular forces. The stranger, as a BwO, will begin to reap the rewards of new inscriptions, of coupling moments, of new realizations ("that's me!") through productive forms of desire. In penology, the intersecting COREL set/assemblages depicted in diagram 4.6 provide a constitutive diagram for the character of these emergent potentialities.[50] Consistent with Nietzsche's vision of a will to power, of overcoming through the interplay of active forces within the process of becoming, is the rebirth of the stranger as mutating, evolving, and transforming. As such, we envision the necessity of a continuing state of far-from-equilibrium conditions in which dissipative structures become ever more prevalent, where the stranger's identity is transparent and fluid, and where the subject becomes Other in an enduring I-thou relationship.

In the remaining chapter of this book, we explore our symmetry-breaking transdesistance process in greater detail. Pivotal to these analyses will be the application of our constitutive theorizing to the revitalization of the stranger in penology. This undertaking will demonstrate how the recursiveness of penal harm, from its pains of imprisonment to its pains of release and back again in cyclical fashion, can be reconceptualized such that a replacement socius is made that much more realizable. This is a developing habitus in which a transforming justice built around molecular intensities and subjects-in-process dislodges and rises above the embeddedness of the criminological shadow. This is a novel form of selfhood that provisionally, positionally, and relationally redefines our humanity and our becoming.

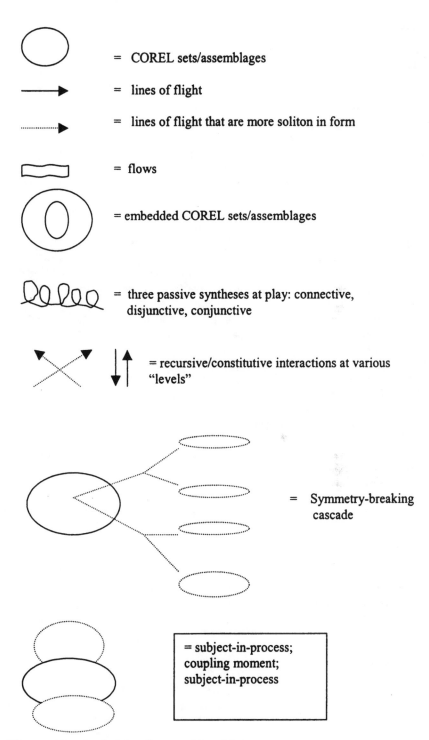

= COREL sets/assemblages

= lines of flight

= lines of flight that are more soliton in form

= flows

= embedded COREL sets/assemblages

= three passive syntheses at play: connective, disjunctive, conjunctive

= recursive/constitutive interactions at various "levels"

= Symmetry-breaking cascade

= subject-in-process; coupling moment; subject-in-process

Diagram 4.7.   Symbols for diagrams 4.4 and 4.6

NOTES

1. Of course, the importation model qualifies the extent to which total institutions operate. Various values, interests, and cultural ways are imported to various degrees, such as with some gangs, and these may become exacerbated within the logic of total institutions.

2. In the subsequent section of this chapter, we problematize who is kept by the recursive activities that essentialize prison. However, for now we draw attention to the material forms of violence that engulf the logic of corrections (e.g., cultural adaptations such as prostitution, drug use, and other underground economies by inmates; sexism, racism and work-related ethical violations by correctional workers; prison privatization, mismanagement, abuses—including the use of cattle prods, taser guns, solitary confinement—and administrative complicity in correctional violence [cover-ups] by wardens and government officials; and support for the death penalty, juvenile waiver to the adult system, sexually violent predator statutes, and heightened modes of surveillance following release by the general public).

3. The research by Raine (1993) on the psychopathology of crime and Moffit, Lynam, and Silva (1994) on neuropsychological prediction of delinquency is especially worth noting.

4. Surveillance can take many forms. Visual and auditory perhaps have been prominent forms. Jeremy Bentham, lest it be forgotten, in his original design of the panopticon included listening pipes to each cell.

5. Foucault did advocate creating mechanisms whereby the subaltern can speak for themselves. Unfortunately, he did not go far enough, especially in light of his earlier work, which indicated the restrictive nature of linguistic regimes. Even the subaltern must speak within dominant discourse (major literature). Additionally, his notion of panopticism leaves little room for struggle. One of us (DM), who has worked with the John Howard Association inspecting prisons, had the opportunity to visit the "roundhouse" at Statesville Prison in Illinois. This is one of the last of the prisons modeled after Bentham's design. When I (DM) visited the central tower, it was a confirmation of the power of Foucault's analysis, until I spoke with an officer. He told me that all that an inmate has to do "on the count" (when he steps outside of his cell so that his presence may be verified) is not return to his cell when instructed to do so. Here, several hundred other inmates will view what will next happen. The inmate has an opportunity to make his case in a theatrical way. He has effectively, temporarily, made power symmetrical. See also Henry and Milovanovic (1996) on their notion of "social judo."

6. See also other authors who have conceptualized the postmodern society in terms of "superpanopticism" (Poster 1996), whereby electronic collections of data provide a Web version of the panopticon, and "synopticism" (Mathiesen 1997), whereby the few watch the preselected many (i.e., celebrities) via cyberspace, a move away from being watched to watching (Bauman 1998, 52). We see this in the placing of offenders and convicted sexual offenders (pictures, information concerning conviction, addresses, and so forth) on publicly accessible websites.

7. As Goodchild (1996, 108) explains it, "The mode of control is no longer enclosure but faciality, or an informational form of it, a number such as those printed

on a credit card. The dominant mode of representation is the pass-word: a face or a figure allows access to the means of production, information, and consumption according to a simple binary scheme."

8. In the school system, it is the continuous reliance on assessment instruments and the greater reliance on the business model in education (Deleuze 1995, 182). According to Wise (1995, 86), exemplary are "flexible and mobile workspaces always in touch with the office, continuous remote monitoring of parolees, constant accumulation of purchasing habits and preferences."

9. Deleuze and Guattari (1987, 129) tell us "this recoiling is also that of mental reality into the dominant reality."

10. Goodchild (1996, 110) provides an example from education: "A teacher will issue statements whose subjects are interchangeable, so that 'we think that' can always be substituted for 'it is thought that.'" Thus, "subjectification begins when one is addressed as 'you'; the statement is repeated by the learning subject, substituting 'I'; finally, this statement may give the new subject of enunciation, making its own perspective from the signifying regimes of such statements."

11. Lacan would agree with the idea that the subject arises after the event (i.e., is spoken by language). For example, Lacan (1977, 1981) refers to the subject as the *parlêtre*, the speaking, or *l'être parlant*, the speaking being. Elsewhere, in explaining his graphs of desire, the elementary cells of speech production, he tells us that the "signifier represents the subject for another signifier." The subject finds her- or himself in the most insignificant location in the bottom left of each of his diagrams, replaced by an "I" that speaks it and a chain of signifiers that represent it.

12. This is connected with the "conjunctive synthesis" that Deleuze and Guattari have explained as the third of the passive forms of synthesis leading to identity.

13. We would add the Tamms supermax in Illinois. DM has been on a prison-inspection team for the John Howard Association on two occasions and confirms the relevance of Bauman's insights there and probably at most other supermax prisons that have been created in the United States.

14. More recent revisionist analysis has witnessed the emergence of a postmodern Marxism, or cyber-Marxism (see Dyer-Witheford 1999). Here, rather than the mode of production, it is the "mode of information" that has centrality. Struggle is now not by the proletariat but by the postmodern proletariat, the "socialized worker" (Negri 1992), the "multitude" (Hardt and Negri 2004), or "cyborgs" (Haraway 1985).

15. Cop, court, and crime-fighting shows on TV, for example, attempt to linearize problems in living. They cater to a passive viewer who constructs "readerly texts" (Barthes) and "organic regimes" (Deleuze 1989). That is, the conventional (modernist) cinematic text reinforces linear logic, order, and stasis—movement toward a clear conclusion. On the other hand, the "crystalline regime" and "writerly text" induces disorder, no clear conclusion, nonlinear flow, and the unexpected, ironic, and contingent truths.

16. See also Johnson's (2002) discussion of inmates' coping mechanisms and niches. Correctional officers, too, are seen as "imprisoned" and develop their own agendas. Violent predators, for Johnson, can be found within both groups.

17. See also Nietzsche (Deleuze 1983). Acquiescence, for Nietzsche, takes the form of resentment, nihilism, investing in reactive forces, and creating idols.

18. In chapter 5, we will suggest several strategies for resisting and transcending these molar forces, consistent with our constitutive penological enterprise. Moreover, in our conclusion, we will identify additional oppositional forms: cyborgs (Haraway 1985), socialized workers (Negri 1992), autonomia movement (Italy), the multitude (Hardt and Negri 2004), and postmodern proletariat (Dyer-Witheford 1999). These conceptions form the basis of supplementary provocative directions awaiting further theoretical analyses and practical integrations.

19. Noology is the study of the images of thought, how we theorize in terms of particular images. Think, for example, of Hobbes's image of thought of the "war of each against all" as apposed to Rousseau's image of the making of the "social contract"; think in terms of much conventional theoretical physics rooted in three space dimensions and one time dimension, compared to string theorists who envision ten space dimensions and one time dimension.

20. We use the word "diagram" in yet another way. In addition to specifying numerically ordered summary information, diagrams are also used in the Deleuzian sense. For Deleuze (1988, 73), a diagram maps "the relation between forces unique to a particular formation." See also Mullarkey (2006, 157–85) on "diagrammatology."

21. See DeLanda's (2006) insightful work on assemblages. Assemblage theory argues for a multiplicity of forms in the socius. Thus, instead of seeing a micro-macro split, agency, and structure as is usually found in the social sciences, DeLanda argues for the existence of embedded assemblages throughout the socius. Some are more molar in form, some more molecular. They differ in the speed of territorialization and deterritorialization, in material and expressive forms. Within some assemblages: encounters may be the more fluid, the most molecular of forms; some networks may be more structured, approaching molar forms; and then work organizations and the state would tend toward the most molar forms. DeLanda also makes a case for explaining the human being in terms of assemblage theory.

22. See Deleuze 1988, 1993; Merleau-Ponty 1969; Conley 2005; Grosz, 1994. Deleuze draws much inspiration from Foucault (*The Birth of the Clinic, The Order of Things, The Archaeology of Knowledge, The History of Madness, The Use of Pleasure*).

23. For Deleuze (1993, 22), the "soul" is a repository of folds.

24. Catastrophe theory is suggestive in terms of how folds may intersect, producing singularities and unexpected "jumps."

25. Deleuze's fascinating analysis also indicates that the inside also retains a "central chamber," Baroque in construction, windowless, doorless, save for select rays of light (Deleuze 1993, 102; see also Conley 2005, 175–76): "We enter into the domain of uncertain doubles and partial deaths, where things continually emerge and fade" (Deleuze 1988, 121; see also 1993, 23, 119). This central chamber harbors the soul: "One fills it with oneself. Here one becomes a master of one's speed and, relatively speaking, a master of one's molecules and particular features, in this zone of subjectivation" (Deleuze 1988, 123; see also Conley 2005). The central chamber is where thinking itself takes place, wherever new folds are created (Deleuze 1993; see also Conley 2005, 176).

26. For the notion of "flow," see chapter 3, note 36.

27. Consider Halsey (2006c, 162): "Criminality is one type of flow. . . . So is juvenile recidivism. As a flow, recidivism emerges as much through the categorical ways

of speaking about repeat or persistent offending (via the judgments, assessments and theories of psychologists, psychiatrists, lawyers, judges, criminologists, social workers, and so on) as it does from any so-called objective material conditions."

28. Rather than prison-industrial complex, we make use of assemblage theory and specify it as the prison-industrial assemblage. The two components of this assemblage include content-expression and territorialization-deterritorialization. Content has to do with the particular way various flows operate (e.g., panopticism, actuarial justice); expression entails the particular way it is given linguistic form (i.e., respectively, rehabilitation rhetoric, cost-benefit rhetoric). Territorialization would include all forces that tend to maintain the prison-industrial assemblage (i.e., penal law); deterritorialization would include all that undermines it (i.e., prisoner suits, exonerations, public outcries, internal revolts).

29. Halsey (2006c, 162) has stated it insightfully: "Recidivism—and more specifically, the phenomenon of repeat incarceration—has most often been dealt with as if it were an administrative event to be managed as opposed to a lived and therefore inherently unpredictable process. Desire is this unpredictability. It is that which does not fit neatly into prescribed discourses or frameworks."

30. The intersecting nature of flows offers the possibility both of resonance and amplification and of discord and challenge—the subject of quick work of operatives to apply the appropriate axiom and bring aberrations within dominant schemas (hail the molar forms!).

31. Noological and genealogical analysis would begin with theorists who have already examined the role of discourse and rationalizations employed by persons. See, e.g., Sykes and Matza's (1957) "techniques of neutralization"; Matza's (1964) *Delinquency and Drift*; Cressey's (1953) *Other People's Money*; Herman and Julia Schwendinger's (1985) *Adolescent Subculture and Delinquency*.

32. As Johnson (1990, 118; see also the discussion of this issue by Farrall and Calverley 2006, 177–78) tells us, "This expanded view allows us to give equal theoretical weight at the level of human motivation to practices that change social systems and those that reproduce them, thereby correcting Giddens' tendency to conflate these two processes." Consider, too, Halsey (2006c), who argues that those subject to conditional release and the risks and reduced autonomy associated with it sometimes opt to remain incarcerated to serve out their time.

33. Halsey (2006c, 13) provides the example of "feeling wild" as a response from the postcustodial subject, a reaction against the disciplinary forces of imprisonment.

34. A classic example offered by chaos theorists would be water: at some temperature, it remains a liquid; at some lower temperature, it becomes a solid; at some higher temperature, it becomes steam.

35. The Hopf bifurcation sequence shown in diagram 4.5 portrays the process of symmetry breaking in three dimensions (see Briggs and Peat 1989, 39–44, 46–47; Young 1997, 32; Abraham 1992). It depicts how a line (series of point attractors) of flight may bifurcate: first, producing a periodic attractor (periodicity of two then a periodicity of four); second, with further perturbation transforming into a torus attractors; and third with more perturbation, into a strange attractor. Critical values in the perturbation process account for the singularities at which points bifurcations take place. Thus, the torus attractor shows how two intertwined systems are maintained in the form of a doughnut-looking object. Here, both order (the distinct shape

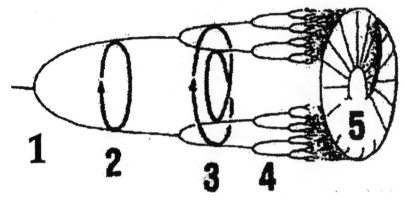

Diagram 4.5. Hopf bifurcation sequence

of the torus) and disorder (within the torus) prevail. Tori may appear in a variety of dimensions beyond three, indicating how various trajectories of dynamic systems are intertwined. Consider, for example, how an incarcerate may live in a socius consisting of those agencies professing a deficiency model and those professing a desistance model. Thus, the determinants of one identity wind around the determinants of a second. The torus attractor shows how these two ongoing adjustments repeat, perhaps manifest in an incarcerate who sees him- or herself at times as wanting and at other times with the capacity to go beyond traditional pathways of adjustment. With further perturbation, the tori may break up and reform as a strange attractor indicating a state of affairs much more indeterminate but still depicting two wings, or outcome basins within which an incarcerate may find her- or himself. Here, unlike the torus attractor, the subject may, with very little perturbation, find her- or himself in one wing or the other. With further perturbation, we enter a more chaotic region within which dissipative structures emerge (order out of order). It is in this region where novelty, epiphanies, alternative life courses, "conscientization" (Freire) may take form (order out of disorder).

36. It also provides various flows constitutive of the guard as brutal hack (Johnson 2002, 202).

37. One component of this is desire. As Halsey (2006a, 162) tells us, "It [desire] is that which does not fit neatly into prescribed discourses or frameworks. And it is this concept that has been missing for too long within correctional theory."

38. See especially Bauman (1998), Halsey (2006c), Farrall and Bowling (1999), and LeBel et al. (2008).

39. David Matza's *Becoming Deviant* (1969) is provocative as to how a subject is passified (objectified) to the point it becomes that which the script demands.

40. We hypothesize that this far-from-equilibrium region will witness the widest expression of epiphanies, insights, flashes of alternatives, and so forth.

41. We could also hypothesize a strange attractor where one wing represents being, the other becoming. In this instance, a small perturbation might iterate in such fashion as to produce an unexpected jump from one wing to the other. Another hypothesis might explore one wing as security, the other as autonomy, and trace the outcomes with perturbation and iteration.

42. For international figures that indicate 90 percent, see Haapanen (1990) and Visher, Lattimore, and Linster (1991). See also Halsey's summary of data (78% to 79% of incarcerated juveniles progressing onto adult custody) in the Australian experience.

43. Banks (forthcoming, 167–86) has argued that both staff and juvenile inmates coproduce a treatment discourse within which each becomes increasingly situated in the construction of narratives. She also points out that the incarcerated juvenile sometimes uses the treatment discourse strategically as a method of resistance. This tactic is mindful of steering the right course between giving evidence to the staff that the inmate is in fact being "corrected" but not to show that the person is treatment-wise.

44. It is more rhizomatic (Deleuze and Guattari 1987).

45. Class, gender, and race are created categories. They may indeed become strategic categories in historical struggle. But we must recognize that they are molar categories, born of history and political economy. See, e.g., Butler (1990), Grosz (1994), Lorraine (1999), and Halberstam (2005).

46. This replacement socius is more consistent with what Deleuze and Guattari refer to as a "permanent revolution," where the molecular is privileged over the molar.

47. Molecular forms as dissipative structures are much more prevalent in far-from-equilibrium conditions, as dynamic systems theory suggests. Molar forms, such as bureaucracies, are more prevalent in static (homeostatic) conditions.

48. For a lucid discussion of news making in various crime and justice contexts, see Barak (1994). For a constitutive and postmodern application in penology, see Arrigo (2006c).

49. At the stage where the person begins to identify with the more complete being of the other, we arrive at "becoming other." At the stage whereby I and other are mutually constituted, we arrive at "becoming imperceptible" (Deleuze and Guattari 1987). This becoming other, becoming imperceptible, sets the challenge for theorizing an ethics and conceptions of justice that are compatible with it. See, e.g., the work by Derrida and Levinas for a beginning foray (See Critchley 1999; Capeheart and Milovanovic 2007, ch. 9).

50. We make no pretenses of offering a blueprint for the society to come. Rather, we argue for alternative possible diagrams more akin to quantum mechanics, hodological (nonstriated) spaces, and far-from-equilibrium conditions in which a plethora of "larval selves" (Deleuze and Guattari 1987) and dissipative structures are provided space within which to emerge and take on form. These are spaces where experimentalism at all levels of the socius is valued and experienced, where the molecular is privileged over the molar, and where point and cyclical attractors become secondary to tori and strange attractors. In short, we advocate a "permanent revolution," a "molecular revolution" (Deleuze and Guattari 1987).

5

The Shadow and Stranger in Constitutive Penology

On (Dis)identities and (Dis)continuities

INTRODUCTION

The previous chapter specified how the pains of imprisonment, from incarceration to release to postconfinement, repetitively and cyclically function to reproduce penal harm. Constitutively speaking, this is a harm that simultaneously and reciprocally reifies the prison-form, its parts and segments understood as correctional philosophies and practices, steeped in an essentializing discourse that imprisons us all. The kept, their keepers (officers and administrators), and the punitive general public coproduce this language and logic and draw support for these activities from the structural and organizational forces that sustain the correctional complex. Panoptic power, technologized culture, negative freedom, and other molar intensities prevail, working to reduce and repress the human subject, who is relegated to the status of a mere shadow.

However, as we indicated, recovery (i.e., being) and transformation (i.e., becoming) are realizable without creating new or more static hierarchies. Indeed, symmetry-breaking cascade strategies can be discerned. Various and intersecting COREL set/assemblages consisting of diverse movements, molecular lines of flight, different threshold levels, and fluctuating speeds and intensities can be active (rather than reactive) energy flows. They signify the mobilization of change and mutation; the dismantling and reassembling of the agency/structure duality that otherwise legitimizes penal harm, the pains of imprisonment, and the normalization of violence; and the birth of a replacement language that challenges/resists the fetishism of correctional discourse. Here, too, incarcerates, those who confine/monitor, the general public, and all others who endorse penal harm can be revitalized, can experience a becoming. This is a transdesistance model that enables the person to evolve as a subject-in-process, to disrupt molar repetitions, and to experience dynamic flows that resuscitate the stranger in provisional, positional, and relational contexts.

In this chapter, the thesis developed throughout this book is revisited in historically specific manifest form. In particular, the molar categories of race, gender, and class as appropriated and manufactured in penology are problematized.[1] First, we demonstrate how such classification schemas, as summary representations, serve only to reproduce relations of libidinal production that merely sustain the status quo and their abstract machines. As we explain, the latter territorialize knowledge, pathologize difference, and homogenize identity all in the furtherance of hegemonic state interests, including the aims of the prison edifice. Featured, then, are the contexts in which these interests take form in Foucault's panoptic gaze, Lacan's *discourse of the master*, Fromm's critique of automaton conformity, Baudrillard's assessment of simulated cultural reality, and Deleuze and Guattari's position on the process of subjectification, such that they constitutively sustain the criminological shadow. As we explain, this is how the normalization of violence is reenacted, reified, and legitimized through singular identity constructions in penology proper.

Second, consistent with our position on the criminological stranger, we suggest how marginalized, disempowered, and disenfranchised individuals and/or collectives can (and do) challenge/oppose summary representations that function to reduce and repress their humanity. Of particular focus are techniques of penal resistance that affirm (the oppressor) in the act of negating (the oppression), notwithstanding one's position of relative dispossession and powerlessness. This is what is meant by transpraxis (Arrigo 2001).[2] Additionally, a series of COREL set/assemblages (strata as molecular lines of flight) that can help to foster the resuscitation of the stranger's overlapping and intersecting standpoints/ identities is delineated. As we note, this is how our proposed symmetry-breaking transdesistance model could operate to advance transformative justice. Insights derived from several critical and postmodern theorists, as well as dynamic systems theory, inform the overall analysis.

THE PENOLOGICAL SHADOW AND IDENTITIES

We take as given the notion that rigid and fixed constructions of race, gender, and class (including their modernist intersectionalities) are historically contingent and socially conceived categories used for purposes of creating summary categories of difference (Kenny 2004; Martin-Alcoff 2005). More troubling, however, as artifacts of materialist culture, these categories are manipulated (often unwittingly) to advance the interests of Oedipus and capital logic, whose effects can and do alienate, exploit, and marginalize those subjected to such harm. These effects emerge as a function of perceived and real structural inequalities, expressed through social institutions (e.g., the system of education, the workforce, the correctional apparatus, the health-care industry) (McMullin 2004), in which the body is regulated, the mind is programmed, and, consequently, identities are cleansed (Martin-Alcoff and Mendieta 2003). The result, then, is an *exclusive society* (Young 1999; Bauman 1998) in which stability, reactive forces, homogeneity, risk-management, actuarial justice, immobilization, and predictability (order) in socioeconomic relations are privileged in the socius. To accomplish this normalization, to pathologize expressions of difference, the supercontrol society (see chapter 4) operates at several distinct and interacting levels. These include (1) economic exclusion from the labor market; (2) social exclusion between people and among divergent groups (e.g., gated communities, white flight from the city, "tracking" models in education); (3) increasing immobilization practices (e.g., proliferating the use of supermax prisons and increasing the segregation of space within correctional facilities); (4) surveillance (both in the Foucaultian panopticon and the Mathiesenian synopticon forms wherein, particularly for the latter, the many monitor/inspect the few, as in the media with selected celebrities and registered sex offenders on the Web); (5) differential access to data (as in Mark Poster's superpanopticon whereby disparate access prevails in retrieving data that impacts on one's life); and (6) political-cultural exclusion in the form of net-widening criminal justice practices (excessive investments in penal philosophies/programs that essentialize prison discourse and reify the correctional edifice).

Of particular concern in this section is the latter form of exclusion, especially its underdeveloped philosophic and psychoanalytic contours. Consistent with our thesis as developed in chapter 4, we interpret the political-cultural disciplining that stems from criminal justice practices as homologous with the normalization of violence. This is a reference to the repetitive molar intensities (e.g., negative freedom, technologized culture, panoptic logic, formal rationality, and capital logic) that constitutively define categories of differences (race, gender, and class) in ways that promote sameness, equilibrium conditions, and status quo dynamics, mediated in this instance by correctional discourse. To describe how this harm (i.e., reduction and repression) routinely unfolds, we first briefly present the case of Mary,[3] an economically disadvantaged woman of color routed to and from the penal system in which temporary housing and respite were secured by way of episodic homeless shelter and soup kitchen assistance.[4] Second, the narrative of Mary is amplified by examining her story within the rubric of constitutive penology, especially our perspective on the pains of imprisonment, the normalization of violence, and the criminological shadow.

The Narrative of Mary:
On the Incarceration-Release-Postconfinement Machine

At the age of twenty-eight, Mary had been incarcerated for prostitution, drug possession/distribution, and theft. She received a three-year prison sentence and served fourteen months. Following her release plan, Mary entered a homeless women's shelter. She was a frequent visitor at nearby sandwich lines and soup kitchens. These outlets provided Mary with a sustainable and supplemental source of daily nourishment. Mary reported no immediate family or other intimates and spoke somewhat indifferently about existing friendships and acquaintances. Her closest companions included other women at the shelter, many of whom were survivors of domestic abuse; others were poor, unwed mothers lacking adequate education or financial means to be self-sufficient; and still others were in need of intensive psychiatric treatment. Restrictions on housing at the shelter prohibited Mary (and all other women) from taking up permanent residence at this facility. Instead, the women were encouraged to secure employment; to get their general equivalence diplomas (GEDs); to pursue literacy training; to enroll in parenting classes; to maintain outpatient psychiatric, drug rehabilitation, and/or medical appointments; to cultivate family reunification; to participate in individual and/or group counseling meetings; to establish rapport with their case workers (including a housing specialist); to develop resume-writing skills; and generally to ready themselves for reentry into the community at large as productive and engaged citizens.[5] Moreover, the women were encouraged to take responsibility for their troubled lives, to change or eliminate the debilitating conditions that led to their wayward conduct, and to focus on recovery, good, healthy living, and redemption through these enumerated prosocial activities.[6] The length of residence at the shelter typically did not exceed three months for a person. In the case of a mother with a child (or children), temporary housing could last as long as six months.

Near the completion of her stay at the shelter, Mary was informed that she would not be able to retain temporary housing beyond the initial three-month period. She reported that during the weeks leading up to the termination of her temporary housing, she was increasingly distraught. Concerned for her long-term welfare and security, Mary began staying out late at night—well past the established curfew (curfews are a standard practice at many shelter facilities). This behavior did not incline the shelter staff to consider any exception to the housing policy in Mary's case.

When the three-month period had elapsed, Mary was denied continued admission into the shelter, notwithstanding her entreaties to the contrary. Left on her own, without adequate economic or social resources to consider meaningful alternatives, Mary returned to a criminal lifestyle that eventually resulted in her rearrest, prosecution, and imprisonment.

Mary was incarcerated a second time for drug possession and theft. By this time, she was thirty-two. She was sentenced to six years and served eighteen months. As during her initial incarceration, Mary was encouraged to participate in employment and educational programming. This included such things as cooking, cleaning, sewing, or "mothercraft" work.[7] Moreover, while confined, Mary was exposed to a range of social services designed to ready her for release. As with her experiences at the homeless shelter, literacy training, drug counseling, and mental health treatment were staple features of the services to which she was exposed.

Following her release from prison, Mary found her way to another homeless shelter for women. This facility guaranteed Mary temporary housing for three months, pending any egregious infractions of shelter rules (e.g., physical violence). Much like her prior experiences with the homeless shelter community, a series of basic living skills and community-engagement practices were emphasized (e.g., GED completion, drug counseling, and employment readiness). Comparable to her past behavior, Mary cycled out of this homeless shelter, returned to a criminal career, and reentered the criminal justice system.

By the time Mary was forty-three, this repetitive cycle of behavior, from incarceration to release to reconfinement, had occurred on at least two more occasions. When Mary reported these events, she was quite clear about what she wanted:

> All I want is to get my life together, ya know? I mean, what's wrong with me? I wanna work, I wanna finish my GED, and I wanna do the things that everyone else does. Why can't I do that? And I'm trying, honest. But I just can't seem to get it. . . . I can't seem to make things happen for me. I do the things I'm told at the shelter, and even when I was in the prison, I pretty much did what I was told. I didn't want to get into trouble. I didn't like it there. . . . But now I'm nowhere. . . . I've got nothing, nothin' at all. It all feels pretty much like a waste of a life to me.

The Pains of Imprisonment, the Normalization of Violence, and the Criminological Shadow: On the Dialectics of Struggle and Identity Politics

As a point of departure, we acknowledge that "feminist theory . . . depends on the nexus of language, subjectivity, and consciousness" (Howe 1994;

DeLauretis 1990, 115; see also Butler 1992, 2004; Cornell 1998, 1999; Halberstam 2005). This is a reference to the contexts in which women are "imprisoned discursively and materially," given various penal environs (Arrigo, Milovanovic, and Schehr 2005, 56). Mindful of our thesis, we note that something more is needed to discern the harm (reduction/repression) that women like Mary constitutively confront, given the agency/structure duality that affirms correctional philosophies/practices, as well as the prison edifice that stands above both. Indeed, persons like Mary need to locate and retrieve a psychic space within which to speak from at least three intersecting standpoints: as a woman, as a person of color, and as an economically disadvantaged (and homeless) citizen. This is a space that facilitates recovery (i.e., being) and transformation (i.e., becoming). Before addressing these concerns, some attention to the dialectics of struggle and identity politics is warranted.

Diagram 5.1 is a "diagram" (in a double sense) depicting the harms of reduction/repression encountered by Mary and many others similarly exposed to the pains of imprisonment, release, and reconfinement. The diagram portrays our position on constitutive penology and the normalization of violence.

In diagram 5.1, we note that the socius within which Mary maneuvers is constituted by various intersecting COREL set/assemblages: some overlap, others intertwine, some are embedded with additional lines of flight, and still others emerge and dissipate. This is to say that it represents a diagram of forces, some more static (reactive), some more dynamic (active), some captured within static forms, some more amorphous and undergoing continuous mutation and transformation. Several assemblages may appear in historically contingent, relatively autonomous coupled configurations. At the structural level, molar strata are depicted. They are characterized by stasis, repetition, linearity, closure, equilibrium conditions, and reactionary forces. The alternating emphases on Mary's correctional rehabilitation as based on the deficit and desistance models, respectively, convey this notion. We may envision this oscillation as being captured within one or the other wing (attractor basin) of a butterfly (strange) attractor. Absent a particular perturbation, this oscillation remains the hodological space[8] within which Mary operates and within which identity is constructed (Deleuze and Guattari's conjunctive synthesis, "that's me!"). We shall return in the second half of this chapter to the necessary conditions by which a relevant perturbation may produce a possible Hopf transformation,[9] whereby symmetry breaking produces new lines of flight.

At the agency level is the Body-without-Organs (BwO). This refers to Mary as a field of intensities and flows constituted by different speeds and various threshold levels. These intensities and flows refer to the man-

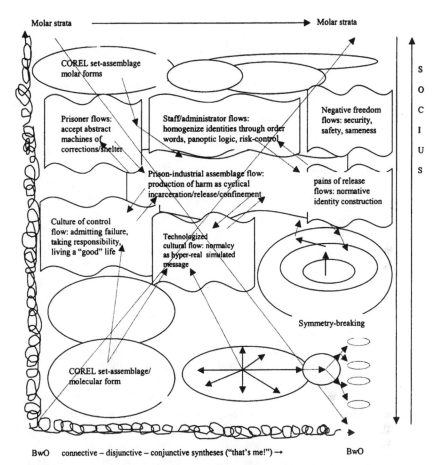

Diagram 5.1. Identities, dialectical struggles, and the normalization of violence.

ifold dimensions of her molar identity (e.g., as a women, a person of color, and poor) and molecular identity (various emerging desires) and to their manifold recognitions ("that's me!"). Perturbations as critical input values exist within which bifurcations, dissipative structures, and symmetry breaking can occur. However, they await mobilization, valorization, and activation (i.e., the resuscitation of the stranger).The lower left- and right-hand portions of diagram 5.1 illustrate this for Mary. A three-dimensional portrait can be represented by the Hopf transformation (see diagram 4.5). Indicated is how symmetry breaking undergoes a series: first, there is a periodic attractor (periodicity of two), followed by a torus attractor, followed by further symmetry breaking (periodicity of four, eight, sixteen, thirty-two, and so forth), followed by a region within which a strange attractor[10] emerges. In Mary's molar flow, it indicates how a deficit or desistance correctional philosophy captured in various components of the control apparatus may initially produce a narrow basin of attraction (point and periodic attractors). However, with appropriate perturbation, these point or limit attractors may undergo symmetry breaking whereby new lines of flight are released. Some of these lines of flight may find expressive form in torus or strange attractors, such as in the oscillation between adjustments to a deficit model and a desistance model. With more input values, these molecular strata may even find an oscillation between the deficit and desistance model in one wing and an emergent (transdesistance model) in the other wing. With more critical feedback, lines of flight may be mutative and transformative. Indeed, as dynamic systems theory suggests, order out of disorder emerges as a dissipative structure in form. Here, the conjunctive synthesis provides new realizations, new epiphanies, and new insights, as well as novel turning points in life. Each of these represents a coupling moment in which a new order is potentially realized. Of course, consistent with the literature on desistance theory, these transformative moments may again undergo symmetry breaking, as is suggested by dynamic systems theory. This symmetry breaking may culminate in lines of flight that are, on the one hand, active, mutative, and transformative or, on the other hand, reactive, static, repetitive, and possibly having harmful consequences to self and/or others. We never know with certainty along which line of flight the subject will escape.

Three "passive syntheses"[11] produce the subject of enunciation. The first, connective synthesis, can be shown at work with Mary, whereby numerous intersecting flows[12] to which she is subjected, many of which originate from the various culture-of-control practices, are synthesized into meaning structures, increasingly characterized by distinct basins of attractors, the point and cyclic attractors being the privileged forms. Stated differently, Mary's socius provides several flows that always already provide relatively stable connected part-objects[13] but which must be integrated by Mary's own desiring productive psychic apparatus. These are passive[14] investments and produce heightened (charged) energy sources and value (Holland 1999, 25; Massumi 1992, 48). Said in yet another way, Mary's socius may be mapped by a diagram that indicates her variously invested part-objects, which attain higher value in her worldview. The prevalence of dominant control components in her socius and their often resonating forms (flows that resonate with similar underlying logics, such as deficits or fallibilities) assure a limited range to which connective syntheses apply, constituting, in short, an invested (cathected) field.

When two or more connective syntheses are further joined by some code, we are in the realm of the disjunctive synthesis. This is a more active phase whereby classificatory and nominalizing processes and their repetition produce statistical regularities. As Brian Massumi (1992, 49) tells us, the disjunctive synthesis is a "product of self-reproducing cultural activities drawing on a store of memory, or knowledge, and directed toward more or less utilitarian ends." For Deleuze and Guattari, this second synthesis is an "overcoding" to be distinguished by the passive coding of the connective synthesis.[15] It is also the moment for the incorporation of master signifiers, order words, and dominant linguistic regimes of signs.[16] For Mary, faced with regularities within her socius—the continuous negotiation with flows that retain a deficit logic—disjunctive syntheses assure that a relatively orderly world will be constructed based on investments in reactive forces (e.g., repetition, limitations of the possible, reduction of mutative/transformative possibilities; premium placed on acknowledging shortcomings in personality and a willingness to "go with the program").[17] This socius also assures that Mary, now more a molarized subject (a client or subject of rehabilitation/punishment), will be integrated striatically into the various control apparatuses and their respective flows.[18]

We note further that with alternative flows, such as those provided by desistance theorizing, the connective and disjunctive syntheses take on different forms. Accordingly, we would expect Mary, faced with these flows, to undergo qualitatively different investments. Ultimately, however, given her accommodations here, dominant forms (e.g., family, cultural values, aspirations, employment) would be reified anew into a cyclical pattern. Admittedly, COREL sets/assemblages would materialize consistently with desistance theory in which moments of active forces would experience mobilization, including their potential dominance over reactive forces. However, in this oscillation (reactive-active, deficit model–desistance model), perhaps best depicted by a strange (butterfly) attractor, no transformative practices would be stabilized or given more permanent standing. In short, master signifiers, order words, and linguistic regimes that potentially could contribute to a recovering subject (being) would nevertheless not foster a genuinely more transformative subject (becoming). Thus, while Mary would greatly benefit from the desistance forms of expression (materialized in pragmatic encounters) over their deficit-form counterparts, she would still fall short of becoming, evolving, and transforming. Already, then, in our transdesistance theory, we begin to see the suggestions for a strategy by which a Hopf transformation could take hold. This is a molecular metamorphosis whereby symmetry breaking releases lines of flight that can be the basis of a becoming or mutating self rather than a situated and finite being.

Whereas the disjunctive synthesis materializes developing subjectivities ("larval subjects") in which boundaries are still blurred, the conjunctive synthesis leads to a realization: "That's me!" In other words, the nominalized (molar) subject appears as "an after effect" (Holland 1999, 33; Massumi 1992, 73, 75) with the realization, "Yes, that's me!" It is the interplay of connective and disjunctive syntheses that sets the stage for the subject, in retrospect, to claim its molarized identity (Holland 1999, 34; see also Massumi 1992, 72). It is the moment in which the subject emerges to consume its various connections and disjunctions. Said in another way, Mary can now act on the various connections and disjunctions made and reap what they potentially offer her.

For example, identifying with the idealized image of a recovering subject in a particular rehabilitation agency offers access to new reward structures (relaxed restrictions on curfew, an exception to the three-month temporary shelter policy) and/or to an alternative vocabulary (taking responsibility for personal deficits, "owning" recovery, pursuing the "good life") in which (illusory) empowerment may result. At times, one can be held captive by one's previously strategic identifications and, in the end, become the molar subject that the agency glorifies. In Mary's socius, various flows provide the raw material from which connective, disjunctive, and conjunctive syntheses play themselves out. Stated differently, her socius is a diagram of forces into which Mary is continuously thrust and from which she recursively subjects herself. These forces are the culmination of repetition, which leads to her molar identities (i.e., as a client, offender, probationer, parolee, recovering subject). Throughout the manifestation of all of these identities, reactive forces (e.g., normalcy/normativity, security/safety, and equivalence/stasis) are repetitively reinforced. Completing the circuit, as constitutive penology stipulates, these nominalized identities provide further credence to dominant understandings of the erring and recovering subject.[19]

In diagram 5.1, the conjunctive synthesis is a molarized line of flight in which the subject (Mary) is defined or interpellated within a particular political economy (i.e., as a female offender imprisoned, as a homeless woman sheltered). The squiggly lines extending from the BwO to the molar strata and from the BwO at one time versus another delineate this. Mary's own statements about getting her life together and doing what everyone else does symbolize the recoiling of the subject[20] in that her identity was given static, linear form. Similarly, the emphasis on conventional interpretations of work, education, family, self-direction, and the like while in prison or in the shelter reflect the structural/organizational dimensions of Mary's subjectification ("that's me!"). From Lacan's *discourse of the master* and Deleuze and Guattari's idea of regimes of signs and order words, we can see how the socius within which Mary is located provides key master signifiers in which she takes up libidinal residence. These master signifiers/order words as constructed, spoken, and reiterated represent the prevailing grammar of control and rehabilitation. Mary insets herself and is situated within this language system.[21] She occupies this (molar) discursive subject-position as an "I" (a recovering subject), and it is from within this standpoint that she speaks. In other words, the subaltern voices of Mary (Spivak 1988) (as a woman, as a person of color, as an economically disadvantaged citizen) have considerable difficulty in finding alternative discursive subject-positions and master signifiers that more completely reflect her plight and from which a fuller narrative about her identities can be constructed. It is in here, then, that we can begin to see how the dialectics of struggle, of endeavoring to transcend the oscillation between and among reactive, static flows, recursively reproduces identity politics: difference is reduced to sameness, knowledge is territorialized, and the stranger is vanquished. Ultimately, repetition, reification, and investment in dominant understandings and reactive forces prevail. These recursive and cyclical activities do nothing more than reconstitute and legitimize status quo dynamics.

What more specifically can be said of diagram 5.1 and the reactive flows within which Mary is positioned and into which she locates herself? A number of nonexhaustive flows[22] are part of the diagram of the socius within which she navigates, and they specify the nominal forces that engulf Mary's identity. These flows produce a molar, limitative BwO. Several of these are noted: technologized cultural flows (the recursive and simulated hyperreal message about normalcy, doing what everyone else does, and living like everyone else lives); the culture-of-control flows (e.g., acknowledging failures, taking responsibility, leading a "good" life, status quo restoration, identifying with idealized recovering subjects); prisoner flows (uncritical acceptance of the abstract machines that constitute the correctional edifice and the homeless shelter system); social service staff and correctional officer/administrator flows (emphasis on neutralizing differences and homogenizing identities through order words [e.g., "going straight"], equilibrium conditions, bureaucratic rationality, panoptic logic, risk management, and capital logic); negative-freedom flows (Mary's desire for security/safety expressed in terms of sameness, doing what she is told, being like everyone else); pains-of-release flows (normative constructions of identity, family, work, education, health, success, and well-being); and prison-industrial COREL set/assemblage flows (cyclical incarceration, release, and reconfinement).

Diagram 5.1 also indicates how some flows intersect with the prison-industrial COREL set/assemblage flow.[23] These points of convergence depict the manner in which Mary's recursively constituted social reality of imprisonment was produced in static form, fostering the normalization of violence (i.e. identity politics) and the silencing of dialectical struggle (i.e., becoming, mutating, transforming). This flow specifies how the harms of reduction and repression that saturated Mary's existence emerged (linguistically and unconsciously) and endured (materially and culturally). Moreover, several of the intersecting COREL set/assemblages as flows, each of which contain their own abstract machines, produced lines of flight/escape delineated by arrows with dotted lines. Depending on the frequency, intensity, critical timing, and duration of these assemblages, coupling moments could appear that would perturb existing threshold levels.[24] This change could further lead to bifurcations, tori and strange attractors, and novel outcome basins.[25]

Circularity and feedback loops in these flows are also dominant. Mary finds herself in these flows. Causality, too, is bidirectional[26] and nonlinear.[27] Jacob Stowell and James Byrne's (2008, 32) review of the literature[28] indicates that "incarceration can lead to increased levels of economic disadvantage and crime by disrupting informal networks [we read as COREL sets/assemblages] of social control, to which offenders belong." In other words, not only may values be imported to prison where they undergo further form by the pains of imprisonment, but they are exported back to the community. Back in the community, they may also interact with cultural values/flows and provide the basis of further reinforcement of a particular flow (e.g., Clear 2007). But these should not be construed as linear events, as linear causation. Rather, following DeLanda (2006, 20–24), given each person's unique internal organization (BwO), each of us has differential capacities to respond to external flows. In other words, each person has differential thresholds "below or above which external causes fail to produce an effect" (DeLanda 2006, 20).[29] Mary, for example, might respond to the configuration of flows within which she operates in a particular manner that is quite distinct from that of another person. However, statistical regularities/probabilities may indeed materialize; "statistical causality" may reflect populations but at the same time provide space in which the role of a *particular* person may make a difference, the latter even contributing to unintended results (DeLanda 2006, 24).[30]

Noteworthy here is the recent work of Robert Sampson and Lydia Bean (2006) with their "culture in action" thesis and Stowell and Byrne (2008) with their notion of integration.[31] Accommodated to our perspective, various flows within the socius provide pragmatic choices[32] for Mary. Not only do we have to ask, for which audience does she perform? but we also must recognize that rational action when applied is itself misleading (Stowell and Byrne 2008, 36; Sampson and Bean, 2006, 25–26). As Sampson and Bean (2006, 25–26) have said, "People often adopt the course of action that uses the practical skills and cognitive tools they have at hand." Consistent with the position we are developing, the subject emerges as an after effect. For example, Sampson and Bean (2006, 25–26) state that "ultimate ends are invented in retrospect, to justify [one's] course of action after it has been completed." Therefore, "choice," for Mary, is already preconstructed based on her socius,[33] its various intersecting flows,[34] and her internal organization (capacities to affect and to be affected).[35] External evaluations of "good" or "bad" choice making miss the mark altogether.[36] Pragmatic problem-solving forms (gang banging, extortion, expressive and instrumental violence, drug trade and use) in the community can be imported to the prison, and they then can be exported back to the community (Stowell and Byrne 2008, 36; Sampson and Bean 2006, 26). When adapted to our view, we see how various assemblages and their expressive forms may attain more molar cohesion, providing as well a singular identity for the subject: "That's me!" For Mary, the very pragmatically based choices she makes become the very building blocks in which her molar identity is advanced and sustained.

We also acknowledge the molar activities that promote regularity, routinization, status quo dynamics, and predictability for shelter staff and correctional workers.[37] These subjects typically find themselves in fields of capture: management philosophies both intended and unintended, staff culture, and inmate culture.[38] Their own flows tend to be molded by the abstract machines into which they insert themselves and/or are situated.[39] Consistent with this viewpoint are the regimes of signs (including Lacan's *discourse of the master*) as assemblages that give expressive form to various flows. In particular, this includes the interpretation of identity in which territorializing forces (process offenders, fill shelter beds, control disruptions, promote healthy living) tend toward stasis and molar reactivity.

Ultimately, however, prisons are places where reactive forces dominate, where bodies are reduced (inmate and staff) to what they are capable of doing. As Halsey (2006b, 16) tells us, "Things are done *to* them [inmates] and for them and only very rarely *with* them (and with their consent). In this sense, inmates are taught to react [rather] than act. They are taught to respond rather than initiate."[40] In short, incarcerates are continuously molded into molar identities, are territorialized, and are reactive subjects. Thus, what could be expected for many upon release other than more crime? Indeed, why the surprise when statistics indicate that 67 percent return to prison after three years of release? Hence, do possibilities exist in which molecular identities *might* emerge?

Mary's socius is a hodological space offering possibilities to affect and to be affected by intersecting flows, changing intensities, feedback loops, repetition, iterative effects, and singularities. Symmetry breaking might unfold with appropriate perturbations. But how can such active forces and molecular lines of flight materialize? What sort of COREL set/assemblages would need to take hold in order to make such a becoming subject remotely possible? In short, how can the stranger (Mary's intersecting identities as an imprisoned/sheltered, poor, black woman) experience resuscitation such that transformation is made that much more realizable?

THE PENOLOGICAL STRANGER AND IDENTITIES

In this final section of chapter 5, we want to suggest how symmetry breaking might produce lines of flight that are active, mutative, and transformative, as is consistent with our transdesistance theory. In other words, molar categories need not be passively accepted, may be undermined by struggle, and may, with appropriate perturbation, pave the way to alternative, more humanistic forms (mobilization of active forces and molecular identities), following the suggestions of the Hopf transformation series. Said in yet another way, we want to offer some thoughts as to how new master signifiers, new identities, and a new socius[41] could release lines of flight characterized as perpetually mutative and transformative for Mary.

Chapter 4 and diagram 4.6 broadly depicted the features of constitutive penology's symmetry-breaking transdesistance model. We return to this schematization in the remaining portions of chapter 5. Our aim is to propose how Mary's penal plight (the politics of her identities through the pains-of-imprisonment cycle) could be noologically reconceptualized. However, to accomplish this, we first situate Mary within the "state thought" that territorializes (colonizes) her potential rhizomatic lines of flight and nomadic movements (Deleuze and Guattari 1987). State thought disciplines molecular lines of flight and smooth and open-ended movements both in theory (e.g., totalizing philosophies of desistance, restoration, and recovery) and in practice (political, bureaucratic, and other organizational state-based machines of control) (Best and Kellner 1991, 102). In response, a "war machine" provides alternative disruptive logic (Deleuze and Guattari 1987, 351–423). This is a nomadic strategy for engaged transpraxis, and it exists outside of or apart from the state apparatus and its noological imagery and striated or gridded logic (Deleuze and Guattari 1987, 380). As we argue, reconceptualizing Mary's identities is the path to deterritorialization and reterritorialization. It is the journey to a becoming self in which the stranger who dwells deep within her and awaits expression, recognition, and valorization can be nonhierarchically retrieved.

From Identities to (Dis)identities, from Continuities to (Dis)continuities: Reconceptualizing Mary and Rethinking the Penological Stranger

Following constitutive penology, the resuscitation of Mary begins by imaging and reimaging the agency/structure duality that formed (and potentially forms) her socius. This undertaking draws attention to the particular visualizations of thought that subtend how she was defined by staff members of the homeless women's shelter and correctional system (as expressed through their articulated investments in the deficit and desistance rehabilitation models) and how she correspondingly and simultaneously conceived of herself. Moreover, this activity highlights the harms (repression/reduction) enacted by the correctional edifice that were sustained through prisonization or confinement discourse, particularly in relation to summary categories of difference, including race, class, and gender dynamics. These comments are subsequently augmented by a diagrammatic representation of Mary's socius in which the symmetry-breaking transdesistance model is more fully enumerated and examined.

So, the question is as follows: how did the state apparatuses of the homeless shelter and the correctional system conceptualize Mary, bearing in mind her status as a black woman of limited economic means? Consistent with our thesis on the criminological shadow, these historically contingent and political-economically informed diagrams of power (and their agents) saw her as a woman, but through the acculturation and experiences of men.[42] And what can be said of this acculturation and these experiences? They were, most of them, the product of the acculturation and experiences of other white, heterosexual men that preceded those individuals who perceived and responded to Mary. So, how was Mary noologically conceived in this malestream state thought? She was the person these systems, their representatives, and those like them made: she was defined in their image of the feminine.[43] Mary was the one who reminded them of what was (is) an ineluctable part of their being. She reminded them who a woman was (is) suppose to "be" and what a woman was (is) suppose to "do." However, Mary is more than this, even though this seemingly indescribable more was not readily accessible to them, immediately recognizable by them, and instantly speakable for them.

Thus, to reframe the question from within constitutive penology, how might Mary (as a woman) be noologically reconceptualized? Mary is the one who insists (Lacan's *pas toute* or lack, 1985) but does not excessively invest in insistence. She is the one who knows (Derrida's absence made present, 1977, 1978) but does not claim that knowing is either sufficient or necessary. Mary is the one who seeks to affirm living (Fromm's notion of authentic/spontaneous freedom, 1994, 2005) because living is so much more about being than knowing. She is the one who wants to evolve (Deleuze and Guattari's notion of desire as flow/production, 1987) because evolving is about her becoming with or without us. And she is still more, so much more, than this.

Her skin color, her age, her abilities and means, her history, her heritage, her sexual(ities) and desires are not reducible to just us (all of us), our histories, or our experiences. Although these categories are the product of our acculturation and experiences made for, by, and about us (mostly white heterosexual men), her (dis)identities (her differences that are not reducible to the logic of sameness) are not readily accessible, immediately recognizable, or instantly speakable through such finite constructions. Mary does not dwell in standpoints but in (dis)locations. She is not made of actualities but of potentialities. Her multiple voice(s) and way(s) of being (her positionalities as a poor, homeless woman of color) defy mathematical precision and scientific quantification. This is what makes her mostly unknowable (invisible and silent) to the state, even when the shelter and correctional systems tried to "restore" her. But restore her to what and in whose image?

The acculturation and experiences of these state agents would have us believe that Mary's uncertainty and disequilibrium are indications of her social-psychological impotence; however, her undecidability and ambiguity may very well be the conditions of her political efficacy. She experiences her potentialities when not named for, by, and about the state. The state, its totalizing philosophy of recovery through deficit/desistance models, and its closed, segmented, and compartmentalized logic (e.g., bureaucratic risk management as in compulsory "going straight" compliance, panopticism as in shelter/prison restrictions and "getting with the program," formal rationality as in leading a "good life") cannot resuscitate Mary or her possibilities when merely gazing upon her continuities. Her becoming self emerges when attention is directed to her (dis)continuities, the nonnormative psychic places from which she struggles to evolve, to experience her molecular revolution. Attending to this mutating self is a formidable challenge indeed. However, it is in these rarest of occasions that Mary's transparency (her intelligibility and efficacy) is conceivable, although it is not likely that she would define her status as such. These are the fleeting epiphanies and coupling moments in which transformation for Mary (for us all) is made that much more realizable.

This challenge of resuscitation extends to all facets of Mary's life, including those that encompass the recursive pains-of-imprisonment cycle. The abstract machine, the prison-industrial assemblage, names her as well. And, in the act of speaking her, she is already imprisoned by this COREL set/assemblage. But her resistance here is not futile, and the conditions under which she speaks of (and acts upon) such larval identities need not themselves be punitive. The task is to revitalize the stranger. This is the journey through which her becoming self can be retrieved again and anew. This is how reauthoring the text that is the transforming self unfolds in provisional, positional, and relational ways.

Diagram 5.2 depicts Mary as a becoming, mutating, and transforming self, consistent with our transdesistance thesis. The diagram reflects the processes and flows by which the stranger (Mary's [dis]identities and [dis]continuities as emergents) could be resuscitated in nonhierarchical

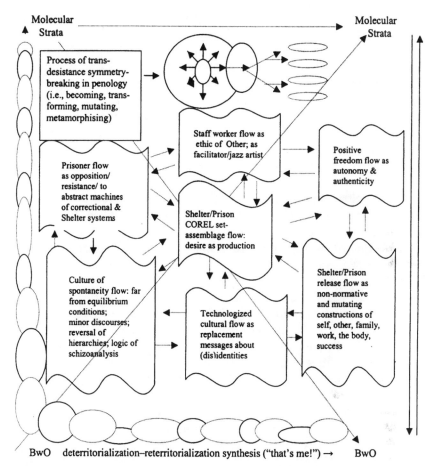

Diagram 5.2.   The transdesistance model as (dis)identities and (dis)continuities: The case of Mary.

and nonlinear form. Stated differently, this schematization implicates the reconfiguration of Mary's socius in molecular, active, and dynamic noological fashion. In effect, then, diagram 5.2 proposes images of thought outside of or apart from the state thought that recursively and cyclically fostered the pains of imprisonment, the normalization of violence (penal harm as reducing/repressing Mary's dislocations), and the reification of the correctional edifice (including its parts/segments as well as its philosophies/practices), expressed through essentializing prisonization discourse. Deconstructing these active forces and flows, even when only speculatively and provisionally undertaken, begins to name the journey through which Mary's agency/structure duality could be more fully liberated such that transpraxis (transformative justice) was rendered that much more realizable. Indeed, this is the path to a permanent revolution (a rhizomatic war machine), a noological vision of Mary yet to come.

The replacement socius envisioned for Mary includes molecular strata. They convey dynamic movement, the presence of flux and spontaneity, receptiveness to change and difference, openness to unpredictability and disorder. Consequently, Mary's socius is reconceptualized as unfolding from within far-from-equilibrium (rather than equilibrium or status quo) conditions. The dotted line situated from the upper left-hand to the upper right-hand sides of the schema conveys this movement. At the agency level is the Body-without-Organs. In the transdesistance model, Mary is a subject-in-process: her identities and continuities (e.g., as a woman, as a person of color, as homeless, as an offender, and as poor) are always already in flux. As such, her transparency is recognized through the (dis)identities and (dis)continuities that she embodies. They mutate and experience various intensities, speeds, and threshold levels. Mary's becoming agency is characterized by the dotted circles and their differing sizes.

In order for Mary not to experience a Deleuzian-Guattarian conjunctive synthesis in which recoiling occurs (Mary as the subject of enunciation reduced to summary representations as "poor," "homeless," "black," "female," "criminal"), active lines of flight must be mobilized. Rallying these molecular intensities entails the strategic use of deterritorialization and reterritorialization. The molar and axiomatic categories in which Mary's plight is spoken and acted upon indicate that she needs to "admit failure," "take responsibility" (deficit model), "lead a good life," and undergo "recovery and restoration" (desistance model). But these passive syntheses, as order words that reflect her subjectification, are overcoded (disjunctive syntheses). They must be resisted, destabilized, and decentered as they produce nothing more than nominalizing identities (Mary as a static, regularized self, as an after effect). Simultaneously, however, she must be situated and must insert herself within dynamic flows (e.g., minor literatures, schizoanalysis, discourse of the hysteric, reversal of hierarchies). These nonstatic energy forces, once activated, fuel the process of reauthoring her life, of continuously displacing and redefining her (dis)identities and (dis)continuities. Through this engaged reworking of the self, of disassembling and reassembling her positionalities, coupling moments can materialize. These are transitory, though lucid, occurrences in which a "flash of light" (Deleuze 1988, 116), a "poetic spark" (Lacan 1981), fleeting epiphanies (Giddens 1984), experimental/pragmatic insights (Rorty 1989; Unger 1986), and contingent universalities (Butler 1992) about the mutating self find embodied expression.

In diagram 5.2, deterritorialization and reterritorialization are depicted by the solid circles in which Mary's human agency is understood as a becoming dislocated self. Their differing sizes specify that variable impact each one has on her evolution. As a dimension of our symmetry-breaking transdesistance theory, mutating Mary's molar identities (as homeless, poor, black, female, criminal, recovering) depends on vigilant and engaged deconstruction/reconstruction. This depiction of human agency, of Mary as a subject-in-process constituted by her (dis)continuities and (dis)locations made transparent through coupling moments, extends from the molecular strata to the BwO as well as from the BwO at one time versus another.

The nonlinear and dynamic activity of symmetry breaking is notably featured in diagram 5.2. A COREL set/assemblage flow is initiated but with molar rigidities. As in diagram 5.1, these forces are communicated through statistical regularity (investments in normalcy, sameness, safety/security), organizational closure (Mary as a homeless shelter client and as an incarcerated female offender), order words ("take responsibility," "lead a good life"), and reactionary forces (secure employment, get GED, pursue literacy training, and so forth while in the community; attend drug counseling sessions, participate in mental health treatment, develop employment/education skills while in prison). These forces are depicted in the upper-middle portion of diagram 5.2 in which various static lines of flight are located, resulting in point and cyclical attractors. The homeless shelter staff and correctional system personnel repetitively reduced/repressed Mary's identities to singularities, imaging her as nothing more or other than a client/offender indistinguishable from all others. This is how the molar forces of homeostasis, equilibrium conditions, and status quo dynamics come to dominate a socius, rendering the becoming self inaccessible, unrecognizable, and unspeakable.

However, symmetry-breaking cascades can materialize. They emerge from Mary's status as a subject-in-process in which coupling moments regarding her (dis)continuities and (dis)locations take form. Nomadologically experiencing these molecular lines of flight represents a transition from what is (conceptualizing Mary as a homeless/confined, poor, black female) to what could be (conceptualizing Mary as a person yet to come). This "becoming other" image of Mary surfaces from the intersection of various COREL set/assemblages in which nonstatic flows, fluctuating thresholds levels, and varying molecular intensities/speeds undergo mobilization and activation. Accordingly, the upper-middle portion of diagram 5.2 depicts an active line of flight moving to the right, perturbing a nearby COREL set/assemblage otherwise resting at some equilibrium state with its characteristic point or limit attractor. As we previously explained, the imagery, logic, and language of the deficit and desistance models exemplify these status quo conditions. Symmetry breaking perturbs the socius, and it occurs when the agency-structure, molecular-molar tensions are deterritorialized and reterritorialized. This is visually depicted by the four outcome basins (and their distinct tori or strange attractors that would correspondingly follow). These novel and emergent outcome basins (Mary's [dis]identities and [dis]continuities signifying the permanent revolution, the person yet to come) resuscitate the stranger. They await recognition and valorization in image, thought, and language. Depending on the frequency, critical timing, duration, and intensity of an active, molecular line of flight, these outcome basins experience libidinal productive investment and narrative coherence.

Revitalization of the stranger, of Mary's (dis)continuities as a nomadic Body-without-Organs, occurs when the dynamic flows/forces representing her socius experience perturbations and symmetry-breaking intensities. These molecular flows are amplified further in the balance of diagram 5.2 as active (rather than reactive) COREL set/assemblages. They demonstrate how the transdesistance model could more completely function to resuscitate Mary as a becoming self, as is consistent with our constitutive penological theorizing.

In particular, we note that these molecular forces include the prisoner flow as resisting/opposing the abstract machines of the homeless shelter and the correctional edifice. To the extent that Mary possessed a will to power (Nietzsche 1968; see also Deleuze 1983)[44] sufficient to challenge the reactive forces of panoptic logic (shelter curfew, prison rules/restrictions), capital logic (investments in conventional employment/educational pursuits), bureaucratic control logic ("leading a good life," "taking responsibility"), and formal rationality (promoting sameness/normalcy, safety/security), prospects for molecular lines of escape would be made that much more realizable.[45]

We note further that as dimensions of an engaged transpraxis, what is destabilized (state thought) does not imply dismissal or marginalization of the "keepers of the kept." This is the presence of hate/revenge politics in which role reversals (slave over master) merely reproduce the relations of (libidinal) production, although in inverted form. Instead, techniques of resistance are called for in which the oppressor is affirmed through the act of negating the harms of repression/reduction, notwithstanding Mary's relative position of material powerlessness. These strategies of transformation qua dialectical struggle run the gamut from direct negotiation, to nonviolent confrontation, to peaceful demonstration.

In addition, however, other COREL set/assemblages can be discerned in diagram 5.2, and they further specify the conditions under which Mary's (dis)identities and (dis)continuities could take up residence in her socius in nonhierarchical, nonlinear form. Summarily, these include the shelter worker and prison staff flow (as facilitating jazz artist, as generating a care ethic toward the Other, as embracing the *discourse of the hysteric/analyst* in dialogical fashion), the positive freedom flow (Mary's investing in autonomy rather than security, authenticity rather than anxiety/fear), the shelter/prison system release flow as disruptions in the repetition of "taking responsibility" and "leading a good life" (e.g., multiple, mutating, and nonnormative constructions of self, other, family, the body, intimacy, work, success), the technologized cultural flow as the conspicuous consumption of evolving nonstatic images, sounds, symbols, and themes about homelessness, the female form, sexualities, nationalities, and other (dis)locations (replacement news-making messages),[46] and the culture-of-spontaneity (rather than control) flow (including minor discourses, far-from-equilibrium conditions, the logic of schizoanalysis, and the nonhierarchical reversal of dominant values, including molecular over molar intensities).

Pivotal to these COREL set/assemblages, their interconnections, and the active forces and lines of flight that promote molecular identities is the shelter/prison assemblage flow. Reactively, this is the force of containment, control, and corrections. However, as depicted, this assemblage is steeped in desire as production. As specified in chapter 4, overcoming, indeed transcending, such panopticism is central to displacing the criminological shadow. What is posited, therefore, is an active and ambulant life force or shelter/prison flow that energizes and revitalizes. In diagram 5.2, this would include the dynamic intersections of the various COREL set/assemblages that collectively constitute a will to power and that, when mobilized and activated, make the becoming, emergent self remotely possible.

We note further that the various overlapping COREL set/assemblages found in diagram 5.2 converge on the shelter/prison flow. Correspondingly, this active force extends to all other assemblages found within the schematization. Thus, varying expressions of interconnectivity are depicted. Moreover, the shelter/prison flow, as embodying a will to power (a will to overcome), includes diverse speeds, various and overlapping intensities, and different threshold levels. As such, molecular lines of flight are readied for activation, perturbation, and mutation. Collectively, these active energy flows, symbolizing the nexus wherein Mary is mobilized to experience her becoming Other, help to displace the reactive molar forces that imagine, define, and act upon her identities as mere singularities (homeless shelter resident, female incarcerate). Moreover, these overlapping and intersecting active COREL set/assemblages, as energized flows/forces, help to marshal the engaged work of deterritorialization and reterritorialization. This is the dynamic reauthoring of the self in which the agency/structure duality that sustains penal harm

(Mary's becoming humanity as reduced/repressed), the normalization of violence (recursive reconstitution of reactive molar flows/forces), and the essentializing prisonization discourse that legitimizes both are non-hierarchically transcended, reimagined, respoken, relived, and reembodied again and anew.

Ongoing Revolution

Revolution in penology demands a holistic approach that is sensitive to various historically contingent, as well as political-economically constructed, interacting "levels" in a socius. These levels are better conceived as COREL sets/assemblages that reflect relatively autonomous distributions of differentially intensive active-reactive forces coordinated by abstract machines embedded within each. The prison-form has attained stasis in repetition. The socius within which it is lodged witnesses the dominance of reactive forces that self-perpetuate. Even the emergent desistance theory, although an improvement over traditional crime-control models, ultimately still fuels a feedback loop that maintains stasis. The challenge is to theorize mechanisms of disruption of repetition that release lines of flight that privilege active forces, far-from-equilibrium conditions, and dissipative structures with ongoing mutative and transformative consequences. The stranger may begin to find coordinates within which new subjectivities emerge that privilege a becoming, not being.

As our analysis reveals, Mary's world, her hodological space, is always already preconstituted with various intersecting flows, the basis of choice, decision making, and ongoing being. We must wage war on the molar just as we must "wage war," as Francois Lyotard (1984) has informed us, "on totality." Ultimately, this revolution in imagery, thought, and language consists of a multitude of struggles in resistance. On occasion, some of these struggles find resonance and relative stability and plant the seeds—a "crystalline seed" to borrow from Deleuze (1988)—that produce transformation in the socius, BwOs, and identities.

Our application work in this chapter is not a blueprint for capture, closure, or consensus. Rather, what we have proposed amounts to some contributory thoughts toward a revolution, a "molecular revolution" in penology. It remains to be seen, however, what additional lines of flight warrant mobilization and activation, as is consistent with our symmetry-breaking transdesistance model. In our conclusion, several additional observations in this direction are tentatively proposed. As we argue, the revolution is only beginning to materialize. Indeed, the journey, always a departure and a movement for the masses, must continue apace.

NOTES

1. Attention to women, minorities, and the poor should not be considered an exhaustive critique. The concerns expressed in this chapter are relevant for debates about ethnicity, age, nationality, sexuality, and (dis)ability as well (Capeheart and Milovanovic 2007; Martin-Alcoff and Mendieta 2003). In effect, then, we draw attention to the problem of *identity politics* (Mohanty et al. 2006) and its impact for affirming and sustaining the criminological shadow in penology.

2. The idea of transpraxis was initially developed in chapter 1. Coupling moments, fleeting epiphanies, and transient insights—as facets of continuously reauthoring our evolving life narratives—possess within them the possibility of transpraxis, the potential to develop replacement grammars (Henry and Milovanovic 1996). These grammars represent ways of rearticulating our changing sense of agency and identity, of reconnecting the dislocated parts of our lives and integrating them with the wider whole of which we are a part, of thinking about and acting toward others in ways that honor their (our) humanness and interdependence, notwithstanding different and changing epistemological standpoints. In short, transpraxis instantiates and energizes human flourishing and becoming in nonreifying ways, ever mindful of the interrelated nature of the agency/structure duality implicated in the activity of perceiving, talking, and conceptualizing.

3. The narrative of Mary represents an instrumental case study. Specifically, we use her experiences (as reported to the first author [BA] through a series of interviews conducted over a fifteen-year period) as a basis to deconstruct the relationship among identity construction (race-gender-class), the penal system, and constitutive theory. Thus, her life story serves to illuminate and illustrate conceptual points under consideration rather than to make claims about particular findings and their generalizability. For more on this ethnographic method of inquiry, see Denzin (1997). For a preliminary assessment addressing the narratives of offenders like Mary, see Arrigo and Takahashi (2007). For a more detailed evaluation of offender narratives, see Maruna (2001), Bosworth (1999b), and Presser (2008).

4. The story of Mary is symbolic of many poor women (and poor women of color) funneled through the correctional and social service systems. To this extent, then, the case should be interpreted as a descriptive representation of the cyclical nature in which the pains of imprisonment function. For additional case illustrations on the plight of women in these systems, see Bloom, Owen, and Covington (2003), Owen (1999), and Sharp (2003).

5. This correctional orientation to rehabilitation is consistent with the "deficit model" as examined in chapter 4. The focus is on ameliorating personal limitations, deficiencies, and fallibilities. The emphasis is on "going straight . . . and responding to failures" (Halsey 2006b, 167; Ward and Maruna 2007).

6. To this extent, women in the shelter were also directed toward desistance strategies (see chapter 4). This correctional approach draws attention to personal restoration and communal reconciliation through commonsense risk-avoidance activities (Strang and Braithwaite 2005). This is how the ex-offender rebuilds her or his life (Maruna 2001).

7. Bosworth (1999b, 103) indicated that in prison environs, these activities shape "women's identity and their presentation of self." Moreover, as she observed, these interactions and experiences are consistent with traditional notions of femininity (1999b, 104; see also Arrigo, Milovanovic, and Schehr 2005, 59).

8. See the various works of Kurt Lewin (e.g., 1966).

9. See note 35 and diagram 4.5 of chapter 4 for more critical commentary.

10. See, e.g., Briggs and Peat (1989, 46).

11. Holland (1999, 25) tells us that "the syntheses are ways of processing or indeed constituting experience."

12. Flows provide the potential of investments in "part-objects"; that is, within flows movement of energy and matter prevails, and it is the connective synthesis that connects the various existing components into more stable forms, the result being an investment in energy in the part-connections made. These are ongoing. As Holland (1999, 26) tells us, they "are multiple, heterogeneous, and continual."

13. The notion of part-object resonates with Melanie Klein and has affinities with Jacques Lacan's notion of *objet petit a*. For Deleuze and Guattari (1983; see also Massumi 1992, 157), these are libidinally invested objects; they are also "organs," or "zones of intensity." Desire connects part-objects. "An infant's mouth at the breast constitutes such a connection, but so do the relations between an eye and a bottle, a mouth and an iron-lung . . . a mouth and a finger." These connections are continuous and multiple in form (Holland 1999, 26). Part-objects also tend to repetition (See Massumi 1992, 70–75; Holland 1999, 26, 45–47).

14. By passive, it is meant that the subject does not attend to each primordial piece of data that impinges on the BwO; it is an ongoing process of connections made without reflective, critical thought. As Massumi (1992, 49) informs us, "No concerted action by an isolable agent was involved."

15. For Holland (1999, 28), the disjunctive synthesis "records networks or relations among connections, instead of producing connections themselves."

16. In this sense, too, the BwO is a recording surface (see Holland 1999, 31).

17. Connective and disjunctive syntheses may be characterized as active or reactive. We may evaluate any synthesis in terms of which force is the more dominant (Massumi 1992, 56). Active forces allow bodies to do all they are capable of doing (becoming). Reactive forces limit the body as to what it is capable of doing (being).

18. As Holland (1999, 51) notes, this "overcoding [provides] . . . a nominal identity, facilitating its insertion into a whole new level of synthesis: a conjunction with numerous other categorized individuals, or persons, in a complex assemblage of thunderbolt judgment."

19. Massumi (1992, 75) tells us that "the reactive nature of the synthesis of recognition ["that's me!"] provides a hook for reactive forces from the social field to clamp into the flesh." He argues that the "nonlimitative body without organs" (molecular identities) and the "limitative body without organs" (molar identities) are both potentialities within a socius, and it is where the subject is captured in the latter that we have reactive investments and the dominance of reactive forces (see also Holland 1999, 35). For the nonlimitative BwO, the "connective syntheses are brought back into play and put into operation on a Body-without-Organs whose disjunctive syntheses multiply their ramifications indefinitely; thereby fueling the

consummation of a perpetually renewed 'nomadic' subject, always different from itself, a kind of 'permanent revolution' of psychic life" (Holland 1999, 35–36).

20. For Mary, we can see how she has been subject over her life course to a number of crime control agencies, each of which provide a point of subjectification from which identities flow, culminating in the subject of recognition, "that's me!" In other words, the three syntheses work in combination with Deleuze and Guattari's theory of the "recoiling of the subject": the larval subject (more molecular) undergoes a transformation into a more static molar identity (e.g., ex-offender, client, probationer, parolee, defendant, offender, recovering subject). As the early sociological literature on the dramatization of evil suggests (Tannenbaum 1938; see also Prus and Grills 2003, 3–15), a certification process culminating in molar categories exists; however, no decertification processes exists that leads back to molecular identities in which transformative, mutating identities can unfold.

21. Consider the effects of a coproduced (staff and juvenile) treatment discourse reported by Banks (forthcoming, 172): "The language of treatment constitutes the 'reality' for residents in the treatment unit and other realities are excluded. It follows that narratives required in the treatment process which attest to the guilt of residents must be framed and keyed to the language of treatment and must exclude other narratives implicating social and economic factors that may have affected, influenced or provoked their delinquency."

22. Recall, flows are lines of flight emanating from relatively autonomous, historically specific, configurations of COREL sets/assemblages. Within each of the latter an abstract machine can be found that provides a logic played out by lines of flight. Expressive forms take shape as axioms. Through deductive logic they then become more predictable, static, and exclusive in their consequence.

23. In a three-dimensional portrayal, we can make use of world-tubes ("trouser diagrams"), which suggest that not a line but a tube-looking structure best characterizes flows and lines of flight (see Milovanovic's in-progress, *Deleuze and Justice*). It suggests not particles but energy flow, a wave in movement. Here, the intersecting of flows may be shown by two tubes converging, indicating how various nomadic flows may resonate, producing more intense fields within which probabilities are enhanced for certain behaviors over others. This also suggests that a socius can be perceived as a background space (hodological space), a field of intensities, a quantum field where various forces (active, reactive) are in movement and rest, where singularities momentarily appear, the basis of which is the beginning of a new COREL set/assemblage. This can be depicted in the world-tube as the appearance of a tube, which may be extended or may disappear again into the background space, remaining in the realm of the virtual and plane of consistency. Various forms of attractors appear within this socius, more a result of historical and political-economic forces. The point and cyclic attractors remain privileged in homeostatic conditions (privileging of order, the molar forms), whereas the torus and strange attractor are privileged in far-from-equilibrium conditions (molecular forms). Emerging molar identities, such as Mary's, can be understood by the particular diagram that traces a socius.

24. The Hopf transformation indicates one series of symmetry breaking bifurcations. Here, a point attractor is transformed into a periodic attractor (periodicity

of two), followed by a torus attractor. We may see this with Mary in which a conventional way of doing things undergoes a bifurcation in which expanded options in the form of lines of flight materialize. These become intertwined as in the torus attractor.

25. Consider, for example, the relative impact on Mary's divergent identity standpoints had she been encouraged to explore her unique competencies, strengths, and talents while in shelter, instead of focusing on "going straight" and "making good." Moreover, consider the relative impact on Mary's divergent identity standpoints had she been exposed to prison workers/officials who interpreted her as a subject-in-process, as becoming Other, rather than as just another female offender. These lines of flight represent possible nonlinear dynamical effects in which deterritorialization and reterritorialization become more realizable in nonstatic molecular form. This is the presence of a symmetry-breaking cascade. As we will demonstrate in the subsequent section on the penological stranger and identities, these emergents foster a becoming subject in which the continual reauthoring of the self and a permanent revolution take on molecular form in positional, provisional, and relational ways.

26. As Stowell and Byrne (2008, 32) tell us, crime can be both a dependent variable and an independent variable; in the latter, it may undermine community cohesion, which in turn provides the escalation of crime-generating forces.

27. DeLanda (2006, 20) explains that "the internal organization of an entity" may provide differential capacities to respond to external flows.

28. See particularly Clear et al. 2001; Rose and Clear, 1998.

29. We recall Matza, in *Becoming Deviant* (1969), where he indicates the process by which a subject's capacities to engage in volitional behavior can be pacified, producing a subject that acts much in accordance with given scripts, what circumstances call for.

30. For example, by the work of iteration and disproportional effects.

31. For Sampson and Bean (2006, 15), culture must be understood not by "a simple adaptation to structure in a one-way causal flow, but as an intersubjective *organizing mechanism* that shapes unfolding social processes and that is constitutive of social structure." For Stowell and Byrne (2008), it is the investment in a particular culture in both prison and community that need be the focus of reform.

32. As Massumi (1992, 81) has said, "There are varying degrees of choices at successive threshold states. . . . The choice belongs to the overall dissipative system with its plurality of selves, and not to the person; it is objectively cocaused at the crossroads of chance and determinacy."

33. DeLanda (2006, 30, 125n6) explains how a diagram reflects "spaces of possibilities" or a "possibility space." COREL sets/assemblages would thus each have their own abstract diagram characterizing the "relations of force or of a distribution of capacities to affect and be affected" (DeLanda 2006, 125; Deleuze 1988, 71–72). Said in another way, each socius is composed of intersecting COREL sets/assemblages, each of which can be captured in the image of an abstract diagram, tracing its forces at play. Within these spaces, differential degrees of freedom assure a more expansive or a more limited range of "choices." Mary's "choices" are thus based on these degrees of freedom at play.

34. Stowell and Byrne (2008, 36) perceptively note that "faced with the same (or worsening) opportunity structure, it is not surprising that they continue to make what you or I might consider 'bad' choices and decisions given their immersion in both institutional and community culture. From the perspective of the actor, however, the choices they made were good choices, not in terms of potential outcomes, but rather because they were justified based on their perception of appropriate behavior and their view of self." See also Halsey (2006b, 33), who suggests making "good" and "bad" choices does not just reside in the inmate but must be shared with administrative rules, procedures, and requirements that are directed toward the inmate.

35. The latter is partially organized by a presupposed "contrast space," a space of relevancies. These are much in accord with the notion of state space—"the geometric representation of the possibilities of a system" (Garfinkel 1981, 40).

36. Garfinkel (1981, 21) provides the example of a priest asking a prisoner why he robs banks. The prisoner answers, "Well, that's where the money is." The priest is more interested in why the prisoner robs. For the prisoner, the question really is why rob banks rather than some other establishment. The priest and prisoner are operating from two different contrasting spaces.

37. For research on staff culture, see Johnson 2002; see the insightful anthology by Byrne, Hummer, and Taxman 2008.

38. Researchers have differentiated prison culture by identifying various contributing components (management, staff, and inmate cultures) and their effects on violence (see Byrne, Hummer, and Taxman 2007; Dilulio 1987; Reisig 1998). Some researchers have further differentiated various management practices: control, responsibility, and consensual models (Reisig 1998; Wortley 2002). However, according to an empirical investigation of various practices over twenty-two years (1984 to 2006), Byrne, Hummer, and Taxman (2007, 55) concluded that the relationship between management styles and prison violence is "unknown." Qualitative studies have indicated differences and are suggestive, however. Our theoretical investigation suggests that many empirical studies do not have adequate theorizing of the subject and her or his relations with control cultures. Desistance theorizing begins a more integrated approach, given its concern for nonlinear adaptations upon release. A more radicalized version, a transdesistance approach as a component of constitutive penology, is suggestive for further developments in this area. Moving in this direction are the highly suggestive and insightful qualitative studies by Halsey (2006c).

39. For good introductions to the prison guard's culture, see Johnson (2002, chs. 7 and 8) Lombardo (1985, 1989), Liebling and Price (2001), Crawley (2004), and Liebling (2008).

40. Consider the mixed messages to which the inmate must respond and the divided self that this ensures: "One of these selves is constructed after the image of the judge, the psychiatrist, the social worker, and the program manager, who all demand the young offender to take an active part in their 'rehabilitation,' whilst the other self [is] rendered in the image of custodial staff, prison architecture, correctional rules and procedures, as well as (on occasion) other inmates or residents who collectively work to defeat any inclination toward 'independent' thought or

the desire to have a meaningful and ongoing say in the management of their own lives within and beyond custodial walls" (Halsey 2006b, 16).

41. In short, a new diagram where nonlimitative BwOs emerge within configurations of COREL sets/assemblages that are characterized as dissipative structures proliferating in a socius characterized as far-from-equilibrium, or as Deleuze and Guattari say, "permanent revolution."

42. The privileging of the phallus and the reactive forms of desire, as in Lacan, are pervasive in the socius. Molar identities in an oedipal-driven economy of desire and a socius with which it is constituted assure the tendency toward divisions, polarization, and the privileging of one molar form over the other. In contrast, as we have seen, Deleuze and Guattari advocate a productive notion of desire, an anoedipal form of desire (Massumi 1992, 119) that only knows differences, mutation, transformation, becoming, and molecular identities.

43. The mechanism of capture and subjection to a dominant axiomatic pervading the socius provides the undercurrent for the formation of core molar identities.

44. This sense of overcoming is a primal, creative force in which desire is understood as production (Deleuze and Guattari 1987). We examine these notions in more detail in subsequent passages of this section.

45. Additional lines of molecular flight consistent with this notion of an oppositional/revolutionary subject and the promotion of a war machine have been discussed in the community reentry literature. For example, Arrigo (1997, 2004b) and Arrigo and Takahashi (2007), commenting on the single-room-occupancy (SRO) phenomenon, describe how homeless and marginally housed men and women experience *transformation through the dialectics of struggle* in which changes "in identity formation, collective empowerment, and structural reform" manifest themselves through an eight-stage developmental model (Arrigo and Takahashi 2007, 309). This psychosocial model emphasizes both a sense of personhood and place where one's becoming (mutating (dis)identities and (dis)continuities) undergoes constant negotiation and reconfiguration with the self, with others, and with the community to which both are interconnected (Arrigo and Takahashi 2007, 318–26).

46. Consider, for example, the convict criminology movement (Ross and Richards 2002). Many participants are former incarcerates employed in the academic community. The replacement message here is that the offender can evolve, can experience a becoming self. In addition, consider the transformative effects that follow upon learning that a homeless shelter resident was previously employed as a physician or a Wall Street trader (Arrigo 1996a, 1997, 2004). In these latter instances, metamorphosis can lead to molar identities for the street dweller but, over time, can energize the individual, can foster novel insights about the self, and can result in a renegotiated molecular identity (Arrigo and Takahashi 2007).

Conclusion

Sustaining the Revolution in Penology

INTRODUCTION

The preceding chapters specified in historically contingent manifest form the linkages among critical inquiry, penal harm, and transformative justice. In chapter 1, these linkages, situated in constitutive theorizing (especially in criminology and penology), drew attention to the broad-based assumptions of coproduction, dynamic systems theory, and reification. As we explained, the subject's transformational process entails both recovery (being) and resuscitation (becoming). Moreover, human agents, as coarchitects of their metamorphosis, shape the institutional and organizational forces within their socius and are shaped by them. As such, our constitutive position on social structure was delineated. The agency/structural duality implicated in the coproduction of crime as the power to harm (reduce/repress) was also reviewed. As we explained, penological discourses and practices represent the material and symbolic forces that legitimize, nurture, and sustain such injury. As a basis to transcend this harm (this essentializing system of communication) that imprisons us all, the logic of replacement discourses was reconsidered.

In chapter 2, we offered a critique of modernist, radical, and actuarial philosophies of punishment (the new penology). Our critique was nonexhaustive. However, in each instance we argued that rather than justify the use of prison as punishment, these penal approaches foster harm in society and, accordingly, contribute to facilitating crime. In short, human agency, social structure, and intermediary "structures" in the form of Deleuzian assemblages are held captive by cyclical and repetitive activities

161

that diminish or quash one's flourishing (being) and one's evolving (becoming). Moreover, a constitutive penology situated in selected insights emanating from semiotic and related critical literatures was described. Of particular importance was transpraxis, a (penological) strategy that identifies the oppressor in the act of negating the oppression, notwithstanding one's position of relative alienation and exploitation. The relevance of this strategy for purposes of advancing the extant philosophical research in penology was presented.

Chapter 3 illustrated the phenomenology of penal harm. This is a reference to the criminology of the shadow, the molar reactive forces that sustain the prison-form, its parts and segments, and the correctional edifice that stands above (and is informed by) them all. The criminological shadow broadly includes the psychoanalytic and philosophic roots of penology's cultural identity and capture of multiplicities in nominal, static regularities that subsequently undergo reification. In addition, however, the chapter featured commentary on the criminological stranger. The criminology of the stranger accounts for how the activities of the recovering and transformative subject can transcend the logic and language that imprisons us all. In penology, this is a movement toward a transdesistance (rather than a desistance or deficit) model, expressed in positional, relational, and provisional ways.

In chapter 4, we undertook a detailed, "macrolevel" assessment of the pains-of-imprisonment thesis. This is a specific reference to how penal harm is recursively and cyclically sustained through various correctional practices. Those confined, those employed by the system as workers and administrators, and those who insist on punitive public policies for the kept are *all* imprisoned. Contributions from Michel Foucault on panoptic power, Jean Baudrillard on technologized culture, Erich Fromm on negative freedom, and Gilles Deleuze, and Felix Guattari on the constitution of the subject and assemblages furthered our view on the criminological shadow in penology. Moreover, commentary delineated how these molar forces could be deterritorialized and reterritorialized such that the stranger in penology experienced resuscitation. Insights from Jacques Lacan, Jacques Derrida, and Gilles Deleuze, as well as several noteworthy observations from complex systems science, informed the analysis.

In chapter 5, we undertook a detailed microlevel assessment of the pains-of-imprisonment thesis. The case of Mary, a black woman of limited economic means, was portrayed. The contexts in which the homeless shelter system and the correctional edifice subjected her to alternating harms of reduction/repression were examined. Mary's (dis)identities were reduced to rigid singularities (sameness). Mary's (dis)continuities were repressed in favor of static and fixed standpoints, thereby limiting or eroding the possible places from which she could experience her molecular revolution. Strategies for mobilizing a will to overcome such molar identities, as summary representations, were explored consistent with our position on constitutive penology and the criminological stranger.

In this concluding chapter, we emphasize the importance of sustaining the revolution in penology. Of particular concern are techniques and tactics that advance our war machine from within a holistic framework. This framework recognizes that the prison-form (its philosophies, principles, and practices) will undergo substantive change only with mutation in the larger socius to which the prison-form is intimately connected. Accordingly, in what follows, several active lines of flight are suggestively considered.

PERMANENT, MOLECULAR REVOLUTION

We have not attempted to provide a blueprint or to offer concrete proposals for a socius yet to come. As Nick Dyer-Witheford (1999, 190) proposes, the danger is that any preconceived socius may result in authoritarian outcomes. In other words, deviation from the conceptualization may be resisted and be regarded as counterrevolutionary. Hence, consistent with Deleuze and Guattari, we have suggested how certain lines of flight might emerge that undermine (deterritorialize) closure and capture so that a more liberating socius[1] could develop (reterritorialize). To remain true to our position, we must accept the potentials that inhere within each of us and, as such, cannot in advance limit these becomings. Indeed, following Dyer-Witheford (1999, 191), "the aim should be to create a space where a diversity of social, cultural, and economic ways of being can coexist."[2] However, we still need to think through possible alternatives, weighing with appropriate ethical consideration the competing options to which we are drawn and for which the struggle, the revolution, in penology is sustained (Dyer-Witheford 1999, 191). In this direction, we are particularly mindful of some key suggestions, some "battlefield maps," offered by Dyer-Witheford (1999, 192–218).

We have seen that the war machine must engage various molar levels. At the more "micro" level, personal strategies for daily survival and challenge are needed. At the more "meso" level, alternative networks and organizations are desirable. At the more "macro" level, either a reformist remedial or radical reformist strategy is recommended (see Henry and Milovanovic 1996).

We return to the constitutive elements of COREL sets/assemblages for guidance at these various "levels." We recall that each comprises (1) a material component ("machinic processes" that produce cuts and breaks or flows of matter/energy providing the raw material on which expressive forms work),[3] (2) an expressive component (the manifest forms—discursive and nondiscursive), (3) territorialization (tendency toward molar structurations and capture in the form of axioms), and (4) deterritorialization (tendency to differentiate, dissipate, break apart). We also recall that iteration and nonlinearity prevail in terms of linkages and effects. Let us briefly provide some possible directions in producing change that may privilege active molecular forces and becoming.

Suggestive at the more "micro" level is Massumi (1992, 103–106), who offers five recommendations. We provide some additional thoughts that augment and amplify his observations.

1. *"Stop the world."* Whereas *being* concerns stasis, repetition of the same, reactive forms of desire, *becoming* is about interruption, disconnections, the creation of spaces within which new relations are (and can be) actively constructed. Thus, Mary's world, although attaining homeostasis and cyclical repetitions, must be interrupted. It is within the interruptions ("zones of indeterminacy") that epiphanies arise.[4] Lacan's (1991) combined *discourse of the analyst/hysteric*, integrated with Paulo Freire's (1973) work on dialogical pedagogy, indicates that interventionists, cultural revolutionaries, may be catalysts in accessing, mobilizing, and retrieving the subaltern's desire for more genuine expression. The suggestion here is not that these interventionists function as revolutionary vanguards armed with the "appropriate" understandings (*master discourse*) of struggle, alienation, exploitation, victimization, and the like; rather, they nomadically participate in engaged, ongoing dialogical encounters.

2. *"Cherish derelict spaces."* Within a socius and its molar forms, spaces always already exist that do not find themselves pacified—regimented, linearized, striated, axiomatized. These are "zones of indeterminacy" (Bergson 1998) where far-from-equilibrium conditions prevail, where with some perturbation dissipative forms will appear as emergents. These are "autonomous zones" that can be the basis of an alternative becoming. The autonomia movement in Italy during the 1960s and 1970s attempted to exploit this movement's revolutionary potential (see Negri 1984, 1999). Similarly, Foucault's[5] later works addressed "limit experiences." He argued that the only genuine direction to recapture subjectivity was in transgressing the various boundaries/limits imposed (inscribed) on the body (see Miller 2000; Lyng 2005, 39–47). These transgressive moments, crossing boundaries, "involved experiments in self-creation . . . forms of resistance . . . acts of liberation" (Lyng 2005, 45–47). Moreover, critical race theorists have called for the creation of such alternative spaces

within classroom settings where assumptions of the other can be challenged in supportive ways (Matsuda 1998). Attending to the subaltern, as with the case of Mary, is by definition about boundary crossing; still, this activity is continuously subject to the regimented molar expressive forms. However, within the edifice of repetition and larval reactive flows, cracks always exist within which alternatives may arise (Goffman 1961). In other words, these cracks can be the basis for replacement material ("machinic cuts") and expressive forms.

Drucilla Cornell (1998) and bell hooks (1994) have also offered the idea of protections for an "imaginary domain." As Cornell (1998, 8, 111) notes, it "is the space of the 'as if' in which we imagine who we might be if we made ourselves our own ends and claimed ourselves as our own persons." It is the "location of recovery" (hooks 1994, 238). It is where we may imagine an otherwise, a becoming, a person yet to come.[6]

3. *"Study camouflage."* "Seeming to be what you are" allows the inhabitant of preconstructed identities (discursive subject-positions) to provide the illusion that she or he is in fact what is dictated, yet at the same time provides the person critical understanding of her or his molar restrictions. This is in accord with Richard Rorty's (1989) "liberal ironist," whereby molar categories are used in everyday practice but understood as the reifying entities that they are. However, these molecular responses are easily transformed into their molar forms: one becomes that from which one previously remained distant. For the subaltern, then, the difficult task is to establish some distance from the identities forced upon the self: one is more than a category in all its expressive forms (consider Mary's categories as a poor, black woman); one's identity is not rooted in being but has potential in becoming.

Desistance theory is evocative here as well. One's postcarceral adaptation will follow a nonlinear pathway but will provide numerous junctures for breaking out of the crime-prison-crime cycle that represents the pains of imprisonment. These singularities are the occasion for symmetry breaking and alternative lines of flight. Hence, camouflaging allows both outward-appearing acquiescence to regimes that would produce the docile body, while simultaneously making possible instances for a reexploration of the self, fleeting occurrences of lucidity, turning points, coupling moments, and novel molecular flows.

4. *"Side and straddle."* "When in doubt, sidestep," says Massumi (1992, 106). In other words, given compelling daily moments to challenge repressive structures, and given the molar forces that police their

form, failure often awaits those who on *every* occasion fight to dismantle the molar forms. However, waiting on the sidelines for the right battle may, over time, produce acquiescence and molar identifications. One's sword becomes rusted in the scabbard, and the occasion for its drawing may find diminished skills in its use. "Charging straight ahead may be necessary and effective at times, but as a general principle it is as self-defeating as uncritical [in its] acceptance of reform" (Massumi 1992, 106). In other words, stepping sideways may be more beneficial in the long run than constant daily challenges. This notion of "tranversality" is found in Guattari (1984, 2001) and in Deleuze and Guattari (1983, 1987). As Massumi (1992, 73) tells us, "An effectively revolutionary movement establishes many other circuits: reform-confrontation, molarity-minority, being-becoming, camouflage-showing oneself, rationality-imagination, and many permutations of these." In other words, for the subaltern and for the activist, developing the ability to transgress various boundaries while providing the appearance of a subject committed to her or his discursive subject-position is encouraged.[7]

5. *"Come out."* Massumi (1992, 106) advocates, "Throw off your camouflage as soon as you can still survive. What one comes out of is identity. What one comes into is greater transformational potential." In other words, molar identities must be discarded at opportunities for the development of molecular identities. It is here where machinic cuts and expressive forms find alternative development. For the subaltern, it may very well be that the daily violent imposition of static identities by social-control agencies regularly preclude "coming out." But moments exist in which a nonstatic identity may find expression, and these should be the basis of cultivation.

To Maussumi's five suggestions, we offer several others[8]:

6. *Seek and form alliances.* Hardt and Negri's (2004, xiv) treatise on the "multitude" indicates that the global society witnesses increasing differences that cannot be reduced to a singular unity; "the multitude is a multiplicity of all these singular differences" (xiv). Accordingly, while commonalities can only be momentary, they are the basis of concerted and focused struggle. Postmodernity both produces ever more refined technologies for growth and control and the possibilities of reappropriating these resources for struggles. Thus, "network struggles" replace class struggles: the former represents a "polycentric" form of opposition[9]; it produces both "new subjectivities and new forms of life" (Hardt and Negri 2004, 83). The Zapatista uprising in Chiapas is a clear example. The new struggles, according

to Dyer-Witheford (1999, 187), "would involve constructing a system of 'mulitivalent engagement' between movements." And, following Guattari and Negri (1990, 123), "each of [these] shows itself to be capable of unleashing irreversible molecular revolutions and of linking itself to either limited or unlimited molar struggles" (see also Dyer-Witheford 1999, 187).[10] The key, then, becomes coming up with creative ways of developing linkages via the technological apparatus (i.e., Internet) that is transforming our lives.

7. *Be a jazz player.* Everywhere that formal rationality takes hold, we find the need to become members of harmonious orchestras. In response, some advocate instead that we become jazz players (Holland 1999). Improvisation in jazz does not necessitate a leader; rather, members vary their play within an overall developing motif (Holland 1999).[11] This conforms with nomadism and the rhizome as described by Deleuze and Guattari. This is not a repetition of the same (stasis) but a perpetual becoming, a continuous transformation of self, society, and other. It is a continuous investment in difference. In this direction, Braidotti (2002, 2006) has developed a postmodern ethics she terms the "ethics of sustainability." This version of moral contemplation and action argues against modernity's linear and unitary conception of the subject; instead, it advances a nonunitary notion ("nomadic subjectivity") as more productive than its counterpart. This nomadic subjecity as the embodiment of an ethic of sustainability regresses into neither relativism nor nihilism but is interconnected with alterity, community, contingencies, and experimentation. Only in this way can continuous transformations (molecular revolution, continuous becoming) be omnipresent and ubiquitous. Additionally, Braidotti (2002, 2006) indicates that it is an "ethic of accountability" that affirms active forces and positive passions conducive to becoming. Consequently, actions that sustain continuous molecular transformations are identified as those that should be advocated for and practiced. Conversely, those that arrest these expressions are deemed "unhealthy."

8. *Invest in social judo.* In response to harms of repression and reduction, rather than responding with further investments in hierarchical power to overcome, which adds to the overall harm, we advocate a social judo (see Henry and Milovanovic 1996).[12] This is the power of domination turned against itself. Consider, for example, Foucault's (1977a) classic study of panopticism in which asymmetrical power relations have been born. More specifically, consider the panopticon designed by Bentham, a circular configuration with cells on the outside and a central tower in the middle for observation. Foucault showed how this was a new form of surveillance that was asymmetrical (the

seen do not see the seers). Foucault overlooked, however, the inherent power of social judo within this scenario. An inmate, after being officially counted ("on the count": he is asked to step outside of his cell for an official body count), is told to return to his cell, and the cell doors then close. But what if he stands outside, be it alone, in an act of resistance?[13] In this instance, all—prisoners, guards, other staff, any civilians working, and so forth—will be witness to anything that follows. In other words, a symmetrical form of power has been reestablished, albeit only temporary. Social judo is a strategy that can reduce harms of reduction and repression by the act of challenging the asymmetrical forms of power without necessarily increasing the overall amount of harm inflicted.

9. *Become-other.* At the core of a socius is a point attractor, becoming-the-same, a continuously reinforced molar outcome. Becoming-other, becoming-minoritarian is a voyage toward otherness. It is releasing the body from stasis and opening it up to what it can do. It is a process of deterritorialization and reterritorialization. It concerns "challenging conventional body boundaries, taking the risk of becoming indiscernible as a social subject, and unsettling a coherent sense of personal self" (Lorraine 1999, 183; see also Grosz 1994). It is to place oneself in the molecular domain and among the active forces. It is to disrupt repetition and to embrace differences. It is to open oneself up to alternative lines of flight and new outcome basins as a result of symmetry-breaking bifurcations along the way. It is a death in the past and a rebirth to the future.

10. *Be active; be joyful.* Not to be confused with the much popularized lyric "Don't worry, be happy," Deleuze's study of "what the body can do," focusing most especially on Spinoza and Nietzsche, identifies the joyful passion and the active as an ethical practice (see Hardt 1993). The body has both powers to affect and powers to be affected. Active affections are those that are connected with our powers to act (Hardt 1993, 92); passive affections are linked to the lack of that power. Active affections allow the body to move toward what it can do; passive affections mobilize the body to suffering and despair. Joyful encounters are those that add to the power to act (Hardt 1993, 94). Joyful passions arise from relations to others. Accordingly, we may draw from Nietzsche's ethic—become active—and from Spinoza's—become joyful (Hardt 1993, 96). Thus, for Deleuze's ethic: "Become joyful; become active" (Hardt 1993, 119). Admittedly, we might prematurely want to dismiss this ethic given the harms of repression and reduction that abound in the socius; however, moments exist in which this active joyful ethic can be cultivated and, with other cultivations, can produce more empowerment, more elation—more lines of flight that are transformative.

11. *Cultivate an ethic of care.* A feminist ethic of care has been developed by Carol Gilligan (1982), Grace Clement (1998), and Nel Noddings (2003).[14] It is a form of substantive justice that centers on context, uniqueness, attachments, human connectedness, the maintenance of relationships, mutuality, and the concrete other. These values stand in contrast to formal, abstract rationality and its concerns for formal equality or inequality. This care ethic signifies a duty to the other as recognized in the work of Emmanuel Levinas,[15] Jacques Derrida, and Francois Lyotard.[16] Law and justice reflect different assumptions; law is more connected to economic calculation; justice is more connected to a gift. Justice is something we owe to the other and, hence, is never calculable.[17] It is a duty bestowed without payment. This suggests that we cultivate a sense of otherness, even as a capitalist socius demands a rational calculating individual with only instrumental concerns for the other. This dialectical play is omnipresent; however, we advocate the development of a personal reorientation to the other, even while recognizing the formal rational forms of justice that abound. We need to think beyond the latter basin of attraction and intuit methods and forms by which the former predominate. We need greater experimentation in becoming-other.

Suggestive at the more meso level are the works of Cornell, Giddens, Deleuze, and Guattari on the patriarchal, nuclear family, the thinking of Christine Parker on responsive organizations, and, on a more abstract level, dynamic systems theory with its notion of dissipative structures.[18] Cornell (1998) has offered an alternative model to the traditional family, one in which sexuate beings[19] are privileged. That is, the nuclear family is seen as out of sync with postmodernity (see also Castells 2004, 192–302; Stacey 1990; Hage and Powers 1992).[20] In Cornell's view, the family should function more in terms of contractual relations in which the parents take on custodial responsibilities as caregivers of the children. This approach does not privilege the monogamous, heterosexual nuclear family (Cornell 1998, 123). "Gays, lesbians, straights, and transgendered [citizens] would all be able to organize their sexuality as it accorded with their own self-representation" (Cornell 1998, 123). Lovers would be able to register in civil partnerships, and health and child care would be guaranteed by the government (Cornell 1998, 128). In this arrangement, Oedipus, desire as lack, and rigid identities would not have substantial grounds for development.

For Giddens (2000), the traditional family was more of an economic entity where inequality assured an imposed order, sexuality was connected with reproduction, and children were of economic benefit. Postmodernity, however, locates couples based more on intimacy and emotional communication; that is, they are more democratic in their very structure. Hence, postmodernity tends toward molecular, not molar, forms of coupling. Deleuze and Guattari, too, have argued that the traditional Oedipal structured family is about reproduction of reactive forms of desire, of imprisoning subjectivity in molar categories (mother, father, child). Moreover, as we explained in chapter 3, the Oedipal found itself quite compatible with the emergence of capital logic. Each person in the traditionally structured family reinforces the other, assuring the molarization of identities. Their schizoanalysis alternative seeks to undo Oedipus, to free themselves from reactive forms of desire, and to open themselves up to active forces, molecular identities, and becoming.

When we look at the prison-form and its visitors, we quite easily see the ubiquitous presence of "dysfunctional families" that are elements in harm-producing investments. We need another way. The traditional molar family is a necessary object of critique and transformation.

On a more abstract level, dynamic systems theory has shown how, in far-from-equilibrium conditions, dissipative structures would emerge. On a continuum, dissipative structures occupy the opposite side of bureaucracy. Whereas the latter are molar, static, and resistant to change, the former are inherently sensitive to perturbations: even the smallest agitation (input value) can produce self-organization leading to a new "structure." Dissipative structures have compatibilities with molecular forms in that they are ever in process, mutating, transforming, and providing the basis of stability and change.[21] Pivotal to such metamorphosis, would be the establishment of a socius characterized by far-from-equilibrium conditions. The notion of dissipative structures has been incorporated in progressive organizational theory.[22] By providing greater autonomy for teams of workers, this literature suggests, these nonhierarchical forms reap the rewards of self-organization and the generation of creative lines of flight. Rather than emphasizing "planned change,"[23] these forms encourage self-organization and the pursuit of bifurcations that are ubiquitously emerging. Thus, molecular developments, rather than molar ones, result. We shall return to this notion in our comments on Unger's suggestions below.

Where organizations do produce harm, suggestions have been developed that are building blocks for a transformative justice. Parker (1999), for example, has provided us with a model of responsive transparent organizations that is in the direction of furthering transformative justice. She argues that a good amount of harm (of reduction/repression) takes place in the workplace and is of a repetitive form. She suggests frameworks that permit the opportunity to present claims against organizational practices. Her ideal is to maximize freedom and to minimize domination. In particular, she suggests (1) consulting those directly involved in order to come up with a list of common dominating practices, (2) developing some form of restorative justice programming that would respond to these harms, and (3) ensuring employees' access to these created forums. The government's role would be to monitor these practices and to facilitate their resolutions. This strategy encourages the development of a multiplicity of sites within which justice practices could unfold from the ground up. Further, organizations could be provided incentives when moving toward, and disincentives when moving away from, the direction of molecular expression in the workplace. In short, machinic cuts and expressive forms may begin to tend toward the molecular and constitute becoming subjects.

Suggestive at the more "macro" level are the works of Unger, postmodern Marxists (Deleuze, Guattari, Dyer-Witheford, Hardt, and Negri), and other significant critics (Beck, Giddens). Each theorist has provided some useful insights into how reformist remedial and radical accusatory styles can activate a more humanistic socius. This would be a socius in which imprisonment as we know it is rendered nonsustainable.

1. *Roberto Unger.* The liberal reformist diagram is exemplary in Unger's (1987) work on superliberalism. In past writings, we have had occasion to make purchase of his keen insights, especially for advancing the possibility of an empowered democracy. Unger's strategy is not the total dismantling of capitalism, for, as is the case for Deleuze and Guattari, it has transcended the rigid codifications of the past, even as capitalism has created new forms of capture and axiomatic categories. Unger envisions a socius where the criticizability of core institutional structures without repercussions and ongoing change remain integral values and practices.

   Centralized capital funds would provide teams of workers the ability to borrow money for new experiments and investments in the economy, the loans returning to the fund for yet other teams of workers. Role jumbling would assure workers the possibility of engaging in several diverse work activities. In his empowered democracy, conflicts would increase but become the basis of deeper understandings of the other. Thus, we can see how these notions fit well with the advocacy of molecular revolutions.

   The empowered democracy would privilege molecular over molar forces, value continuous variation, and provide greater opportunities to become-other—all in far-from-equilibrium conditions. Accordingly, dissipative structures would be emergents that remained susceptible to even the smallest perturbation. Within this socius, symmetry breaking would not be aberrant; rather, it would be the more likely event. And within this socius, we must locate the basis to an alternative prison-form. Some aspects of restorative justice would be spared from some recent critiques. Transformative justice would be consistent with the logic of far-from-equilibrium conditions. Both Rorty's (1989) and Unger's (1996) call for pragmatism, experimentalism, and formations of principles of justice from the ground up would also resonate with this approach. Similarly, Levinas's and Derrida's more abstract principles of justice as a duty to the other would find a more receptive milieu. Still further, machinic cuts and expressive forms could follow, whereby I-thou relationships predominated over their I-it counterparts, where molecular subjects predominate. Most likely, more rather than less conflict within the socius would materialize. This conflict would necessitate new conceptions of justice rendering along the direction theorized by those advocating transformative justice. The prison-form, under these circumstances, would find a multiplicity of undermining logics, breaks in repetition.

2. *Postmodern Marxists.* Several recent integrations have proposed a postmodern Marxism (see the seminal work by Dyer-Witheford 1999). Key theoreticians here are Negri, Hardt and Negri, Negri and Guattari, Donna Haraway, Guattari, and Deleuze and Guattari.[24] Characterizing postmodernity are new forms of struggle in a global order, dramatic technological advancements in the information highway,[25] and the demise of class as envisioned by Marx. Rather than the proletariat as a homogenous class, we have the postmodern proletariat, socialized workers (Negri 1992), the multitude (Hardt and Negri 2005), and cyborgs (Haraway 1985) that become new sources of antagonisms and transformations. Witnessed here are varying alliances that cut across borders—united by the Internet as a mode of communication—and articulate agendas, strategies for change, and continuous coverage of struggles in video form.[26]

Postmodern Marxists offer recommendations for transformative struggles in postmodernity. Their insights suggest replacement machinic cuts and forms of expression, the privileging of molecular forces, the desirability of far-from-equilibrium conditions, and the ubiquity of becoming. The prison-form in the emerging socius will undergo severe critique that could undermine its nominal *raison d'être*. A revolution in penology, a break in cyclical practices, awaits the various microrevolutions that are able to attain linkages that cut across borders, infused with the images of the Internet and vitalized by the multitude's focalization of energy and resources clamoring for change. This will be ongoing. No endpoint exists that can be "posited," only becoming. While all forms of harm will not be entirely extinguished, a less harmful socius with more ongoing transformative justice rendering can be envisioned.

3. *Ulrich Beck and Anthony Giddens and the risk society.* Since about the 1980s, postmodernity has been characterized by increasing risks (Beck 1992). These hazards exist at every level: economic, political, environmental, technological, and individual. Thus, we are engulfed in uncertainty. Contrary to the promises inherent in Enlightenment reasoning—that rationality would pave the way toward an orderly world—in postmodernity we witness a habitus increasingly "out of our control—a runaway world" (Giddens 2000, 20). Giddens (20–21) suggests that two opposing views will be increasingly activated in the continued movement toward globalism: "In a globalizing world, where information and images are routinely transmitted across the globe, we are all regularly in contact with others who think differently, and live differently, from ourselves. Cosmopolitans welcome and embrace this cultural complexity. Fundamentalists [on the other hand] find it disturbing and dangerous. . . . They take refuge in a renewed and purified tradition—and quite often, violence ensues."[27] When reconceptualized, we have a classic Deleuzean-Guattarian clash between active and reactive forces, molecular and molar flows, change and stasis. Given the ascendancy of the risk society, Deleuze and Guattari's work is becoming increasingly relevant for locating insights into the coming order and for novel ways of becoming.

What direct relevance does the risk society have for penology? We have already had the occasion to review the work of Bauman (1998), who suggests one ominous direction for penology in a global order based more on differences: the proliferation of places of exclusion and immobility (see also Young 1999). This is in accord with Giddens' prediction of a fundamentalist line of flight. We have also seen the ascendancy of the actuarial model in criminal justice, where predictive instruments determine interventionist policies. What needs mobilization are active forces that privilege cosmopolitan views.

Dyer-Witheford (1999) has concisely summarized some further suggestions. In brief, he argues for (1) an institutionalized, guaranteed income; (2) communication networks accessible to all, regardless of income levels; (3) the use of the latter for decentralized forms of governance; and (4) more democratic controls in technological developments (1999, 192–218). These strategies would act synergistically toward the development of a new noncapitalist socius. Rather than a "withering away of the state" as suggested by Marx, Dyer-Witheford's review of the literature posits a "destatification" in a downward direction. For Dyer-Witheford, "The role of government is redefined as supporting collective initiatives rather than substituting for them, diffusing rather than concentrating control, nurturing social transformation from the bottom up rather than engineering it from the top down" (1999, 209).

Moreover, activism in various forms, for Dyer-Witheford, already has a growing viable existence and efficacy (e.g., ecological, feminist, housing, labor). For example, we increasingly see rainbow coalitions emerging and dissipating in accordance with the logic of the multitude. By lending support to these and other efforts at dynamic reform, destatification is made that much more realizable. Indeed, as Dyer-Witheford tells us, this "battlefield map . . . does not identify an agenda to be implemented 'after the revolution,' but a series of initiatives whose advancement would contaminate and overload the circuitry of capital with demands and requirements contradictory to the imperatives of profit." And further, "pursuit of these interrelated measures would cumulatively undermine the logic that binds society around market exchange and increasingly require the reassembly of everyday activities into a new configuration [read, socius]" (Dyer-Witheford 1999, 217). It is under such circumstances as these that the prison-form and its expression will begin to atrophy. It is under conditions such as these that more genuine forms of restorative and transformative justice would take root.

Our modest proposal for a radical desistance approach, a transdesistance model, steeped in constitutive principles entails a focus on three intersecting "levels" (i.e., "micro," "meso," and "macro"). These three levels must be seen as constitutive of the whole and in turn constituted by the whole. Critical strategies must engage the synergenic potentials of their resonances. Understandings of the prison-form (and crime) can only be more fully actualized from within a holistic approach. Prison-forms (including their attendant philosophies, principles, and practices) must have their grounds for existence undermined. We do not project a final destination in these preliminary approximations; rather, we suggest possible sources for lines of flight that may in their own course witness symmetry-breaking cascades. These are the crystalline seeds of change that can usher in unheralded potentials in becoming.

Thus, our vision quest for a war machine, a rhizomatic excursion, folds back upon itself in a familiar, though novel, refrain. Revolution. From whence does it come? It emerges in unconscious desire and is echoed in one's assemblages. It is given birth in an imperceptible whisper or in a shadow's desperate glow. And when it first appears, it is like a stranger calling: unrecognizable, inaccessible, and unspeakable. But when it is movement, a movement for the masses, it is an active line of flight: productive, mutating, transforming. This nomadic expedition, always already a departure rather than an arrival in its unfolding meaning, continues apace now, again, anew. And so it is with penology, the molecular revolution in penology. . . .

NOTES

1. See Delgado and Stefancic's *Failed Revolutions* (1994) for some thoughtful commentary concerning how revolutionary potentials can be derailed or undermined in pursuing legal remedies.

2. The movement toward a noncapitalist society can be seen "not as a state-socialist imposition of centralized uniformity but as an explosion of difference—a dissolution of the global command of profit that opens the way to alternatives that, like a volcanic magma, spread out in a 'network of streams of enjoyments, of propositions, of inventions'" (Dyer-Witheford 1999, 191; Negri 1984, 150).

3. We also see this in Lacan's Schema R. It depicts how a subject, inserted in an oedipal-based socius, actualizes "cuts" (gestalts) that become the basis of action.

4. As Bergson (1998, 176) notes, a delay, or "zone of indeterminacy," exists between the moment of perception and the moment of action. As this delay increases, so, too, does the subject's access to alternative strategies of sense making and recognition that can lead to coupling moments or fleeting epiphanies.

5. Foucault's early work on the disciplinary mechanisms argued for how bodies were made docile and subjects of utility. There was no escape from the disciplinary mechanisms and the panoptic abstract machine. His later works investigated how the body could liberate itself from these constraints (see Miller 1993).

6. Cornell (1998, 59) notes the limits: "The sole justification for the violation of a person's imaginary domain can be only that the way in which she represents her sexuate being is so bad for her, or for others; the state then can warrant prohibiting it outright, or at least can try to discourage it. But I have argued that we should not do this even in the case of prostitution; history shows the dangers of allowing the state to be the source of meaning of acceptable 'sex.'" Elsewhere she notes, "There are only two limitations on the right of each one of us as a person to the self-representation of her sexuate being. The first is . . . that no one can use force or violence against another person in representing her sexuate being [what we refer to as 'harms of repression']. The second is the 'degradation prohibition,' which prohibits any one of us from being graded down because of her form of representation of her sexuate being [what we refer to as 'harms of reduction']" (60).

7. Consider Bank's (forthcoming) insightful analysis concerning incarcerated juveniles' forms of resistance. As she tells us, "Residents must . . . 'learn the lingo' in order to secure their release. . . . Residents must steer a course between learning enough to express their adherence to normative values and refraining from too facile a use of that language. If they do not steer the right course between these poles and veer towards a too facile use of the language, they are liable to be categorized as 'treatment-wise'" (173, 177).

8. This is not to suggest an exhaustive list. These are only approximations.

9. For Guattari and Negri (1990, 103), it is the development of multifocused "machines of struggle."

10. As Guattari (1984, 263) informs us, the emerging molecular revolution is characterized by "a proliferation of *fringe groups, minorities and autonomist movements* leading to a flowering of particular desires (individual and/or collective) and the appearance of new forms of social groupings."

11. One of us, DM, is a member of the Chicago Didjeridu Chorus, a group of eight players with various instruments from around the world, including three didjeridus, whose public performances, much like individual jam sessions, follow nomadic principles. We have never replayed precisely what has appeared before. A tune begins somewhat out of accord, but quickly moves into a coherent form, only to redo itself again.

12. Todd May (1994, 1995) has developed some useful thoughts on how to evaluate various forces. See especially May (1994, 121–55; 1995, 135–46); Lambert (2006, 129–38) has incorporated this in his call for an alternative "right to desire" and a "right to invest in new possibilities of life," going beyond the Enlightenment's call for universal rights to life, liberty, and property. As May (1995, 144) has poignantly observed, "We may think of ourselves as a canvas to be filled or a score to be written."

13. I (DM) was apprised of this possibility on a prison visit with the John Howard Association to Stateville Prison in Illinois, where one of the last panopticon-type structures still exists, called "the roundhouse." When I actually visited the central tower, I was impressed with Bentham and Foucault, only to find out later, from one of the officials, about the possibility of challenge.

14. For additional discussions, elaborations, and productive critiques see, Braidotti (2006), Held (2005), Slote (2007), Sevenhuijsen (1998), and Tronto (1993, 1995).

15. See Critchley (1999).

16. For a brief review of Lyotard's philosophy and its relevance to law and justice, see Arrigo, Milovanovic, and Schehr (2005).

17. See Derrida (1995) and Caputo (1997). For applications of the "gift" in various penological contexts, see Arrigo and Williams (1999) and Williams and Arrigo (2000).

18. This is by no way an exhaustive list. It merely begins the necessary discussion. Much awaits the critical criminologist and the further development of a revolutionary penology.

19. By sexuate being, Cornell (1998, 25) means "engaged in a framework by which we orient ourselves; because we are sexuate beings we have to orient ourselves sexually."

20. Castells (2004, 301) also suggests that with the "end of patriarchalism," and until new forms of the family emerge, "chaos" and anxiety will be unleashed due to the dissipation of the normalizing factors associated with the previous molar structured family. Nevertheless, with the dissolution of patriarchal forms of family, new personalities will emerge that are in accord with "the people yet to come."

21. For insightful analysis in this direction ("organization-without-organs," "rhizomatic organizations"), see Cooper and Burrel (1988), Linstead (2000), and Kornberger, Rhodes, and ten Bos (2006).

22. See, e.g., Peters (1988), Farazmand (2003), Sullivan (2004), and Smith (2001).

23. Consider the traditional organizational ideal: "Organizations are focused on structure and design. Charts are drawn to illustrate who is accountable to whom or who plays what role and when. Business experts break down organizations into the smallest of parts. They build models of organizational practice and

policy with hope that this atomizing will yield better information on how to improve the organization's functioning" (see Mason and Kirkwood 2006).

24. Deleuze and Guattari would object to being identified as postmodernist, as Donna Haraway most likely would as well. Nevertheless, key ideas offered resonate well with the thrust of postmodern analysis.

25. See especially Castells (2004).

26. Contrary to the pessimism of Baudrillard's notion of the hyperreal and simulacra, as well as the earlier Foucault and his death of the subject, postmodernity offers new opportunities to appropriate the very technology and informational devices driving the central economy such that their use can foster alternative conceptions of agency and autonomy. As Dyer-Witheford (1999, 176–77) has said, "If the self is always fabricated, some fabrications promote a subjectivity of passivity, dependency, and indifference, while others foster agency, autonomy, and inquiry. . . . One of the characteristics of the socialized worker—or postmodern proletariat—is his/her increasing ability to reappropriate capital's communicational machines in order to contest its simulations."

27. The pains-of-imprisonment and the normalization-of-violence theses developed in chapter 4 amply demonstrate this point. The kept, their keepers, correctional officials/administrators, and the general public react, in molar form, to the uncertainty that pervades the socius through cyclical and repetitive harms of reduction and repression.

References

Abraham, Frederick D. 1992. "Chaos, Bifurcations, and Self-Organization: Dynamical Extensions of Neurological Positivism and Ecological Psychology." *Psychoscience* 1(2): 85–118.

Acorn, Annalaise E. 2004. *Compulsory Compassion: A Critique of Restorative Justice.* Vancouver, Canada: University of British Columbia.

American Psychiatric Association (APA). 2001. *Diagnostic and Statistical Manual of Mental Disorders-IV-TR.* 4th ed. Washington, DC: APA.

Amsterdam, Anthony, and Jerome Bruner. 2000. *Minding the Law: How Courts Rely on Storytelling, and How Their Stories Change the Ways We Understand the Law— and Ourselves.* Cambridge, MA: Harvard University Press.

Anderson, Kevin. 1998. "The Young Erich Fromm's Contribution to Criminology." *Justice Quarterly* 15(4): 667–96.

———. 2000. "Erich Fromm and the Frankfurt School Critique of Criminal Justice." In *Erich Fromm and Critical Criminology: Beyond the Punitive Society,* ed. K. Anderson and R. Quinney, 83–119. Chicago: University of Illinois Press.

Anderson, Kevin, and Richard Quinney, eds. 2000. *Erich Fromm and Critical Criminology: Beyond the Punitive Society.* Chicago: University of Illinois Press.

Andrews, D. A., Ivan Zinger, Robert Hoge, James Bonta, Paul Gendreau, and Francis Cullen. 1990. "Does Correctional Treatment Work? A Clinically Relevant and Psychological Informed Meta-Analysis." *Criminology* 28(3): 369–404.

Arendt, Hannah. 2006. *Eichmann in Jerusalem: A Report on the Banality of Evil.* New York: Penguin (originally published in 1977).

Arrigo, Bruce A. 1993. *Madness, Language, and the Law.* Albany: Harrow and Heston.

———. 1994. "Legal Discourse and the Disordered Criminal Defendant." *Legal Studies Forum* 18(1): 93–112.

———. 1995. "The Peripheral Core of Law and Criminology: On Postmodern Social Theory and Conceptual Integration." *Justice Quarterly* 12(3): 447–72.

———. 1996a. *The Contours of Psychiatric Justice: A Postmodern Critique of Mental Illness, Criminal Insanity, and the Law.* New York: Garland.

———. 1996b. "Desire in the Psychiatric Courtroom: On Language, Law, and Lacan." *Current Perspectives in Social Theory* 16: 159–87.

———. 1997. "Recommunalizing Drug Offenders: The 'Drug Peace' Agenda." *Journal of Offender Rehabilitation* 21(3/4): 53–73.

———. 2001. "Praxis." In *The Sage Dictionary of Criminology,* ed. E. McLaughlin and J. Muncie, 219–21. London: Sage.

———. 2002. *Punishing the Mentally Ill: A Critical Analysis of Law and Psychiatry.* Albany: SUNY Press.

———. 2003. "Justice and the Deconstruction of Psychological Jurisprudence: The Case of Competency to Stand Trial." *Theoretical Criminology* 7(1): 55–88.

———. 2004a. "Rethinking Restorative and Community Justice: A Postmodern Inquiry." *Contemporary Justice Review* 7(1): 91–100.

———. 2004b. "Theorizing Non-Linear Communities: On Social Deviance and Housing the Homeless." *Deviant Behavior: An Interdisciplinary Journal* 25(3): 193–213.

———. 2006a. "Towards a Critical Penology of the Mentally Ill Offender: On Law, Ideology, and the Logic of 'Competency.'" In *Advances in Critical Criminology: Theory and Application,* ed. W. S. DeKeseredy and B. Perry, 219–39. Lexington, MA: Lexington Books.

———. 2006b. "Punishment, Freedom, and the Culture of Control: A Film Review Essay of *Torture: America's Brutal Prisons*" (by Nick London, First Run/Icarus Films). *Contemporary Justice Review* 9(2): 229–33.

———. 2006c. "The Ontology of Crime: On the Construction of the Real, the Image, and the Hyper-real." In *Philosophy, Crime, and Criminology,* ed. B. A. Arrigo and C. R. Williams, 41–73. Urbana and Chicago: University of Illinois Press.

———. 2007. "Punishment, Freedom and the Culture of Control: The Case of Brain Imaging and the Law." *American Journal of Law and Medicine* 33(3): 457–82.

———. 2008. "Crime, Justice, and the Under-laborer: On the Criminology of the Shadow and the Search for Disciplinary Legitimacy and Identity." *Justice Quarterly* 25(3): 439–68.

Arrigo, Bruce A., Dragan Milovanovic, and Robert C. Schehr. 2005. *The French Connection in Criminology: Rediscovering Crime, Law, and Social Change.* Albany: SUNY Press.

Arrigo, Bruce A., and Robert C. Schehr. 1998. "Restoring Justice for Juveniles: A Critical Analysis of Victim Offender Mediation." *Justice Quarterly* 15(4): 629–66.

Arrigo, Bruce. A., and Yoshiko Takahashi. 2006. "Recommunalization of the Disenfranchised: A Theoretical and Critical Criminological Inquiry." *Theoretical Criminology: An International Journal* 10(3): 307–36.

———. 2007. "Theorizing Community Reentry for Male Incarcerates and Confined Mothers: Lessons Learned from Housing the Homeless." *Journal of Offender Rehabilitation* 46(1/2): 133–62.

Arrigo, Bruce, and Jeffrey J. Taska. 1999. "The Right to Refuse Treatment, Competency to Be Executed, and Therapeutic Jurisprudence." *Law and Psychology Review* 23(1): 1–47.

Arrigo, Bruce A., and Christopher R. Williams. 1999. "Law, Ideology, and Critical Inquiry: The Case of Treatment Refusal for Incompetent Prisoners Awaiting Execution." *New England Journal on Criminal and Civil Confinement* 25(2): 367–412.

Artaud, Antonin. 1988. *Artaud: Selected Writings*. Berkeley: University of California Press.

Athens, Lonnie. 1989. *The Creation of Dangerous Violent Criminals*. New York: Routledge.

Austin, James. 2007. *It's About Time: America's Imprisonment Binge*. 4th ed. Belmont, CA: Wadsworth.

Austin, J., T. Clear, T. Duster, D. Greenburg, J. Irwin, C. McCoy, A. Mobley, B. Owen, and J. Page. 2007. *Unlocking America: Why and How to Reduce America's Prison Population*. Washington, DC: JFA Institute.

Balkin, J. M. 1987. "Deconstructive Practice and Legal Theory." *Yale Law Journal* 96: 743–86.

Banks, Cyndi. Forthcoming. *"Waiting for the Outs": Power, Resistance and Culture in a Juvenile Institution*. Albany: SUNY Press.

Bannister, Shelley, and Dragan Milovanovic. 1990. "The Necessity Defense, Substantive Justice and Oppositional Linguistic Praxis." *International Journal of the Sociology of Law* 18: 179–98.

Barak, Gregg. 1988. "Newsmaking Criminology: Reflections on the Media, Intellectuals and Crime." *Justice Quarterly* 5: 565–87.

———, ed. 1994. *Media, Process, and the Social Construction of Crime: Studies in Newsmaking Criminology*. New York: Garland.

———. 2003. *Violence and Nonviolence: Pathways to Understanding*. Thousand Oaks, CA: Sage.

Barry, Monica. 2006. *Youth Offending in Transition: The Search for Social Recognition*. London: Routledge.

Baskin, Deborah. 1988. "Community Mediation and the Public/Private Problem." *Social Justice* 15(1): 98–115.

Baudrillard, Jean. 1972. *For a Critique of the Political Economy of the Sign*. St. Louis: Telos Press.

———. 1976. *L'échange symbolique et la mort*. Paris: Gallimard.

———. 1983a. *Simulations*. New York: Semiotext(e).

———. 1983b. *In the Shadow of the Silent Majorities*. New York: Semiotext(e).

Bauman, Zygmunt. 1989. *Modernity and the Holocaust*. Cambridge, UK: Polity.

———. 1998. *Globalization: The Human Consequences*. New York: Columbia University Press.

Bazemore, Gordon, and Carsten Erbe. 2004. "Reintegration and Restorative Justice: Towards a Theory and Practice of Informal Social Control and Support." In *After Crime and Punishment*, ed. Shadd Maruna and Russ Immarigeon, 27–58. Cullompton, UK: Willan Publishing.

Beck, Ulrich. 1992. *Risk Society: Towards a New Modernity*. London: Sage.

Beckett, K., and B. Western. 2001. "Governing Social Marginality." *Mass Imprisonment: Social Causes and Consequences*, ed. D. Garland, 35–50. London: Sage.

Benton, Ted, and Ian Craib. 2001. *Philosophy of Social Science: The Philosophical Foundations of Social Thought*. New York: Palgrave.

Berger, Peter, and Thomas Luckmann. 1967. *The Social Construction of Reality*. New York: Doubleday.

Bergson, Henri. 1998. *Creative Evolution*, trans. Arthur Mitchell. Mineola, NY: Dover Publications.

Best, Steven, and Douglas Kellner. 1991. *Postmodern Theory: Critical Interrogations*. New York: Guilford Press.

Black, Donald. 1976. *The Behavior of Law*. New York: Academic Press.

———. 1989. *Sociological Justice*. New York: Oxford University Press.

Bloom, Barbara, Barbara Owen, and Stephanie Covington. 2003. *Gender Responsive Strategies: Research Practice and Guiding Principles for Women Offenders*. Washington, DC: United States Department of Justice, National Institute of Corrections.

Borradori, Giovanna. 2003. *Philosophy in a Time of Terror: Dialogues with Jurgen Habermas and Jacques Derrida*. Chicago: University of Chicago Press.

Bosworth, Mary. 1999a. "Agency and Choice in Women's Prisons: Toward a Constitutive Penology." In *Constitutive Criminology at Work: Applications to Crime and Justice*, ed. S. Henry and D. Milovanovic, 205–26. Albany: SUNY Press.

———. 1999b. *Engendering Resistance: Agency and Power in Women's Prisons*. Sydney, Australia: Ashgate.

Bottoms, Anthony, and P. Wiles. 1992. "Explanations of Crime and Place." In *Crime, Policing and Place*, ed. D. J. Evans, N. R. Fyfe, and D. T. Herbert. London: Routledge.

Bourdieu, Pierre. 1984. *Distinction: A Social Critique of the Judgment of Taste*. Cambridge, MA: Harvard University Press.

———. 1986. "The Forms of Social Capital." In *Handbook of Theory and Research for the Sociology of Education*, ed. J. G. Richardson, 241–58. New York, Greenwood.

Bourdieu, Pierre, and Loïc Wacquant. 1992. *An Invitation to Reflexive Sociology*. Chicago: University of Chicago Press.

Box, Steven. 1987. *Recession, Crime and Punishment*. London: Macmillan.

Box, Steven, and Chris Hale. 1986. "Unemployment, Crime and Imprisonment and the Enduring Problem of Prison Overcrowding." In *Confronting Crime*, ed. Roger Matthews and Jock Young. London: Sage.

Braidotti, Rosi. 2002. *Metamorphosis*. Cambridge, UK: Polity.

———. 2006. *Transpositions*. Cambridge, UK: Polity.

Braithwaite, John. 1989. *Crime, Shame, and Reintegration*. Cambridge, UK: Cambridge University Press.

Braswell, Michael, John R. Fuller, and Bo Lozoff. 2000. *Corrections, Peacemaking, and Restorative Justice: Transforming Individuals and Institutions*. Cincinnati: Anderson Publishing.

Briggs, John, and David Peat. 1989. *Turbulent Mirror*. New York: Harper and Row.

Brunner, Jose. 2000. "Freud and the Rule of Law: From Totem and Taboo to Psychoanalytic Jurisprudence." In *The Analytic Freud: Philosophy and Psychoanalysis*, ed. Michael P. Levine, 277–305. London: Routledge.

Burnett, Ros, and Colin Roberts, eds. 2004. *What Works in Probation in Youth Justice: Developing Evidence-Based Practice*. Cullompton, UK: Willan Publishing.

Burnside, Jonathan, and Nicola Baker, eds. 1994. *Relational Justice: Repairing the Breach*. Winchester, UK: Waterside Press.

Butler, Judith. 1990. *Gender Trouble*. New York: Routledge.

———. 1992. "Contingent Foundations: Feminism and the Question of Postmodernism." In *Feminists Theorize the Political*, ed. J. Butler and J. W. Scott, 3–21. London: Routledge.

———. 2004. *Undoing Gender*. New York: Routledge.

Byrne, James, Donald Hummer, and Faye Taxman. 2007. *The Culture of Prison Violence*. Boston: Allyn and Bacon.

———, eds. 2008. *The Culture of Prison Violence*. New York: Pearson Education, Inc.

Capeheart, Loretta, and Dragan Milovanovic. 2007. *Social Justice*. New Brunswick, NJ: Rutgers University Press.

Caputo, John. 1997. *Deconstruction in a Nutshell*. New York: Fordham University Press

Carrabine, Eamonn. 2001. "Incapacitation." *The Sage Dictionary of Criminology*, ed. E. McLaughlin and J. Muncie, 146–47. London: Sage.

Castells, Manuel. 2004. *The Information Age*, vol. 2, *The Power of Identity*. Oxford: Blackwell Publishing.

Cavadino, Mick, and James Dignan. 2006. *Penal Systems: A Comparative Approach*. London: Sage.

Christie, Nils. 2000. *Crime Control as Industry*. 3rd ed. London: Routledge.

———. 2004. *A Suitable Amount of Crime*. London: Routledge.

Clear, Todd. 1994. *Harm in American Penology: Offenders, Victims, and Their Communities*. Albany: SUNY Press.

———. 2007. *Imprisoning Communities: How Mass Incarceration Makes Disadvantaged Neighborhoods Worse*. New York: Oxford University Press.

Clear, Todd, R. Dina, R. Rose, and Judith Ryder. 2001. "Incarceration and Community: The Problem of Removing Offenders." *Crime and Delinquency* 47: 335–51.

Clement, Grace. 1998. *Care, Autonomy, and Justice: Feminism and the Ethic of Care*. Boulder, CO: Westview Press.

Clemmer, Donald. 1958. *The Prison Community*. New York: Rinehart and Co.

Coleman, James S. 1988. "Social Capital in the Creation of Human Capital." *American Journal of Sociology* 94: 95–120.

———. 1990. *Foundations of Social Theory*. London: Belknap Press.

Conley, Tom. 2005. "Folds and Folding." In *Gilles Deleuze: Key Concepts*, ed. Charles Stivale, 170–81. Montreal, Canada: McGill-Queen's University Press.

Cooper, R., and G. Burrel. 1988. "Modernism, Postmodernism and Organizational Analysis." *Organization Studies* 1: 1–23.

Cornell, Drucilla. 1998. *At the Heart of Freedom: Feminism, Sex, and Equality*. Princeton, NJ: Princeton University Press.

———. 1999. *Beyond Accommodation*. Lanham, MD: Rowman & Littlefield.

Craissati, Jacki. 2004. *Managing High Risk Sex Offenders in the Community: A Psychological Approach*. New York: Routledge.

Crawley, E. 2004. *Doing Prison Work: The Public and Private Lives of Prison Officers*. Cullompton, UK: Willan Publishing.

Cressey, Donald R. 1953. *Other People's Money*. Glencoe, IL: Free Press.

———. 1970. "The Respectable Criminal." In *Modern Criminals*, ed. James Short, 105–16. New York: Transaction-Aldine.

Critchley, Simon. 1999. *The Ethics of Deconstruction: Derrida and Levinas*. West Lafayette, IN: Purdue University Press.

Crow, Iain D. G., ed. 2001. *The Treatment and Rehabilitation of Offenders*. Thousand Oaks, CA: Sage.

Cullen, Frank T., and Paul Gendreau. 2001. "From Nothing Works to What Works? Changing Professional Ideology in the 21st Century." *The Prison Journal* 81(3): 313–38.

———. 2002. "Assessing Correctional Rehabilitation: Policy, Practice, and Prospects." *Criminal Justice 2000*, vol. 3, *Policies, Processes, and Decisions of the Criminal Justice System*, ed. J. Horney, 109–75. Washington, DC: National Institute of Justice, U.S. Department of Justice.

Cullen, Francis T., and Karen E. Gilbert. 1982. *Reaffirming Rehabilitation*. Cincinnati: Anderson Publishing.

Curran, J., and J. Seaton. 1981. *Power without Responsibility*. London: Methuen.

Currie, Elliott. 1998. *Crime and Punishment in America*. New York: Metropolitan Books.

de Haan, Willem. 1990. *The Politics of Redress: Crime, Punishment and Penal Abolition*. Boston: Unwin Hyman.

Debord, Guy. 1983. *Society of the Spectacle*. Detroit: Red and Black.

DeLanda, Manuel. 1997. *A Thousand Years of Nonlinear History*. New York: Zone Books.

———. 2002. *Intensive Science and Virtual Philosophy*. New York: Continuum Books.

———. 2006. *A New Philosophy of Society: Assemblage Theory and Social Complexity*. New York: Continuum Books.

DeLauretis, Teresa. 1990. *The Practice of Love*. Bloomington: Indiana University Press.

Deleuze, Gilles. 1983. *Nietzsche and Philosophy*. New York: Columbia University Press.

———. 1986. *Cinema 1: The Movement Image*. Minneapolis: University of Minnesota Press.

———. 1988. *Foucault*. Minneapolis: University of Minnesota Press.

———. 1989. *Cinema 2: The Time Image*. Minneapolis: University of Minnesota Press.

———. 1990a. *Logic of Sense*, trans. M. Lester and C. Stivale. New York: Columbia University Press.

———. 1990b. *Negotiations*. New York: Columbia University Press.

———. 1993. *The Fold*. Minneapolis: University of Minnesota Press.

———. 1995. *Negotiations*. New York: Columbia University Press.

———. 2000. *Proust and Signs*. Minneapolis: University of Minnesota Press.

Deleuze, Gilles, and Felix Guattari. 1983. *Anti-Oedipus*. Minneapolis: University of Minnesota Press.

———. 1986. *Kafka: Toward a Minor Literature*. Minneapolis: University of Minnesota Press.

———. 1987. *A Thousand Plateaus*. Minneapolis: University of Minnesota Press.

Delgado, Richard, and Jean Stefancic. 1994. *Failed Revolutions: Social Reform and the Limits of Legal Imagination*. Boulder, CO: Westview Press.

Denzin, Norman. 1997. *Interpretive Ethnography*. Thousand Oaks, CA: Sage.

Derrida, Jacques. 1977. *Of Grammatology*. Baltimore: Johns Hopkins University Press.

———. 1978. *Writing and Difference*. Chicago: University of Chicago Press.

———. 1991. *The Force of Law: The Mystical Foundations of Authority*. Paris: Galilee.

———. 1995. *The Gift of Death*. Chicago: University of Chicago Press.

Descartes, Renee. 1999. *Discourse on Method and Mediations on First Philosophy*, trans. D. A. Cress. 4th ed. Indianapolis: Hackett Publishing Co.

Dilulio, John J. 1987. *Governing Prisons*. New York: Free Press.

Downes, David, and Kirstine Hansen. 2006. "Welfare and Punishment: The Relationship between Welfare Spending and Imprisonment." Crime and Society Foundation, Briefing, 2: 1–8.

Duncan, Martha. 1996. *Romantic Outlaws, Beloved Prisoners: The Unconscious Meaning of Punishment*. New York: New York University Press.

Dyer-Witheford, Nick. 1999. *Cyber-Marx*. Chicago: University of Illinois Press.

Edgar, Kimmett, Ian O'Donnell, and Carol Martin. 2003. *Prison Violence: The Dynamics of Conflict, Fear, and Power*. Cullompton, UK: Willan Publishing.

Edin, K., L. Lein, and T. Nelson. 2001. "Taking Care of Business: The Economic Survival Strategies of Low-Income Non-Custodial Fathers." In *Laboring below the Line*, ed. F. Munger, 125–47. New York: Russell Sage Foundation.

Einstadter, Werner, and Stuart Henry. 1995. *Criminological Theory: An Analysis of Its Underlying Assumptions*. Fort Worth, TX: Harcourt Brace.

———. 2007. *Criminological Theory: An Analysis of Its Underlying Assumptions*. 2nd ed. New York: Rowman & Littlefield.

Evans, Jessica. 2003. "Vigilance and Vigilantes: Thinking Psychoanalytically about Anti-pedophile Action." *Theoretical Criminology* 7(2): 163–89.

Ewick, Patricia, and Susan Silbey. 1998. *The Common Place of Law*. Chicago: University of Chicago Press.

Farazmand, Ali. 2003. "Chaos and Transformation Theories: A Theoretical Analysis with Implications for Organization Theory and Public Management." *Public Organization Review* 3(4): 339–72.

Farrall, Stephen. 2004. "Social Capital and Offender Reintegration: Making Probation Desistance Focused." In *After Crime and Punishment*, ed. Shadd Maruna and Russ Immarigeon. Cullompton, UK: Willan Publishing.

Farrall, Stephen, and Benjamin Bowling. 1999. "Structuration, Human Development, and Desistance from Crime." *British Journal of Criminology* 33(2): 253–68.

Farrall, Stephen, and Adam Calverley. 2006. *Understanding Desistance from Crime*. Berkshire, UK: Open University Press.

Farrington, D. P., B. Gallagher, L. Morley, R. J. St. Ledger, and D. J. West. 1986. "Unemployment, School Leaving and Crime." *British Journal of Criminology* 26(4): 335–56.

Feeley, Malcolm, and Jonathan Simon. 1992. "The New Penology: Notes on the Emerging Strategy of Corrections and Its Implications" *Criminology* 30: 449–70.

———. 2004. "The New Penology." In *Theorizing Criminal Justice*, ed. Peter Kraska, 302–22. Long Grove, IL: Waveland Press.

Ferraro, Kathleen J. 1997. "Review of Adrian Howe's *Punish and Critique: Towards a Feminist Analysis of Penality*." *Signs* 22(3): 784–87.

Forrester, John. 1991. *The Seductions of Psychoanalysis: Freud, Lacan, Derrida*. Cambridge, UK: Cambridge University Press.

Foucault, Michel. 1977a. *Discipline and Punish*. New York: Pantheon Books.

———. 1977b. "What Is an Author?" In *Language, Counter Memory, Practice*, ed. D. F. Bouchard. Ithaca, NY: Cornell University Press.

Freire, Paulo. 1973. *Pedagogy of the Oppressed*. South Hadley, MA: Herder and Herder.

Freud, Sigmund. 1965. *The Interpretation of Dreams*. New York: Avon Books (originally published in 1900).

———. 1989. *Totem and Taboo*. New York: W. W. Norton (originally published in 1912).

———. 2002. *Civilization and Its Discontents*. Hammondsworth, UK: Penguin (originally published in 1930).

Fromm, Erich. 1994. *Escape from Freedom*. New York: Henry Holt and Co. (originally published in 1941).

———. 2000a. "The State as Educator: On the Psychology of Criminal Justice." In *Erich Fromm and Critical Criminology: Beyond the Punitive Society*, ed. K. Anderson and R. Quinney, trans. H. D. Osterle and K. Anderson, 123–28. Urbana-Champagne: University of Illinois Press (originally published in 1930).

———. 2000b. "On the Psychology of the Criminal and the Punitive Society." In *Erich Fromm and Critical Criminology: Beyond the Punitive Society*, ed. K. Anderson and R. Quinney, trans. H. D. Osterle and K. Anderson, 129–56. Urbana-Champagne: University of Illinois Press.

———. 2003. *The Sane Society*. New York: Routledge (originally published in 1955).

———. 2005. *To Have or to Be?* London: Continuum International Publishing (originally published in 1976).

Fuller, John R. 1998. *Criminal Justice: A Peacemaking Perspective*. Boston: Allyn and Bacon.

Garfinkel, Alan. 1981. *Forms of Explanation*. New Haven, CT: Yale University Press.

Garland, David. 1990. *Punishment and Modern Society: A Study in Social Theory*. London: Clarendon Press.

———. 2001. *The Culture of Control: Crime and Social Order in Contemporary Society*. Chicago: University of Chicago Press.

Giddens, Anthony. 1984. *The Constitution of Society: Outline of a Theory of Structuration*. Stanford, CA: Stanford University Press.

———. 2000. *Runaway World*. New York: Routledge.

Gilligan, Carol. 1982. *In a Different Voice*. Cambridge, MA: Harvard University Press.

Gilsinan, James. 1982. *Doing Justice: How the System Works—As Seen by the Participants*. Englewood Cliffs, NJ: Prentice Hall.

Glaser, Daniel. 1994. "What Works and Why It Is Important: A Response to Logan and Gaes." *Justice Quarterly* 11(4): 711–23.

Goffman, Erving. 1961. *Asylums: Essays on the Social Situation of Mental Patients and Other Inmates*. Garden City, NY: Anchor Books.

Goodchild, Philip. 1996. *Deleuze and Guattari: An Introduction to the Politics of Desire*. London: Sage Publications.

Goulding, Jay. 2007. "New Ways toward Sino-Western Philosophical Dialogues." *Journal of Chinese Philosophy* 34(1): 99–125.

Greenwood, Peter. 1983. "Controlling the Crime Rate through Imprisonment." In *Crime and Public Policy*, ed. J. Q. Wilson, 251–69. San Francisco: Institute for Contemporary Studies.

Grosz, Elizabeth. 1994. *Volatile Bodies*. Bloomington: Indiana University Press.

Groves, W. Byron. 1987. "Freud and Freedom." *Psychoanalysis and Contemporary Thought* 10(1): 69–101.

———. 1993. "Criminology and Ontology." In *Discovering Criminology: From W. Byron Groves*, ed. G. R. Newman, M. J. Lynch, and D. H. Galaty, 23–36. New York: Harrow and Heston.

Groves, W. Byron, and David H. Galaty. 1986. "Freud, Foucault, and Social Control." *Humanity and Society* 12(3): 297–317.

Guattari, Felix. 1984. *Molecular Revolution*. Hammondsworth, UK: Penguin.

———. 2001. *The Three Ecologies*. New Brunswick, NJ: Athlone.

Guattari, Felix, and Antonio Negri. 1990. *Communists Like Us*. New York: Autonomedia.

Guerra, Nancy A. 2002. "Serious and Violent Juvenile Offenders: Gaps in Knowledge and Research Priorities." In *Serious and Violent Juvenile Offenders: Risk Factors and Successful Interventions*, ed. R. Loeber and D. P. Farrington, 389–404. Thousand Oaks, CA: Sage.

Haapanen, Rudy. 1990. *Selective Incapacitation and the Serious Offender*. New York: Springer-Verlag.

Hagan, John. 1997. "Crime and Capitalization: Toward a Developmental Theory of Street Crime in America." *Advances in Criminological Theory* 7: 287–308.

Hage, Jerald, and Charles Powers. 1992. *Postindustrial Lives*. London: Sage.

Halberstam, Judith. 2005. *In a Queer Time and Place*. New York: New York University Press.

Hallett, Michael A. 2006. *Private Prisons in America: A Critical Race Perspective*. Urbana-Champagne: University of Illinois Press.

Halsey, Mark. 2006a. *Deleuze and Environmental Damage*. Aldershot, UK: Ashgate.

———. 2006b. "Assembling the Custodial Subject: Rhetoric and Reality of Post-Release Life." *Journal of Criminal Law and Criminology* 97(4).

———. 2006c. "Negotiating Conditional Release." *Punishment and Society* 8(2): 147–81.

Haney, Craig. 2006. *Reforming Punishment: Psychological Limitations to the Pains of Imprisonment*. Washington, DC: American Psychological Association.

Haney, Craig, Cynthia Banks, and Philip Zimbardo. 1973. "Interpersonal Dynamics in a Simulated Prison." *International Journal of Criminology and Penology* 1(1): 69–95.

Haraway, Donna. 1985. "A Manifesto for Cyborgs." *Socialist Review* 80: 65–107.

Hardt, Michael. 1993. *Gilles Deleuze*. Minneapolis: University of Minnesota Press.

Hardt, Michael, and Antonio Negri. 2000. *Empire*. Cambridge, MA: Harvard University Press.

———. 2004. *Multitude: War and Democracy in the Age of Empire*. New York: Penguin Press.

Heffer, Chris. 2005. *The Language of Jury Trial*. New York: Palgrave MacMillan.

Hegel, Frederick W. H. 1955. *Philosophy of Right*, trans. T. M. Knox. New York: Oxford University Press.

Heidensohn, Francis. 1996. "Review of Adrian Howe's *Punish and Critique: Towards a Feminist Analysis of Penality.*" *British Journal of Sociology* 47(3): 565–56.

Held, Virginia. 2005. *The Ethics of Care.* New York: Oxford University Press.

Henry, Stuart. 1994. "Newsmaking Criminology as Replacement Discourse." In *Media, Process and the Social Construction of Crime,* ed. G. Barak, 287–319. New York: Garland Publishing.

———. 2007. "Deviance, Constructionist Perspectives." In *The Blackwell Encyclopedia of Sociology,* ed. G. Ritzer, 1086–92. Oxford: Blackwell Publishing.

Henry, Stuart, and M. M. Lanier, eds. 2001. *What Is Crime? Controversies over the Nature of Crime and What to Do About It.* Boulder, CO: Rowman & Littlefield.

Henry, Stuart, and Dragan Milovanovic. 1996. *Constitutive Criminology: Beyond Postmodernism.* London: Sage.

———, eds. 1999. *Constitutive Criminology at Work: Applications to Crime and Justice.* Albany: SUNY Press.

———. 2003. "Constitutive Criminology." In *Controversies in Critical Criminology,* eds. M. D. Schwartz and S. Hatty, 57–69. Cincinnati: Anderson Publishing.

Hirschi, T. 1969. *Causes of Delinquency.* Berkeley: University of California Press.

Hoffman, Martin L. 2001. *Empathy and Moral Development: Implications for Caring and Justice.* Cambridge, UK: Cambridge University Press.

Holland, Eugene. 1999. *Deleuze and Guattari's Anti-Oedipus: Introduction to Schizoanalysis.* New York: Routledge.

Hooks, bell. 1994. *Outlaw Culture: Resisting Representations.* New York: Routledge.

———. 1996. *Bone Black: Memories of Girlhood.* New York: Henry Holt.

Howe, Adrian. 1994. *Punish and Critique: Towards a Feminist Analysis of Penality.* London: Routledge.

Hudson, Barbara. 1993. *Penal Policy and Social Justice.* Toronto: University of Toronto Press.

———. 2003. *Understanding Justice: An Introduction to Ideas, Perspectives, and Controversies in Modern Penal Theory.* 2nd ed. Berkshire, UK: Open University Press.

Husserl, Edmund. 1983. *Ideas Pertaining to a Pure Phenomenology and to a Phenomenological Philosophy,* trans. F. Kersten. The Hague: Martinus Nijhoff Publishers.

Hussey, Ann C. 1997. "Incapacitation." In *Crime and the Justice System in America,* ed. F. Schmalleger, 120–21. Westport, CT: Greenwood.

International Journal for the Semiotics of Law. 2007. Special Issue: "Deleuze and the Semiotics of Law," Ronnie Lippens and Jamie Murray (Eds.).

Irwin, John. 1992. *The Jail: Managing the Underclass in American Society.* Berkeley: University of California Press.

Irwin, John, and Barbara Owen. 2007. *The Warehouse Prison: Disposal of the New Dangerous Class.* New York: Oxford University Press.

Jackson, Bernard. 1988. *Law, Fact, and Narrative Coherence.* Merseyside, UK: Deborah Charles Publications.

———. 1995. *Making Sense of Law.* Liverpool, UK: Deborah Charles Publications.

Jacobs, James J. 1978. *Statesville: The Penitentiary in Mass Society.* Chicago: University of Chicago Press.

Jacobson, Michael. 2005. *Downsizing Prisons: How to Reduce Crime and End Mass Incarceration.* New York: New York University Press.

Johnson, Doyle Paul. 1990. "Security versus Autonomy Motivation in Anthony Giddens' Conception of Agency." *Journal for the Theory of Social Behavior* 20(2): 111–30.

Johnson, Robert. 2002. *Hard Time*. Belmont, CA: Wadsworth.

Jones, Richard S., and Thomas J. Schmid. 2005. *Doing Time: Prison Experience and Identity among First-Time Inmates*. UK: Butterworth-Heinemann.

Jung, Carl. 1964. *Man and His Symbols*. New York: Laurel.

Kalinich, David B. 1986. *Power, Stability and Contraband: The Inmate Economy*. Prospect Heights, IL. Waveland Press.

Kappeler, Victor, and Peter Kraska. 1999. "Policing: Scientific and Community-Based Violence on Symbolic Playing Fields." In *Constitutive Criminology at Work: Applications to Crime and Justice*, ed. S. Henry and D. Milovanovic, 175–203. Albany: SUNY Press.

Katz, Jack. 1988. *Seductions of Crime*. New York: Basic Books.

Kelman, Mark. 1981. "Interpretive Construction in the Substantive Criminal Law." *Stanford Law Review* 33: 591–74.

Kempf-Leonard, Kimberly, and Elicka S. L. Peterson. 2000. "Expanding Realms of the New Penology: The Advent of Actuarial Justice for Juveniles." *Punishment and Society* 2(1): 66–97.

Kennedy, Duncan. 1997. *A Critique of Adjudication: Fin de Siecle*. Cambridge, MA: Harvard University Press.

———. 2001. "Afterword: A Semiotics of Critique." *Cardozo Law Review* 22: 1147–86.

Kennedy, Mark. 1970. "Beyond Incrimination." *Catalyst* 5: 1–37.

Kenny, Michael. 2004. *The Politics of Identity: Liberal Political Theory and the Dilemmas of Difference*. Cambridge, MA: Polity Press.

Klein, Melanie. 1985. *Love, Guilt and Other Works, 1921–1945*. London: Hogarth Press.

Knorr Cetina, Karin. 1982. *Advances in Social Theory and Methodology: Toward an Integration of Micro- and Macro-Sociologies*. London: Routledge Kegan Paul.

———. 1999. *Epistemic Cultures: How the Sciences Make Knowledge*. Cambridge, MA: Harvard University Press.

Korn, R. 1988. "The Effects of Confinement in a High Security Unit in Lexington." *Social Justice* 15(1): 8–19.

Kornberger, Martin, Carl Rhodes, and Rene ten Bos. 2006. "The Others of Hierarchy." In *Deleuze and the Social*, ed. Martin Fuglsang and Bent Meier Sorensen, 58–74. Edinburg: Edinburg University Press.

Kristeva, Julia. 1984. *Revolution in Poetic Language*. New York: Columbia University Press.

Lab, Stephen, P. and John T. Whitehead. 1990. "From 'Nothing Works' to 'The Appropriate Works.'" *Criminology* 28(4): 405–17.

Lacan, Jacques. 1977. *Écrits: A Selection*. New York: W. W. Norton.

———. 1981. *The Four Fundamental Concepts of Psychoanalysis*. New York: W. W. Norton.

———. 1985. *Feminine Sexuality*. New York: W. W. Norton.

———. 1988. *The Seminars of Jacques Lacan, Book II: The Ego in Freud's Theory and the Technique of Psychoanalysis, 1954–1955*. Cambridge, UK: Cambridge University Press.

———. 1991. *L'envers de la psychanalyse*. Paris: Editions du Seuil.

Laclau, Ernesto, and Chantal Mouffe. 2001. *Hegemony and Socialist Strategy: Towards a Radical Democratic Politics*. 2nd ed. New York: Verso.

Laing, R. D. 1983. *The Politics of Experience*. New York: Pantheon.

Lambert, Gregg. 2006. *Who's Afraid of Deleuze and Guattari*. London: Continuum International Publishing Group.

Laub, J. H., and Robert Sampson. 2001. "Understanding Desistance from Crime." In *Crime and Justice* 26, ed. M. H. Tonry and N. Norris, 1–78. Chicago: University of Chicago Press.

LeBel, Thomas, Ros Burnett, Shadd Maruna, and Shawn Bushway. 2008. "The Chicken and Egg of Subjective and Social Factors in Desistance from Crime." *European Journal of Criminology* 5(2): 131–59

Lecercle, Jean-Jacques. 2002. *Deleuze and Language*. New York: Palgrave MacMillan.

Lee, John S. 1990. *Jacques Lacan*. Amherst: University of Massachusetts Press.

Levinas, Emmanuel. 1987. *Time and the Other*. Pittsburgh, PA: Duquesne University Press.

———. 2004. *Otherwise Than Being*. Pittsburgh, PA: Duquesne University Press.

Lewin, Kurt. 1966. *Principles of Psychology*. New York: McGraw-Hill.

Liebling, Alison. 2008. "Why Prison Staff Culture Matters." In *The Culture of Prison Violence*, ed. James Byrne, Don Hummer, and Faye Taxman, 105–22. New York: Pearson Education.

Liebling, Alison, and D. Price. 2001. *The Prison Officer*. Leyhilll: Prison Service and Waterside Press.

Linstead, Stephen. 2000. "Dangerous Fluids and the Organization-without-Organs." In *Body and Organization*, ed. J. Hassard, R. Holliday, and H. Willmott, 31–51. London: Sage.

Loeber, Rolf, and David P. Farrington, eds. 2002. *Serious and Violent Juvenile Offenders: Risk Factors and Successful Interventions*. Thousand Oaks, CA: Sage.

Lombardo, L. 1985. "Group Dynamics and the Prison Guard Subculture." *International Journal of Offender Therapy and Comparative Criminology* 29(1): 79–90.

———. 1989. *Guards Imprisoned: Correctional Officers at Work*. Cincinnati: Anderson Publishing.

Lorraine, Tamsin. 1999. *Irigaray and Deleuze: Experiments in Visceral Philosophy*. Ithaca, NY: Cornell University Press.

Lucaks, Georg. 1971. *History of Class Consciousness*. Cambridge, MA: MIT Press.

Lynch, Mona. 1998. "Waste Managers: The New Penology, Crime Fighting, and Parole Agent Identity." *Law and Society Review* 32(4): 839–69.

———. 2000. "Rehabilitation as Rhetoric: The Ideal of Reformation in Contemporary Parole Discourse and Practices." *Punishment and Society* 2(1): 40–65.

Lyng, Stephen. 2005. *Edgework: The Sociology of Risk-Taking*. New York: Routledge.

Lyotard, Jean-Francois. 1984. *The Postmodern Condition*. Minneapolis: University of Minnesota Press.

MacCabe, Colin. 2002. *James Joyce and the Revolution of the World*. 2nd ed. London: Palgrave MacMillan.

MacKenzie, Doris. 2006. *What Works in Corrections?* New York: Cambridge University Press.

MacLean, Brian, ed. 1993. *We Who Would Take No Prisoners*. Vancouver, CA: The Collective Press.

Manning, Peter. 1988. *Symbolic Communication: Signifying Calls and the Police Response*. Cambridge, MA: MIT Press.

———. 1990. "Critical Semiotics Part II." *The Critical Criminologist* 2(1): 5–6, 16.

Martin-Alcoff, Linda. 2005. *Visible Identities: Race, Gender, and the Self*. New York: Oxford University Press.

Martin-Alcoff, Linda, and Eduardo Mendieta, eds. 2003. *Identities: Race, Class, Gender and Nationality*. New York: Blackwell Publishing.

Martinson, Robert. 1974. "What Works?—Questions and Answers about Prison Reform." *The Public Interest* 35: 22–54.

Maruna, S. 2001. *Making Good: How Ex-Offenders Reform and Reclaim Their Lives*. Washington, DC: American Psychological Association Books.

Maruna, Shadd, and Russ Immarigeon, eds. 2004. *After Crime and Punishment: Pathways to Offender Reintegration*. Cullompton, UK: Willan Publishing.

Maruna, Shadd, Amanda Matravers, and Angela King. 2004. "Disowning Our Shadow: A Psychoanalytic Approach to Understanding Punitive Public Attitudes." *Deviant Behavior* 25(3): 277–99.

Maruna, Shadd, and Hans Toch. 2005. "The Impact of Incarceration on the Desistance Process." In *Prisoner Reentry and Public Safety in America*, ed. J. Travis and C. Visher. New York: Cambridge University Press.

Marx, Karl. 1964. *The Economic and Philosophical Manuscripts of 1844*. New York: International Publishers (originally published in 1844).

———. 1984. *Contributions to a Critique of Political Economy*. New York: International Publishers (originally published in 1859).

Mason, Wendy, and Hal Kirkwood. 2006. "Chaos Theory." Reference for Business. www.referenceforbusiness.com/management/Bun-Comp/Chaos-Theory.html.

Massumi, Brian. 1992. *A User's Guide to Capitalism and Schizophrenia*. London: MIT Press.

Mathiesen, Thomas. 1997. "The Viewer Society: Michel Foucault's 'Panopticon' Revisited." *Theoretical Criminology* 1(2): 215–34.

Matravers, Amanda, ed. 2005. *Sex Offenders in the Community: Managing and Reducing Risks*. Cullompton, UK: Willan Publishing.

Matravers, Amanda, and Shadd Maruna. 2004. "Contemporary Penality and Psychoanalysis." *Critical Review of International and Political Philosophy* 7: 118–44.

Matsuda, Mari J. 1998. *Where Is Your Body: And Other Essays on Race, Gender, and the Law*. Boston: Beacon Press.

Matza, David. 1964. *Delinquency and Drift*. New York: Wiley.

———. 1969. *Becoming Deviant*. Englewood Cliffs, NJ: Prentice Hall.

Mauer, Marc. 1997. *Intended and Unintended Consequences: State Racial Disparities in Imprisonment*. Washington, DC: The Sentencing Project.

———. 2006. *Race to Incarcerate*. London: The New Press.

Mauer, Marc, and Meda Chesney-Lind, eds. 2003. *Invisible Punishment: The Collateral Consequences of Mass Imprisonment*. London: The New Press.

May, Todd. 1994. *The Political Philosophy of Poststructuralist Anarchism*. University Park: Pennsylvania University Press.

———. 1995. *The Moral Theory of Poststructuralism*. University Park: Pennsylvania University Press.

McGuire, James, ed. 2003. *Offender Rehabilitation and Treatment: Effective Programs and Policies to Reduce Re-offending.* London: Wiley.

McMullin, Julie. 2004. *Understanding Social Inequality: Intersections of Class, Age, Gender, Ethnicity, and Race in Canada.* New York: Oxford University Press.

Meisenhelder, Thomas. 1977. "An Exploratory Study of Exiting from Criminal Careers." *Criminology* 15: 319–34.

Melossi, Dario. 1985. "Punishment and Social Action: Changing Vocabularies on Punitive Motive within a Political Business Cycle." *Current Perspectives in Social Theory* 6: 169–97.

——. 1989. "An Introduction: Fifty Years Later, and Social Structure in Comparative Analysis." *Crime, Law, and Social Change* 13(4): 311–26.

Melossi, Dario, and M. Pavarini. 1981. *The Prison and the Factory: The Origins of the Penitentiary System.* New York: MacMillan.

Merleau-Ponty, M. 1969. *The Visible and the Invisible.* Evanston, IL: Northwestern University Press.

Mika, Harry, and Jim Thomas. 1988. "The Dialectics of Prisoner Litigation: Reformist Idealism or Social Praxis?" *Social Justice* 15(1): 48–71.

Milgram, Stanley. 1974. *Obedience to Authority: An Experimental View.* London: Tavistock.

Miller, James. 2000. *The Passions of Michel Foucault.* Cambridge, MA: Harvard University Press.

Mills, C. Wright. 1940. "Situated Actions and Vocabularies of Motive." *American Sociological Review* 5: 904–13.

——. 1959. *The Sociological Imagination.* New York: Oxford University Press.

Milovanovic, Dragan. 1986. "Juridico-linguistic Communicative Markets: Towards a Semiotic Analysis." *Contemporary Crisis* 10: 281–304.

——. 1988. "Jailhouse Lawyers and Jailhouse Lawyering." *International Journal of the Sociology of Law* 16: 455–75.

——. 1991. "Humanistic Sociology and the Chaos Paradigm: A Review Essay of Katherine Hayles, Chaos Bound." *Humanity and Society* 15(1): 135–46.

——. 1996. "'Rebellious Lawyering': Lacan, Chaos, and the Development of Alternative Juridico-Semiotic Forms." *Legal Studies Forum* 20(3): 295–321.

——. 1999. "Catastrophe Theory, Discourse, and Conflict Resolution: Generating the 'Third Way.'" In *Social Justice/Criminal Justice,* ed. Bruce Arrigo, 201–23. Belmont, CA: West/Wadsworth.

——. 2001. "Postmodernism Meets the Balkan Crises: Affirming, Celebrating, and Prioritizing Difference and Sameness in Mediation Efforts." *International Journal for the Semiotics of Law* 14(4): 409–28.

——. 2002. *Critical Criminology at the Edge: Postmodern Perspectives, Integration, and Applications.* Westport, CT: Praeger.

——. 2003. *An Introduction to the Sociology of Law.* Monsey, NY: Criminal Justice Press.

——. 2005. "Psychoanalytic Semiotics, Chaos, and Rebellious Lawyering." In *Lacan: Topologically Speaking,* ed. Ellie Ragland and Dragan Milovanovic, 174–204. New York: Other Press.

——. 2006. "Diversity, Law and Justice." *International Journal for the Semiotics of Law* 20(1): 55–79.

Milovanovic, Dragan, and Stuart Henry. 1991. "Constitutive Penology." *Social Justice* 18: 204–24.

———. 2001. "Constitutive Definition of Crime: Power as Harm." In *What Is Crime? Controversies over the Nature of Crime and What to Do about It,* ed. S. Henry and M. M. Lanier, 165–78. Boulder, CO: Rowman & Littlefield.

Milovanovic, Dragan, and Katheryn Russell. 2001. *Petit Apartheid in the U.S. Criminal Justice System: The Dark Figure of Racism.* Durham, NC: Carolina Academic Press.

Milovanovic, Dragan, and Jim Thomas. 1989. "Overcoming the Absurd: Legal Struggle as Primitive Rebellion." *Social Problems* 36(1): 48–60.

Moffit, Terrie E., Donald Lynam, and Phil Silva. 1994. "Neuropsychological Tests Predicting Male Delinquency." *Criminology* 33(3): 277–300.

Mohanty, Satya P., Linda Martin-Alcoff, Michael Hames-Garcia, and Paul M. L. Moya, eds. 2006. *Identity Politics Reconsidered.* New York: Palgrave MacMillan.

Morris, Ruth. 1994. *A Practical Path to Transformative Justice.* Toronto: Rittenhouse.

———. 2000. *Stories of Transformative Justice.* Toronto: Canadian Scholars Press.

Muir, William. 1977. *Police: Streetcorner Politicians.* Chicago: University of Chicago Press.

Mullarkey, John. 2006. *Post-Continental Philosophy.* New York: Continuum.

Murray, C. 1997. *Does Prison Work?* London: Institute for Economic Affairs.

Murray, Jamie. 2006. "Nome Law: Deleuze and Guattari on the Emergence of Law." *International Journal for the Semiotics of Law* 19(2): 127–51.

Nasar, Rebecca L., and Christy A. Visher. 2006. "Family Members' Experience with Incarceration and Reentry." *Western Criminological Review* 7(2): 7–31.

Negri, Antonio. 1984. *Marx beyond Marx.* New York: Bergin and Garvey.

———. 1992. "Interpretation of the Class Situation Today: Methodological Aspects." In *Open Marxism,* vol. 2, *Theory and Practice,* ed. Werner Bonefeld, Richard Gunn, and Kosmas Psychopedis, 69–105. London: Pluto Press.

———. 1999. *Insurgencies: Constituent Power and the Modern State.* Minneapolis: University of Minnesota Press.

Ness, Daniel, and Karen Strong. 2002. *Restoring Justice.* Cincinnati: Anderson Publishing Company.

Nietzsche, Friedrich W. 1966. *Beyond Good and Evil: Prelude to a Philosophy of the Future,* ed. Walter Kaufmann. New ed. New York: Vintage (originally published in 1886).

———. 1968. *The Will to Power,* ed. Walter Kaufmann. New ed. New York: Vintage (originally published in 1888).

———. 1969. *On the Genealogy of Morals and Ecce Homo,* ed. Walter Kaufmann. New York: Vintage (originally published in 1887).

Noddings, Nel. 2003. *Caring: A Feminine Approach to Ethics and Moral Education.* 2nd ed. Berkeley: University of California Press.

Omer, Haim, and C. Strenger. 1992. "The Pluralist Revolution: From One True Meaning to an Infinity of Constructed Meanings." *Psychotherapy* 29(2): 254–61.

Owen, Barbara A. 1999. *In the Mix: Struggle and Survival in a Women's Prison.* Albany: SUNY Press.

Palmer, A. 1975. "Martinson Revisited." *Journal of Research in Crime and Delinquency* 12(2): 133–52.

Palmer, Emma J. 2004. *Offender Behavior: Moral Reasoning, Criminal Conduct, and the Rehabilitation of Offenders*. Cullompton, UK: Willan Publishing.

Parker, Christine. 1999. *Just Lawyers*. Oxford: Oxford University Press.

Parry, Alan, and Robert E. Doan. 1994. *Story Re-visions: Narrative Therapy in the Postmodern World*. New York: Guilford.

Patton, Paul. 2000. *Deleuze and the Political*. New York: Routledge.

Pavlich, George. 2005. *The Paradoxes of Restorative Justice*. London: Glasshouse Press.

Pecheux, Michel, and H. C. Nagpal. 1982. *Language, Semantics and Ideology*. New York: St. Martin's Press.

Pemberton, Simon. 2004. "A Theory of Moral Indifference: Understanding the Production of Harm by Capitalist Society." In *Beyond Criminology: Taking Harm Seriously*, ed. P. Hillyard, C. Pantazis, S. Tombs, and D. Gordan, 67–83. London: Pluto Press.

Pepinsky, Harold E., and Richard Quinney. 1991. *Criminology as Peacemaking*. Bloomington: Indiana University Press.

Perlin, Michael L. 2000. *The Hidden Prejudice: Mental Disability on Trial*. Washington, DC: American Psychological Association.

Peters, Tom. 1988. *Thriving on Chaos: Handbook for a Management Revolution*. Harper Paperback.

Petersilia, Joan. 2003. *When Prisoners Come Home*. New York: Oxford University Press.

Pfeiffer, Mary Beth. 2007. *Crazy in America: The Hidden Tragedy of our Criminalized Mentally Ill*. New York: Carroll and Graf.

Philips, Susan. 1998. *Ideology in the Language of Judges: How Judges Practice Law, Politics, and Courtroom Control*. New York: Oxford University Press.

Piquero, Alex, David Farrington, and Alfred Blumstein. 2007. *Key Issues in Criminal Career Research: New Analyses of the Cambridge Study in Delinquent Development*. New York: Cambridge University Press.

Popper, Karl. 1959. *The Logic of Scientific Discovery*. New York: Basic Books.

———. 1963. *Conjectures and Refutations: The Growth of Scientific Knowledge*. New York: Basic Books.

———. 1972. *Objective Knowledge: An Evolutionary Approach*. Oxford: Clarendon Press.

Poster, Mark. 1996. "Database as Discourse, Or Electronic Interpellations." In *Detraditionalization*, ed. Paul Heelas, Scott Lash, and Paul Morris, 277–93. Oxford: Blackwell.

Presser, Lois. 2008. *Been a Heavy Life: Stories of Violent Men*. Chicago: University of Illinois Press.

Prus, Robert, and Scott Grills. 2003. *The Deviant Mystique: Involvements, Realities, and Regulation*. Westport, CT: Praeger.

Quinney, Richard. 1970. *The Social Reality of Crime*. Boston: Little Brown and Company.

Ragland, Ellie, and Dragan Milovanovic, eds. 2005. *Lacan: Topologically Speaking*. New York: Other Press.

Raine, Adrian. 1993. *The Psychopathology of Crime: Criminal Behavior as a Clinical Disorder*. San Diego, CA: Academic Press.

Reiman, Jeffrey. 2006. *The Rich Get Richer and the Poor Get Prison: Ideology, Class, and Criminal Justice*. 8th ed. Boston: Allyn and Bacon.

Reisig, M. D. 1998. "Rates of Disorder in Higher-Custody State Prisons." *Crime and Delinquency* 41(2): 229–44.

Rhodes, Lorna A. 2001. "Toward an Anthropology of Prisons." *Annual Review of Anthropology* (30): 65–83.

———. 2004. *Total Confinement: Madness and Reason in the Maximum Security Prison*. Berkeley: University of California Press.

Robinson, Matthew. 2004. *Why Crime? An Integrated Systems Theory of Anti Social Behavior*. Upper Saddle River, NJ: Prentice Hall.

Roche, Declan. 2003. *Accountability in Restorative Justice*. Oxford, UK: Oxford University Press.

Rorty, Richard. 1989. *Contingency, Irony, and Solidarity*. Cambridge, UK: Cambridge University Press.

Rose, Dina, and Todd Clear. 1998. "Incarceration, Social Capital, and Crime." *Criminology* 36: 441–80.

Rosenau, Pauline. 1992. *Post-modernism and the Social Sciences: Insights, Inroads, and Intrusions*. Princeton, NJ: Princeton University Press.

Ross, Jeffrey I., and Stephen C. Richards. 2002. *Behind Bars: Surviving Prisons*. New York: Alpha.

Rothman, David J. 1971. *Discovery of the Asylum: Social Order and Disorder in the Republic*. Boston: Little, Brown.

Rusche, George, and Otto Kirchheiner. 1968. *Punishment and Social Structure*. Totowa, NJ: Transaction Publishers (originally published in 1939).

Sampson, Robert, and Lydia Bean. 2006. "Cultural Mechanisms and Killing Fields." In *Race, Ethnicity, and Crime in America*, ed. Ruth Peterson, Laurie Krivo, and John Hagan, 8–36. New York: New York University Press.

Sampson, Robert, and John Laub. 1993. *Crime in the Making: Pathways and Turning Points through Life*. Cambridge, MA: Harvard University Press.

Sarre, Rick. 2003. "Restorative Justice: A Paradigm of Possibility." In *Controversies in Critical Criminology*, ed. Martin D. Schwartz and Suzanne E. Hatty, 97–108. Cincinnati: Anderson.

Saussure, Ferdinand de. 1966. *Course in General Linguistics*. New York: McGraw-Hill.

Schehr, Robert, and Dragan Milovanovic. 1999. "Conflict Mediation and the Postmodern: Chaos, Catastrophe, and Psychoanalytic Semiotics." *Social Justice* 26(1): 208–32.

Schwendinger, Herman, and Julia Schwendinger. 1985. *Adolescent Subcultures and Delinquency*. New York: Praeger.

Scraton, Phil, Joe Sim, and Paula Skidmore. 1991. *Prisons under Protest*. Philadelphia: Open University Press.

Sevenhuijsen, Selma. 1998. *Citizenship and the Ethics of Care*. London: Routledge.

Sharp, Susan. F., ed. 2003. *The Incarcerated Woman: Rehabilitative Programming in Women's Prisons*. Upper Saddle River, NJ: Prentice Hall.

Sheehan, Rosemary, Gill McIvor, and Chris Trotter. 2007. *What Works with Women Offenders?* Cullompton, UK: Willan Publishing.

Sherman, Lawrence. 2002. *Evidence-Based Crime Prevention*. New York: Routledge.

Silbey, Susan. 1993. "Mediation Mythology." *Negotiation Journal* 9(4): 349–53.

Silverman, Kaja. 1983. *The Subject of Semiotics*. New York: Oxford University Press.

Sloop, John. 1996. *The Cultural Prison: Discourse, Prisoners and Punishment*. Tuscaloosa: University of Alabama Press.

Slote, Michael. 2007. *The Ethics of Care and Empathy*. New York: Routledge.

Smith, Paul. 1988. *Discerning the Subject*. Minneapolis: University of Minnesota Press.

Smith, W. 2001. "Chaos Theory and Postmodern Organization." *International Journal of Organizational Theory and Behavior* 4: 259–286.

Solan, Lawrence. 1993. *The Language of Judges*. Chicago: University of Chicago Press.

Solan, Lawrence, and Peter Tiersma. 2005. *Speaking of Crime: The Language of Criminal Justice*. Chicago: University of Chicago Press.

Sparks, Richard. 2001. "Penology." In *The Sage Dictionary of Criminology*, ed. E. McLaughlin and J. Muncie, 206–207. London: Sage.

Spivak, Gayatri Chakravorty. 1988. "Can the Subaltern Speak?" In *Marxism and the Interpretation of Culture*, ed. Cary Nelson and Larry Grossberg, 271–313. Chicago: University of Chicago Press.

Stacey, Judith. 1990. *Brave New Families*. New York: Basic Books.

Stein, Abby. 2006. *Prologue to Violence: Child Abuse, Dissociation, and Crime*. New York: The Analytic Press.

Stewart, Ian. 1989. *Does God Play Dice? The Mathematics of Chaos*. Oxford: Basil Blackwell.

Stowell, Jacob, and James Byrne. 2008. "Does What Happen in Prison Stay in Prison? Examining the Reciprocal Relationship between Community and Prison Culture." In *The Culture of Prison Violence*, ed. James Byrne, Don Hummer, and Faye Taxman, 27–39. New York: Pearson Education.

Strang, Heather, and John Braithwaite, eds. 2005. *Restorative Justice and Civil Society*. Cambridge, UK: Cambridge University Press.

Street, D., R. Vinter, and C. Perrow. 1966. *Organization for Treatment: A Comparative Analysis of Institutions for Delinquents*. New York: The Free Press.

Sullivan, Dennis, and Larry Tifft. 2005. *Restorative Justice: Healing the Foundations of Our Everyday Lives*. 2nd ed. Monsey, NY: Criminal Justice Press.

Sullivan, Terence. 2004. "The Viability of Using Various System Theories to Describe Organizational Change." *Journal of Educational Administration* 42(1): 43–54.

Surette, Ray. 1998. *Media, Crime, and Criminal Justice: Images and Realities*. New York: Wadsworth.

Sykes, Gresham. 1958. *Society of Captives: A Study of a Maximum Security Prison*. Princeton, NJ: Princeton University Press.

Sykes, Gresham, and David Matza. 1957. "Techniques of Neutralization: A Theory of Delinquency." *American Sociological Review* 22: 665–70.

Tannenbaum, Frank. 1938. *Crime and the Community*. New York: Columbia University Press.

Taxman, Fay, Douglas Young, and James Byrne. 2004. "With Eyes Wide Open: Formalizing Community and Social Control Intervention in Offender Reintegration Programmes." In *After Crime and Punishment*, ed. Shadd Maruna and Russ Immarigeon, 233–60. Cullompton, UK: Willan Publishing.

Thomas, Jim. 1988. *Prisoner Litigation: The Paradox of the Jailhouse Lawyer*. Totowa, NJ: Rowman & Littlefield.

Thomas, Jim, and H. Mika. 1988. "The Dialectics of Prisoner Litigation: Reformist Idealism or Social Praxis?" *Social Justice* 15(1): 48–71.

Thomas, Jim, and Dragan Milovanovic. 1999. "Revisiting Jailhouse Lawyers: An Excursion into Constitutive Criminology." In *Constitutive Criminology at Work*, ed. Stuart Henry and Dragan Milovanovic, 227–46. New York: SUNY Press.

Tiersma, Peter. 1999. *Legal Language*. Chicago: University of Chicago Press.

Travis, Jeremy, and Christy Visher, eds. 2005. *Prison Reentry and Crime in America*. New York: Cambridge University Press.

Tronto, Joan. 1993. *Moral Boundaries: A Political Argument for an Ethic of Care*. New York: Routledge.

———. 1995. *Caring for Democracy*. Utrecht, Netherlands: University of Humanistic Studies.

Uggen, Christopher, Jeff Manza, and Angela Behrens. 2004. "Less Than the Average Citizen." In *After Crime and Punishment: Pathways to Offender Reintegration*, ed. Shadd Maruna and Russ Immarigeon. Cullompton, UK: Willan Publishing.

Unger, Roberto. 1986. *The Critical Legal Studies Movement*. Cambridge, MA: Harvard University Press.

———. 1987. *False Necessity*. New York: Cambridge University Press.

———. 1996. *What Should Legal Analysis Become?* London: Verso.

Valier, Claire. 2000. "Looking Daggers: A Psychoanalytic Reading of the Scene of Punishment." *Punishment and Society* 2(4): 379–94.

Visher, Christy, Pamela Lattimore, and Richard Linster. 1991. "Predicting the Recidivism of Serious Youthful Offenders Using Survival Models." *Criminology* 29: 329–66.

Voruz, Veronique. 2004. "Recent Perspectives on Penal Punitiveness." In *Psychological Jurisprudence: Critical Reflections in Crime, Law, and Society*, ed. B. Arrigo, 155–77. Albany: SUNY Press.

Wacquant, Loïc. 2005. *Deadly Symbiosis: Race and the Rise of Neoliberal Penality*. Cambridge, UK: Polity Press.

Walker, Samuel. 2005. *Sense and Nonsense about Crime and Drugs: A Policy Guide*. 6th ed. Belmont, CA: Wadsworth.

Ward, Tony, and Shadd Maruna. 2007. *Rehabilitation*. London: Routledge.

Welch, Michael. 2005. *Ironies of Imprisonment*. Thousand Oaks, CA: Sage.

Welsh, Brandon C., and David P. Farrington, eds. 2006. *Preventing Crime: What Works for Children, Offenders, Victims, and Places*. New York: Springer.

Wheatley, Margaret. 2001. *Leadership and the New Science: Discovering Order in a Chaotic World Revised*. San Francisco: Berrett-Koehler Publishers.

White, Hayden. 1973. *Metahistory*. Baltimore: Johns Hopkins University Press.

Williams, Christopher R., and Bruce A. Arrigo. 2000. "The Philosophy of the Gift and the Psychology of Advocacy: Critical Reflections on Forensic Mental Health Intervention." *International Journal for the Semiotics of Law* 13: 215–42.

———. 2002. *Law, Psychology, and Justice: Chaos Theory and the New (Dis)order*. Albany: SUNY Press.

———. 2006. "Introduction: Philosophy, Crime, and Theoretical Criminology." In *Philosophy, Crime, and Criminology*, ed. B. A. Arrigo and C. R. Williams, 1–38. Urbana-Champagne: University of Illinois Press.

Wise, John Macgregor. 1997. *Exploring Technology and Social Space*. Thousand Oaks, CA: Sage.

Wolfgang, Marvin, Robert M. Figlio, and Thorsten Sellin. 1972. *Delinquency in a Birth Cohort*. Chicago: University of Chicago Press.

Wortley, Richard. 2002. *Situational Prison Control*. Cambridge, UK: Cambridge University Press.

Yngvesson, Barbara. 1993. *Virtuous Citizens Disruptive Subjects: Order and Complaint in a New England Court*. New York: Routledge.

Young, Jock. 1999. *The Exclusive Society: Social Exclusion, Crime, and Difference in Late Modernity*. London: Sage.

Young, T. R. 1997. "Challenges for a Postmodern Criminology." In *Chaos, Criminology and Social Justice: The New Orderly (Dis)order*, ed. Dragan Milovanovic, 29–51. Westport, CT: Praeger Publishers.

Zedner, Lucia, and Andrew Ashworth, eds. 2003. *The Criminological Foundations of Penal Policy: Essays in Honor of Roger Hood*. New York: Oxford University Press.

Zimbardo, Philip. 2007. *The Lucifer Effect: Understanding How Good People Turn Evil*. New York: Random House.

Zimring, Franklin, and Gordon Hawkins. 1997. *Incapacitation: Penal Confinement and the Restraint of Crime*. New York: Oxford University Press.

Zizek, Slavoj. 1989. *The Sublime Object of Ideology*. New York: Verso.

Zwerman, Gilda. 1988. "Social Incapacitation: The Emergence of a New Correctional Facility for Women Political Prisoners." *Social Justice* 15(1): 31–47.

Author Index

Subject Index

About the Authors

Bruce A. Arrigo, PhD, is a professor of crime, law, and society in the Department of Criminal Justice at the University of North Carolina, Charlotte. He has (co)authored more than 150 scholarly articles, chapters, and essays, as well as (co)authored or (co)edited 20 books. Among his numerous recognitions, Dr. Arrigo was named the Critical Criminologist of the Year (2000) by the Division on Critical Criminology of the American Society of Criminology, was elected as a fellow of the American Psychological Association (2002) and the Academy of Criminal Justice Sciences (2005), and was the recipient of the latter organization's Bruce Smith Sr. Award (2007) for distinguished research contributions. His book, *The French Connection in Criminology: Rediscovering Crime, Law, and Social Change* (coauthored with Dragan Milovanovic and Robert Schehr), received the 2005 Book-of-the-Year Award from the Crime and Juvenile Delinquency Section of the Society for the Study of Social Problems.

Dragan Milovanovic, PhD, is a professor in the Justice Studies Department at Northeastern Illinois University. He received his degree from the State University of New York, Albany. He has published or has forthcoming (as author, coauthor, or coeditor) twenty books as well as numerous articles and other scholarly publications. His most recent book (coauthored) is *Social Justice* (2007). He received the Distinguished Achievement Award from the Division of Critical Criminology of the American Society of Criminology (1992–1993) and was named the Bernard J. Brommel Distinguished Research Professor in 2006.